Granny Brand

HER STORY

Other Books by Dorothy Clarke Wilson

DR IDA

TAKE MY HANDS

TEN FINGERS FOR GOD

HILARY

LONE WOMAN

PALACE OF HEALING

Granny Brand

Brand

HER STORY

Dorothy Clarke Wilson

Paul Brand Publishing
Distributed by
Dick Sleeper Distribution
18680-B Langensand Road
Sandy, Oregon 97055-9427 USA

Paul Brand Publishing
1026 California Lane
Seattle WA 98116

ISBN 0-9643137-1-5

Printed in the United States of America

Acknowledgments

The author makes grateful acknowledgment to the following:
Dr. Paul W. Brand, Granny's son, who arranged the author's trip to the Kollis and Kalryans with Granny, furnished invaluable information through interviews, tapes, letters, as well as comments on the manuscript; and his wife, Dr. Margaret Brand, who provided many interesting anecdotes and other material;

Mrs. David Wilmshurst, Granny's daughter, for interviews in England and the sharing of many reminiscences and personal letters, as well as criticism of the manuscript;

Dr. Ruth Harris, Granny's niece, who with her sister Monica, a nurse, worked closely with Granny, for interviews in both India and England.

Miss Carolyn Weeber, the nurse associated with Granny on the mountains for many years, who provided letters, diaries, personal reminiscences, and most helpful criticism of the manuscript, as well as preparing the meticulously detailed maps used in the book;

Dr. Howard T. Lewis, President of the International Gospel League, who took the mountain trip with the author, provided literature, pictures, and other research materials, with permission to draw heavily on the content of Granny's little autobiography, *Trust and Triumph*, and the author's booklet, *Life for the Mountains of Death*, both published by the League;

Mrs. K. G. Koshi, wife of the former Director of the Vellore Christian Medical College, who also accompanied the author on the mountain trip and assisted in the assembling of a mass of material on Granny's life stored in Vellore;

The publishers of the author's previous book about the Brands, *Ten Fingers for God*, for the use of material in it relating to Granny, some incidents being borrowed almost verbatim;

All the relatives and friends of Granny who have given encouragement, inspiration and—most appreciated of all—assurances that the book faithfully portrays the spirit, life style, and achievements of a most remarkable woman.

Illustrations

Evelyn Brand
Early work on the Kollis
A painting by Evelyn Brand on the Kollis
Paul's childhood home
Jessie and Evelyn Brand, Paul and Connie
Evelyn with her paints
With Dr. Ruth Harris in the boarding home
Ruth Harris with the medical van
Granny on horseback
Dangerous trails; a constant hazard
A native hut where Granny ministered
Carol Weeber and Granny Brand with two friends[1]
The *dholi*, a principal means of mountain travel[1]
With a group of Christians[1]
Astride a hill pony
Granny with her two bamboo sticks

[1] International Gospel League

Foreword

To many people around the world she was known as "Grandmother Brand". To her eleven grandchildren and other relatives and close friends she was simply "Granny". But to thousands of hill people on five mountain ranges of South India she was *Amma*, Mother, *Akka*, Sister, the *doraisani*, honoured lady, who nursed and doctored and taught and scolded and loved them, the living embodiment of the Gospel she shared with them for over sixty years.

I first saw Evelyn Brand in March, 1964. I had come to India to gather material for my book *Ten Fingers for God*, the story of her son Dr. Paul Brand, the noted pioneer in surgery and rehabilitation for leprosy. I wanted to visit the mountain mission station where he spent his childhood. My companions on the trip were Dr. Brand, Susie Koshi, wife of one of the doctors at the Vellore Christian Medical College and Hospital, and Reverend Howard Lewis, of the International Gospel League, which for years had been the supporter of Granny's mountain work. It was arranged that we should meet Granny at a hotel in Salem, about 150 miles from Vellore. She arrived in the evening soon after we did in a car driven by her missionary friend, Regina Hansen.

In spite of all I had heard about her, I was still unprepared. In the dim light of the hotel courtyard she seemed more wraith-like than human. Small of stature, stooped, gaunt, emaciated, she looked as fragile as a dry reed. A fringe of short straight white hair, untidily confined by a ribbon band, gave her deeply wrinkled face a witch-like quality. An ill-fitting dress hung loosely from her bony shoulders. Her feet and limbs were encased in heavy leather sandals and stout braces, and she walked with a slow shuffling gait, clutching two crude unmated bamboo sticks.

9

"Poor creature!" was my first pitying thought. "Not only queer but senile!"

Within minutes I was qualifying these adjectives. Poor, yes, if complete disdain of life's outward trappings can be called poverty. Queer, if the obsession of a Saint Francis or a Schweitzer can be dubbed eccentricity. Senile, if senility can be defined as mere ageing of body. For Granny's mind was as vigorous as her tongue and as keen-edged.

"A hotel!" she spluttered. "Utter unnecessary luxury!" Later in the hotel dining room she expressed further disapproval. "Oh, my dears, think of all the poor people up on my hills who can't eat like this!"

Visiting her room that evening, I was impressed by her utter lack of dependence on *things*. For some reason she needed a pair of scissors, and I produced a small cheap manicure pair.

"Oh!" she exclaimed delightedly. "What a beautiful little pair of scissors!"

"Please keep them," I urged. "I have another."

But she refused. She would probably lose them, and, anyway, what use for a pair of manicure scissors on top of a mountain? I recalled hearing that for many years she had not owned a mirror.

Looking at this shrivelled little creature, I found it hard to believe that sixty years before she was the beautiful Evelyn Constance Harris, belle of a fashionable London suburb, one of nine beautiful and cherished daughters of a doting father, fastidious in dress and person even while playing Lady Bountiful in the slums, dabbling daintily in water-colours or modelling for her admiring friends in a little artists' colony. It was then that I became imbued with the desire to write her story. I knew much about her already, but I must know more. What innate qualities had made her break open that protective cocoon and travel to these "uttermost parts of the earth"? What was the secret of the incredible will and purpose which, at age eighty-five and unable even to walk, kept her riding her little horse over rough mountain trails, fording streams, camping out in a little mosquito-net hut, treating the sick, teaching women better ways of homemaking and men better methods of agriculture, gathering children around her in the evening under the mosquito net and teaching them to read and write and pray—and day after day, unceasingly, telling the story of Jesus? Yes, I had to know.

Before light the next morning we all crowded into another car and travelled south-east across the plain to the range of mountains where Jesse and Evelyn Brand had pioneered in their first mission station. The Kolli malai, they were called, "mountains of death", in those days the spawning ground of deadly malarial fever. As I travelled up the mountain with Granny I thought of the fantastic trip she had made in a *dholi* on her wedding night. Now there was a fairly decent road which, in spite of its seventy-two hairpin bends, was not too frightening. Only twice did my blood chill, when the turns were so abrupt that we had to drive straight to the edge of a sheer drop, back up and start around again, to make the curve. Fortunately I did not discover until later that there was no emergency brake!

This was Granny's world. The higher we climbed the more vibrantly she came alive. Her nostrils dilated. She breathed deeply of the rapidly clarifying mountain air. When we stopped to enjoy the view she was out of the car, hobbling about with the aid of the ill-mated bamboo sticks, overflowing with gratitude.

"*Stottherum*, praise the Lord! Isn't it wonderful, Paul, to be up here again where you can breathe!"

At between three and four thousand feet the road dipped gently downward into a valley. The crags and forests became grassy, rolling hills. Then appeared on either side bright green rectangles of *nangi kadu*, rice fields wrested from the jungle by the sturdy hill men. After the wild vegetation of the steep slopes they were breathtakingly beautiful, seeming to flow through the broad valley like an emerald river. A little farther, and there was our destination, a little settlement of buildings on a hilltop, their white-washed walls and red metal or tiled roofs a surprising contrast to the mud and thatch huts of the villages we had glimpsed on the ascent.

Over the road leading up the hill an archway of greenery and flowers had been erected, and all around it a crowd was waiting. As Granny with her son Paul emerged from the car, they burst into shouts of welcome. With fervent repetitions of "*Stottherum, stottherum!*" she tottered towards them. The bamboo poles seemed extensions of her eager arms outstretched to gather in the motley crowd. Granny had come home.

We explored the little wooden house where Evelyn and Jesse Brand first lived and laboured to create this Christian community. We had dinner in the chapel, sitting bare-footed on strips of straw matting, our backs against the whitewashed walls. The hot rice and curry were served to us on big banana leaves by smiling women in bright clean saris, smooth hair drawn back into neat knots or braids and decorated with flowers. Presently four long strips of matting were laid on the chapel floor, with an aisle down the middle, and the Christian community began to assemble, as decorously as a West End congregation, and seated themselves crosslegged on the strips, boys and men on one side, girls and women and children on the other. I was amazed at the neat, clean appearance of the worshippers, so different from that of many of the villagers I had seen on our way up the mountain. A church service followed, then discussion, much of it concerned with the problem of finding and supporting a new leader for this Christian community the Brands had started long ago.

"And how they do need a leader!" mourned Granny.

That first day of our trip we shared with her some memories of her first fifteen years on the mountains. Then down we came around the seventy-two hairpin turns. We stayed that night near Salem in Regina Hansen's comfortable mission bungalow.

"How can she!" scolded Granny in a pungent aside. "Living down here in this horrible town when she might be working up on the mountains!"

The next morning early we started across the plains, driving perhaps twenty miles to the foot of the Kalryans, Granny's mission field during the previous fifteen years.

"Jesse and I," she explained, "set out to take the Gospel to the people on five mountain ranges. The Kollis were the first. Next came the Kalryans. After that the Pachais. If God gives me time, I shall see that the Gospel gets to all of them."

The new road up the mountain, we were assured, was "jeep-able". The word was but mildly descriptive. Pebbles, stones, boulders, sheer ledges, ruts as deep as small gullies, forty-five degree ascents, centre ridges which would have scraped the belly of an army tank, hairpin bends . . . everything but mud, for this was the dry season. The reddish soil was like powder, the grass rank and brown, the jungle scrub coated with dust. Yet, thanks to Dr. Brand's cool and skilful driving, the road was "jeepable".

Eight miles up new conveyances were waiting: horses for Granny and Mr. Lewis, *dholies* for Susie and me. Having sampled almost every kind of conveyance on my three trips to India, from aeroplane to bullock cart, I welcomed the new experience with relish. The *dholi* was stretched on the ground. Like Granny on her wedding day, I arranged myself on the strips of canvas, set my foot against the front crosspiece of bamboo, disposing of my arched knees with as much modesty as possible, and the four bearers hoisted me to their shoulders. The initial impact was something like that of mounting a camel, but once I became used to the elevation and the jogging pace the motion was not unpleasant . . . as long as we remained on level terrain. But a mountain is not level terrain. I clutched the poles harder as the bearers started up a rocky slope, relaxed with relief at the top, then stared aghast at an even steeper path leading down the other side. Hadn't I heard a story about Granny's being dropped accidentally when riding in a *dholi*? When we came to a ribbon of path with a sheer drop on one side, I turned coward. Deficient though my Tamil was, I managed to make the bearers understand that I wanted to get *down*. Thereafter I walked.

The path wound up and down hillsides, through dry river beds, along the edges of steep slopes, through thickets of rank brown grass and thistles.

"It was a place just like this," commented Granny cheerfully, as the path plunged down a stony stream bed, "where I was once thrown right over the horse's head."

We finally climbed the last steep slope to the hilltop which Granny chose for her headquarters on the Kalryans. There was a rousing welcome here too. We met some of her fellow workers during over fifteen years of working on this second mountain range. Then we were ushered into the small house which was her home for many of those years and would be our shelter overnight. It consisted of two small rooms and a screened porch, with a tiny narrow cooking space and bathing cubicle at the rear. In a corner of the latter, proudly exhibited as a surprise for Granny and freshly installed for the benefit of the American visitors, was —of all things—a bathroom flush unit! There it stood, incongruous in its primitive surroundings, in all its white porcelain glory. I had a mental picture of it, trekking up those sixteen miles of mountain trail on some coolie's head!

Of even more interest to me was the little hut just across the path from the main house, Granny's first home on the Kalryans. Differing little from the huts of native tribes in surrounding villages, it was made of woven bamboo strips overlaid with clay and whitewashed, surmounted by a high thickly peaked thatched roof.

That evening Granny gathered the Christians of the little settlement about her on the veranda for *jebbum,* prayer. Unable to follow the Tamil of the hymns and prayers, I sat on a striped mat with my head against the wall, watching the play of lamplight on the clean, radiant faces, listening to the haunting melodies, the rhythmic clapping of hands, the firm confident voice of Granny talking intimately about these people and their problems with one who for nearly eighty-five years had been her constant companion.

The same motley crowd assembled the next morning to see us off as had welcomed us. It was a farewell for Granny too, for she was now working on her third mountain range, starting the process all over again: the slow making of friends and converts, the hundreds of miles of riding on horseback over stony mountain trails, the camping out under a crude shelter in all kinds of weather

. . . in short, the long slow process of bringing new life to more thousands of needy people.

Do you wonder that I wanted to write her story? Reluctantly, with much persuasion, she agreed. She hated and scorned all publicity, but a book, Mr. Lewis and others urged, would encourage support for the work on her beloved mountains. She came back to Vellore with us, and we spent many hours reviewing the details of her life. I delved into a big trunk and brought back to America a great pile of letters, pictures, diaries, reports, notebooks, and other treasures. Then she reconsidered. Only she herself, she wrote, could write about her life as it had actually been lived. She would write her story herself.

Since I had an obligation to Mr. Lewis and his organisation, I wrote for their use a short booklet called *Life for the Mountains of Death* describing this mountain journey, some of which is included in this Foreword. A few of the highlights of Granny's life, mostly those concerning her children, were of course a part of her son's story, *Ten Fingers for God*, and you will find them repeated here. Granny did write a short story of her life entitled *Trust and Triumph*, published independently by the International Gospel League.

Now that she has written it, I thought, she will be willing to let me write it my way. But, no. She was still reluctant. "Sister," she wrote, "I hope you will understand."

I did understand. Granny was an individualist. She could not trust another person to thrust probing fingers into her thoughts, her emotions, her precious personal relationship with her Lord. Moreover, she feared that too much credit would be given to herself, her own achievements, when all the credit belonged to God—and her beloved husband Jesse. And she had not written the full story in her first little book, she told me. She must write another.

But in recent years she seemed to relent a bit. She began sending me material to piece out what I already had. "Do wait a few more months and let me die," she wrote to me not long ago. "You can write what you like then."

Well, Granny has gone. She died, still almost literally in the saddle, last December at the age of ninety-five. So here is the story that I have waited over ten years to write.

Orono, Maine, U.S.A., 1975   D. G. W.

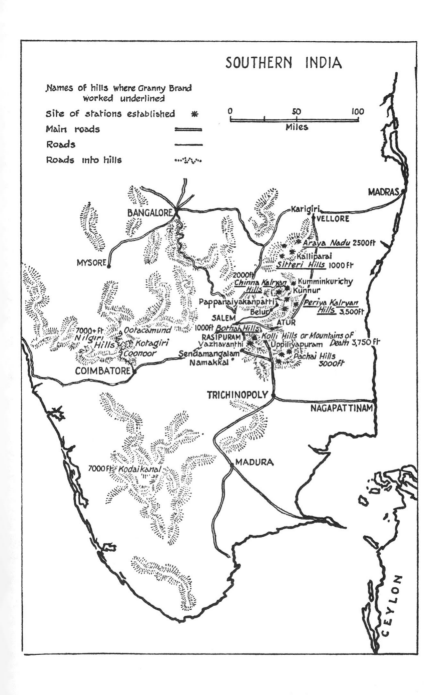

SOUTHERN INDIA

Names of hills where Granny Brand
worked underlined

Site of stations established ✳

Main roads ══════

Roads ─────

Roads into hills ⋯⋰⋮⋱⋯

0   50   100
Miles

MADRAS

BANGALORE

Karigiri
VELLORE

MYSORE

Araya Nadu 2500ft
Kalliparai
Sitteri Hills 1000 Ft

2000ft
Chinna Kalryan Hills   Kumminkurichy
Kunnur

Pappanaiyakanpatti   Periya Kalryan Hills 3,500ft
SALEM   Belur
ATUR

7000+Ft   1000ft Bothai Hills
Nilgiri   Ootacamund   RASIPURAM   Kolli Hills or Mountains of
Hills   Kotagiri   Vazhavanthi   Uppiliyapuram Death 3,750 Ft
Coonoor   Sendamangalam   Pachai Hills 3000ft
COIMBATORE   Namakkal

TRICHINOPOLY

NAGAPATTINAM

7000Ft Kodaikanal

MADURA

CEYLON

One

"How beautiful upon the mountains are the feet of him who bringeth good tidings . . ."

Isaiah 52:7

1

From the beginning she refused to be pressed into a mould. Though ninth among eleven children, nine of them daughters, she was never just "one of those Harris girls". She was always and completely herself, Evelyn Constance Harris, dubbed "Babs" and "Baby" by her older brother Charlie, usually called "Evie" by the rest of the family.

Even in infancy she diverged from the established pattern. Exhausted from bearing eight children, Mother followed the doctor's advice by feeding the newcomer at three months on goat's milk, an innovation indeed for the breast-fed culture of 1879 and one potentially costly.

"You'd never believe what happened!" Evie was told the story later. "One day the goat wandered into the office, and Mother had to put her hand down its throat to get a bank note the foolish thing had swallowed!"

Her child world was small, but beautiful and all-sufficient. It was a house and a garden, a saintly mother, a doting father, eight adored sisters, and two fun-loving brothers. It was tenderness and comfort, peace and security. It was rich in flavour and fragrance and colour, sweetness of lush grapes growing in the big glass greenhouse, golds of plump marrows in the other hothouse that they dubbed "the Pit", tang of gooseberries and currants from the kitchen garden, greens of ferns and vines, pinks and crimsons and corals of begonias and geraniums. Even the ugly black iron fence enclosing the garden was often buried under masses of huge purple lilacs. And, because she was born with the eyes and soul of an artist, the colour far outrivalled sweetness and fragrance.

It was a world of colour, yes, but also of blacks and whites. In the moral judgments of the Harrises there were no greys or sepias. Sin was black and virtue white, and the line between them clearly drawn. Between the cardinal sins, such as theft, rape, murder, blasphemy, and the less flagrant offences discountenanced by Strict Baptists—dancing, card playing, theatre, Sabbath breaking—there was difference only in degree, not in kind. Smoking was tabu. Though Father felt compelled to keep two cigars on an ash tray out of courtesy for guests, the moment the offender departed he would rush back to the library and fling open the windows. All work, even cooking, was prohibited on Sunday. "The servants," insisted Father, "must have as much opportunity to attend worship as we do." But cold meats, cold cherry and gooseberry pies were ample sustenance. And, since some of the teachers of his beloved Sunday School, as well as visiting ministers, were invited for tea, the day offered more excitement than deprivation. In spite of its rigidity, Evie's world seemed neither restrictive nor repressive. Love, not fear, was the heart of its religious as well as its domestic creed.

Of course there was more world outside the walls, a surrounding enclave known as St. John's Wood, a vague encompassing region named London, and beyond that a still vaguer combination called "the world", much of it submerged in heathen darkness. Because of the missionaries who often spoke in Chapel, India and Africa were more real than England, the Poor and the Lost of more human substance than the Queen.

She could do little about the Lost, except put pennies into the missionary offering at church. But for the Poor there was the Giving-Away-Box, into which went broken toys, cast-off dresses, and unwanted possessions of all the children. Even at an early age Evie regarded this medium of charity dubiously. Mother often gave away things she really wanted, and she seemed to have a wonderful time doing it.

"My dear, I can't find my boots," Father might make puzzled complaint.

Mother's smile would be radiant. "Oh, I'm so sorry. A poor man called at the door. His shoes were full of holes. I do hope you understand."

Father did. No doubt he remembered that she had once felt led to take off her own dress to supply the needs of a poor cousin.

The children were not so understanding. "She doesn't give just a tenth, as we've been taught to," worried Grace, who kept the accounts. "She hands out at least a fifth!"

"And to whom?" scolded Minnie, the next youngest. "To any old tramp who comes along! Hoaxers, probably, half of them."

Mother merely smiled. She would rather help ten unworthy people, she explained cheerfully, than miss one true child of God in real need.

When Evie was still a small child, her world was rocked by change. The Great Central Railway appropriated their house and grounds to build railway yards. The family moved to a new home at 3, Cavendish Road. One bleak midwinter day they went back for a last goodbye to the old house. As they entered the conservatory which formed the front entrance, she uttered a low moan of anguish. No one had heated the furnaces. The white shelves were strewn with petals of begonias, like drops of blood. Pain twisted deep into her vitals.

"What a mess!" one of the older girls commented with disgust. "All dead."

"We should sweep them up," said Eunice, the tidy one.

"It's cold." Hope shivered and began to cry. "I wish I hadn't come."

Evie stood, mutely suffering. Only Father shared her pain. Like the passion for colour and beauty, it was part of their special kinship, this intense love of all living things. She would never lose it, nor would she forget this moment. Always it would pain her to see flowers plucked and carelessly discarded. She would still care for them if a flicker of life remained.

In the new home her world slowly righted itself. The house, like the old one, was called "Nethania" which meant "Gift of God". Its high narrow grey brick walls were as tight and secure a shelter. There was a basement room for play, opening on a garden. One walked the old familiar carpets. The huge walnut cabinet in the drawing room held the same treasures: the nautilus shell, the ivory crab, the piece of green Wedgwood with its ring of dancing maidens. There was the same wall clock with the angel on top blowing a trumpet. And of course all over the house were specimens of Father's beloved Martin Ware, the exquisite art pottery produced by the three Martin brothers in a little shed with a home-made kiln.

His joy in watching a perfect creation emerge from the white-hot kiln was exultant; his dismay when the carefully stacked artifices fell to pieces under the fierce heat approaching genuine grief. The brothers were master craftsmen, reluctant to sacrifice their creative genius in commercial reproductions.

"You shouldn't buy that," one of them would advise cunningly, and Father, knowing it was so exquisite they did not want to part with it, would promptly add it to his collection.

Evie fingered the beautiful objects rapturously, tracing the intricate and delicate designs on jars and figurines, "Oh"-ing and

"Ah"-ing over the vibrant blues. She was equally enthusiastic over his other hobby, his precious microscope, which revealed such wonders of nature as the innumerable facets of an insect's eye. They shared, too, a passion for painting, and she nearly burst with pride when one of Father's pictures was hung in the National Gallery.

If there were flaws in the near-perfection of her childhood, they were etched by her own self-conscious little ego. She had one major grievance. She was "one of the little ones". After her seven older sisters—Grace, Minnie, Lily, Rosa, Eunice, Florence, Hope—had come Charlie, the first boy. Then there had been a brief hiatus, followed by herself, Stella, and Bertie. Though the eldest of this trio and consciously much wiser and more mature, she was relegated to the same status. Perhaps her dogged persistence to become expert on stilts, even walking up and down stairs with ease, was an attempt to demonstrate a level of adulthood.

"Send the three little ones to the nursery," someone would say after dinner when serious matters were to be discussed, and she would be bundled off with, as she termed them aggrievedly, the two babies. It was more than humiliation. It was rejection. But there was compensation when on Sunday evenings, while the older children were away at chapel, Mother gathered the "three little ones" about her knee to hear stories of the loving Jesus. Among the numerous scripture passages they learned were the Beatitudes. "Blessed are they that hunger and thirst after righteousness, for they shall be filled." Evie repeated the words with a sudden sweet sense of release. They described her exactly. She felt like Pilgrim in the exciting adventures of *Pilgrim's Progress* when he had felt his burden slip away. From that day she started to think less about her own hurts and frustrations and more about how she could help others.

"Too young," objected more than one sister when she asked to be baptised.

Mother did not think so. And when Evelyn Constance Harris, aged eleven, was baptised, Strict Baptist fashion by immersion, it was with an intense fervour and commitment which were to shape her whole life.

2

IF FATHER HAD one absorbing passion approaching in intensity his religious zeal, it was the ambition to provide sumptuously for his family, not only during their childhood and adolescence but through all their remaining years. None of them, he prided himself, would ever be forced to earn a living. Nothing would have suited him better than to keep them all, especially his nine daughters, under his tight, benevolent roof during his lifetime and thereafter.

"If I hadn't intervened," Mother would admit laughingly, "desirable young men would never have been welcomed into our house."

A prosperous merchant, Father was well able to realise his ambition financially. Comfort and plenty were his children's heritage on both sides of the family. Grandfather Wilson, Mother's father, was an importer of eggs and other commodities from Denmark. The business of both men was conducted with total allegiance to their religious creed. Father rejoiced that his first and last lie had been promptly discovered and punished. In the market where merchants met to fix prices on Mondays, he was the one to whom others came for consultation, sure of an honest estimate. Grandfather Wilson had deliberately forfeited an early job when it was proposed that he work on the Sabbath. And both combined thrift with unswerving honesty.

"Rather starve than borrow," Grandfather would admonish. "I took my watch to the pawnbrokers to pay my bills rather than incur a debt."

It was the Victorian era, when young women of well-to-do families were enshrouded in protective domesticity. Servants cooked and scrubbed for them; maids ministered to personal necessities. Legally the woman had little status. Economically she was utterly dependent on husband, father, or brother. Few paying occupations were open to her—governess, seamstress, in rare instances writer—and the first two of these were tacitly reserved for the genteel poor. Father was by no means unique in his desire to provide generous security for his nine daughters. Only his opposition to their marriage was a bit unusual.

He provided them all with the education considered suitable for young ladies, which included few practical subjects beyond the three R's. Women's "modesty", "refinement", "delicacy", the Victorian era's definitions of male supremacy, required only such additional accomplishments as painting, music, embroidery, perhaps a little French. Father, as well as Mother, had a French background, his father having married a governess in the Royal Household, and he had spent part of his boyhood in France. French, therefore, was considered an essential of education.

Rosa, most brilliant of the girls, became teacher of the "three little ones". For Evie this was a happy arrangement. Rosa shared not only her artistic penchant but her love of nature, and they took long walks around the park where she learned the names of trees and flowers. But it did not last. Evie and Stella were sent to a large girls' boarding school, where they were wretchedly homesick. After two weeks of misery they came home.

The next episode, in a smaller, more informal school at Boscomb near the sea, was more to their liking. They were so close to the sea they could run to the beach in their bathing suits. A guard boat from which they could swim and dive furnished hours of enjoyment. There were steamer expeditions around the Isle of Wight. Still Evie felt burdened and oppressed. Mademoiselle, the French teacher, was her Nemesis. Sweating over exercises, struggling with conjugations when she longed to be preparing for her beloved art course, painting rocks and waves and sunsets, she felt like a caged animal. Though she fumed and rushed about from one task to another with her fierce and abundant energy, she could elicit only disapproving clucks from Mademoiselle. Only the comforting presence of sweet and loving Stella, always her comrade and confidante, kept her from hopeless frustration.

Their next exposure to French was less painful. They spent three months as paying guests at the home of Pasteur Saillens in Boulla Reign near Paris. But what humiliation to find how ineffectual had been all her frenzied efforts for Mademoiselle!

"A pity," was one of the first comments, "that you studied French in England!"

The Saillens' daughter, whom they dubbed "Chère Professeure", gave them thorough tutelage in both language and the marvels of Paris. It was a spiritual as well as a cultural experience, for Saillen was pastor of a Baptist Mission Chapel. Two English boys, also boarding students, were so influenced by the pastor's life and teaching that they asked for baptism. Pasteur Saillens hesitated. "First you must ask your father's permission," he insisted.

A cable gave swift response. "Come home at once." The letter which followed was curtly explanatory. "Baptists in England are a low caste, greatly despised. I will not have my sons disgraced. Religious they can be, but never Baptists."

Evie felt angered, puzzled, and, worst of all, helpless. Did fathers have the right to dictate what their children should believe? Suppose one of Father's children wanted to join the Church of

England, or—stern Huguenot heritage forbid—become a *Catholic*! She felt a vague uneasiness.

She left France with an improved reading ability in French and a moderate facility in speaking it. Languages would never be her forte. Now, back in England, she was able to pursue her best-loved study. She enrolled in the St. John's Wood School of Art. Since painting was within the category of acceptable pursuits for "nice" young women, and the school was just around the corner, in spite of its possible exposure to eligible young men, Father gave wholehearted encouragement.

"Now," she thought, "this uncertainty and restlessness that I've been feeling so long will go away. This is what I was really meant to do."

She plunged into the new activities, attending classes, roaming art galleries, splashing canvases with gorgeous sunset tints. She got up early to go out on the downs to catch the sun rising on the mists, in vain attempt to emulate Turner's "Sun Rising Through Vapour". In fact, Turner became her paragon. She revelled in the crimsons and golds of his Ulysses, his Venice, "city of rose and white, rising out of an emerald sea against a sky of sapphire blue". She obtained a permit to copy in the Tate Gallery, and when all the students had to submit an exhibit, she was awarded a few good marks.

"Of course," a fellow student disparaged, "she copies Turner in the Tate!"

Her joy was marred, not from the belittlement of her achievement but from loss of confidence in human nature. Why must they be so selfish? Like the girl in the big school where she and Stella had spent those tearful weeks. "But don't you pity *me*?" Her wail had resounded through the huge unheeding dormitory. And she, Evie, had been too immersed in her own suffering to listen. But she remembered now. She would always remember that cry. Was that perhaps what being "saved" really meant, not from some vague future punishment, but from *self*?

Evie was model as well as artist. Her classical patrician beauty appealed to the imagination of both students and teachers. One of the latter was a sculptor, and he persuaded her to sit for a head and shoulders. "You look sad," he told her with professional interest. Some of his comments were not so professional. If Father had heard the sweet nothings which escaped his lips, he would have terminated her artistic education then and there. But his daughter had learned discretion. She was naturally flattered, especially when her admirer sent the finished bust to Venice.

The uncertainty and restlessness increased rather than vanished. Colours on a canvas were dead, unchanging. Part of the glory of a sunset was in its constant mutations, its kaleidoscopic shiftings and blendings and crescendos. In spite of her intense interest in lessons depicting movement, subjects remained flat, static. Perhaps if she excelled in portrait painting, like one of her fellow students, Baker, instead of landscape . . . At least she would be working with human beings!

People. More and more she became conscious of them as she moved farther from the tight walls of childhood and adolescence: tortured, worried faces passed in the streets; hopeless eyes peering through windows in the drab slums around the chapel; most of all the vague shadows of millions in far lands who had never heard the gospel story. Missionaries came often to the chapel and later to the Harris home. One was Mrs. Booth, wife of a missionary to India, telling of the dire needs of women in the city of Madras, arousing even more turbulent restlessness. Evie was made a member of a committee to start a women's auxiliary, its purpose to send out a woman missionary to work in the Zenanas, those secluded quarters of Indian homes where no male except a member of family could enter. A young woman, Olive Elliott, applied, and the committee agreed on her appointment. As Evie sat looking at her, young, strong, glowing with dedication and assurance, uncertainty became almost intolerable. Oughtn't it to be she, Evie, who should have been chosen?

Back at her easel the brushes seemed like child's toys. Once she ventured to express the audacious idea to her friend Baker. "Did —did you ever think you would like to be a—a missionary?" she blurted.

The other girl did not seem surprised. "Yes, I've often thought so. In fact, I think I would if God hadn't given me this talent. I am sure he wants me to cultivate it. But of course this may not apply to you at all."

Evie envied her friend. She seemed so sure! Was it because she had more confidence in her ability? But Evie had no mean talent, especially in landscape. No, that wasn't the secret of the difference between them. Life would always be easier for the Bakers of this world. Their wishes could easily be interpreted as God's leading. They were like quiet streams flowing in clearly defined channels toward certain goals. While the Evies— ! She felt like a tumbling torrent, rushing, encountering obstacles, precipices, quicksands, driven relentlessly towards some God-given outlet for her energies, but never able to find it.

3

FATHER'S BENEVOLENT segregation of his daughters was unavailing. One after another eligible bachelors penetrated the protective shield and bore away a bride. It was part of the Victorian cultus for the oldest daughter to stay at home and care for her parents until she married. When Grace, the eldest, became the wife of a well-to-do farmer, Minnie assumed charge of the household. When she married and moved to Bristol, Lily took over her duties. But when Lily married a cousin, the order was interrupted. Rosa, the fifth and most brilliant daughter, became the wife of Richard Robbins, who from a boyhood of extreme poverty was to become, first a successful farmer, later founder and president of the Farmers' Union, finally rising to statesmanship under Asquith and Lloyd George, from which eminence he was to refuse a knighthood.

It was Eunice who stepped into the role of household head, and here the succession ended. Though austerely beautiful and given chances to marry, she refused them all. Gifted with a keen mathematical brain, a phenomenal memory which recorded unerringly the name, birthday, and age of every person on the family tree, and an intellectual curiosity which delved into such variants as astronomy and archaeology, in a later era she might have gone far in a profession. But she had only one desire, to look after her parents to the end of their lives.

Romance suddenly entered the house when an uncle who had settled in Brisbane, Australia, came to London for the Colonial Exhibition, bringing a collection of great opal matrix stones to exhibit—also his son, Charles Frazer. Father immediately added opals to his collective hobbies and filled a cabinet with them. But Charles was a greater attraction to his daughters than opals. They promptly lost their hearts to him. It was Florence, Florrie, on whom he fixed his eyes. When he left, it was with a promise to return as soon as he became established in business and claim his bride.

Evie shared with Florrie the tortures of three years of waiting. Empathy with her sister's unhappiness helped to ease her own frustration. But the three years passed and Charles returned. Though she would have scoffed incredulously at the idea, Evie in her bridesmaid's dress with its puffed sleeves, ruchings, frills, and voluminous tucked skirt, her big plumed hat which so becomingly framed the dark wings of hair and pure cameo-like features, attracted as many admiring glances as the bride. Then suddenly it was over, and Florrie was gone. Charlie and Bertie were both married and raising families. There were only four girls at home, competent Eunice, impetuous, emotional Hope, who sometimes shocked her staid sister by running and whistling, sweet, gentle Stella, and Evie.

Florrie's going left a vacuum which all the old restlessness rushed in to fill. Evie could find no remedy but activity. The pursuit of art seemed more and more a purposeless hobby. Only in one interest did she find partial satisfaction; dispensing charity. Like painting and embroidery, it was considered a proper function of "nice" young women. Even Father approved of his daughter's benevolent sallies into neighbouring slums. In fact, he had often taken them on such expeditions, led them up dingy stairways and through odorous passages, into rooms redolent of poverty, drunkenness, disease. Beside the Giving-away-box, Mother was leader of a society for the benefit of "fallen women". Layettes were made and loaned for a month to each unfortunate mother, who was expected to wash the clothes and bring them back. In spite of her distaste for such largesse (Horrible, giving away old things!) Evie mended ragged garments, collected donations, surreptitiously supplemented the cast-off articles from her own allowance, and poked determinedly into squalid mews and tenements and almshouses. For such expeditions she dressed as carefully as for a fashionable tea. It would have been patronage, she felt, not to look her best. Not until years afterward would it occur to her that the frills, laces, silks, and big flowered hats had been the most invidious forms of patronage.

"She looks lovely," she heard one little boy remark wistfully, "just as if she'd stepped out of a lovely garden."

She visited mission fields vicariously, hungrily absorbing the stories of missionaries returning from outposts in India and Africa, devouring every word of articles and annual reports. One, published early in 1910, was a booklet entitled "How the Gospel First Came to the Mountains of Death", its author a young missionary named Jesse Mann Brand.

She read it with burning fascination. She had heard of young Brand before, a member of the Guildford congregation who had gone out to India three years before. It told of a trip he and Mr. Morling, another missionary, had made up the Kolli Malai, a range of mountains in southern India, where there were tens of thousands of people who had never heard the Gospel.

In imagination she went with them, rising at three in the morning, loading the bullock carts, crossing the plains towards the misty forbidding heights where plainsmen dared not go, so deadly was the scourge of malaria; transferring the baggage to the heads of coolies, climbing, crawling, up, up, through a dense and tangled forest into a world which knew no roads, no vehicles, no beasts of burden; lodging in grain huts and cow sheds, visiting village after village of brown huts with steep thatched roofs; slowly winning the confidence of timid villagers, telling them the story of the great and kind Guru who hated sin but loved sinners, who gave sight to the blind and health to the sick, who blessed little children and wept with the sorrowing, and who finally vanquished death. The people, young Brand wrote, had listened eagerly.

"We believe your Yesu to be the only true Swami," three sober men had told him. "If you will stay with us and teach us, or if you will send others to do so, we will all become Christians."

"But before they can take this step," Evie's eyes remained glued to the words in italics, *"you must send them preachers and teachers. . . ."*

Her heart leaped. If only—! But of course it was impossible. Already she was thirty years old. And, anyway, Father would never consent. The silken threads of dependence, so lovingly woven, had become a strong net from which there was no escape. But she did escape, at least for a while.

4

THERE WERE CRISES in the family. Rosa, the brilliant, the lover of trees and flowers, died, leaving Richard Robbins with two young children. Mother suddenly looked thin and old, the ringlets whitening around her smooth cheeks. Father's step grew slower, his voice raised in family prayers or at chapel service as full of praise, but weaker. The net closed tighter and tighter. Then Florrie came home from Australia bringing her second child, two-year-old Ray, who had a birth mark which needed to be frozen. The journey had been torture because of her seasickness.

"You had better go back with her," Father told Evie. "She needs someone to help care for those two little boys."

The trip was a reprieve. Six weeks each way, six in Australia, three months when life ceased to remain static! It was a feast of beauty. Half the time she was running from one side of the ship to the other, trying to capture the colour on canvas—the snow-covered mountains of Crete, the palms and yellow sands of Egypt, blues of ocean and skies, crimsons and purples of sunsets. And somehow the closer proximity of those dark continents she had visualised, the sight of black glistening bodies swimming out to the ship, of dark-skinned coolies swarming over the decks with head-loads of coal, turned restlessness to hope. If she could get as close as this to them, who knew what miracle might happen!

"Thank you, thank you, God!" she exulted again and again.

But it was the journey back which changed her life. She had been put in the care of a godly couple, who introduced her to a young missionary working in Africa. He kept seeking her out, talking in glowing superlatives about the need for new workers in his mission, especially women who could relate to their dark-skinned sisters.

"Like yourself." He turned to her with intense eagerness. "I've sensed your dedication to the cause. Surely you would be happy to give your life to such a mission."

Under the glowing magnetism of his gaze her blood seemed to stop flowing, then rushed tumultuously to every part of her body. "Yes, oh, yes!" she responded.

The following days were filled with quivering expectation. She had not the least doubt that her prayers of many years were being answered. No matter that she felt little of the mysterious impact of romantic love as she had imagined it! That would come later. Eagerly she absorbed details of his life at his mission outpost, all the time waiting for the climactic moment which should determine her future. Surely he would soon propose marriage.

The moment came, one of rude awakening.

"After we reach England, I hope you will soon have an opportunity to meet my wife. She had to go home on furlough earlier, as you probably know. How happy she will be to know that she may have a companion and co-worker in the field!"

Evie spoke through stiff lips, surprised that any sound came out at all. "I—I would like to meet her. But—please don't get her hopes up until—until I've made up my mind. There are—many difficulties."

As soon as possible she fled to her stateroom, flung herself on the berth, and ground her face into the pillow. Oh—stupid, *stupid*! She pummelled the soundless words with her fists. What a silly little fool, mistaking the recruiting techniques of a devoted missionary, perfectly normal and legitimate, for those of courtship! Restored to partial calmness, she went to the woman into whose charge she had been given and told her the whole story. "My dear, I know just how you feel. I've been through such deep waters myself. And you weren't being stupid. It was a perfectly natural mistake."

"But—what shall I do! Oh, I'm so ashamed! How can I ever face him?"

"You can, my dear, and you will. We're given strength for such things."

Removing the vestiges of tears with cold packs, Evie brushed the soft wings of her brown hair until they shone, put on one of her gayest dresses, and went out to promenade the deck. No one suspected, certainly not the missionary, her shame and disappointment. But during the rest of the journey she did much thinking. Whether the result of this traumatic experience or the new sense of independence fostered by the trip, the Evelyn Constance Harris who returned to England was not the same person who had left it. She was no longer restless or undecided.

It had been autumn when she left Australia. Here it was July and summer. The family was away for its annual vacation, this year in the beautiful Lake District of northern England. She went from the ship almost directly to Keswick, where she had arranged to meet her sisters in the great tent where each July a big religious convention was held. Soon after her arrival in the tent, before meeting her sisters, an invitation to rise was given for all those who felt the call to missionary service.

The decision had already been made. Still she hesitated. Would her sisters be looking around curiously to see if she was there and standing? Probably. But she was not ready to have them know yet. Father must be told first. She stood, yes, but slipped behind a pillar. Back in London, she still temporised. Father was so glad to see her! "Don't go away again," he begged her. "Only four of my girls left now. I can't spare one of you."

Eagerly he showed her a new piece of Martin Ware, a big jar depicting fish swimming among rocks and seaweed. "It's exquisite!" she exclaimed rapturously. "You can actually feel yourself under water." She pored over the microscope, marvelling at the wonders of his new slides, especially the incredible complexity of colours in a butterfly's wing. Now that Rosa was gone, she was akin to him in nature as no other of his daughters. No, she could not tell him yet.

Not that there was any possibility of changing her mind. It would be India, of course. Most of her church's projects were there, and the country's needs had always fired her imagination. Was it pure coincidence that soon after her return a young missionary came to speak in the St. John's Wood chapel? In Evie's book there were no coincidences. All were God's leading.

Jesse Mann Brand. Only after he had begun to speak did the

31

name register in her memory. The man who had gone up into the hills! She listened with mounting excitement as he described his life in Sendamangalam, a town on the plains of southern India.

"The houses are poor and mean; the shops are few and ill-furnished with goods; the great temple car is unimpressive in its dusty decay. But living behind those dull grey walls are *men* and *women* to whom life is as full of interest as to any dweller in London. Children, too, are there in swarms. Day by day the engrossing drama of human existence is being played, sometimes comedy, sometimes tragedy. A missionary above all people must have eyes to see beneath the drab surface of things."

Though the speaker was unaware of her existence, his words seemed directed straight to her. Could you do this, he seemed to be asking, you, a pampered, clean, fashionably dressed city girl? Could you stand bodily contact with filth, disease, poverty, starvation, lice, open sores, dirty clutching fingers? *Yes*! she hurled back in silent defiance. With God's help I can do all those things.

Before going to the mission field in 1907 Jesse Brand had studied for a year at Livingstone College, taking the Missionary Medical Course. In his work in India this meagre medical knowledge had been taxed to the limit. He told of a terrible epidemic of plague which had broken out in his town, when hordes had fled in terror to field huts to avoid the danger. Contagion from the fatal disease was difficult to prevent, he explained, for the fleas on rats at their death would seek other hosts, often human beings. He had urged his workers to leave, but some had stayed with him. There had been cholera too, swift and deadly. All of these emergencies had kept him from pursuing that compelling urge which haunted all his other activities, to minister to those thousands on the Mountains of Death.

"We used to stand on the veranda of the mission house and wonder what lay beyond that long rugged skyline. Dark they were in the morning, silent, eloquent in their mystery, but gloriously crimson at the sun's setting. Who lived there? What sort were those few hill men we had seen, coming down early on a Sunday morning to change their bananas in the shandy for tobacco and salt and other goods?

"Then one day an old man staggered up and sank down on the veranda. His dress was different from that of the plains, a loin cloth tied with a string and a cloth thrown over his shoulders. He looked ill and spent. 'Where are you from?' I asked. He pointed up toward the mountains. He had been travelling two days, crawling down the hill and resting every quarter of a mile. He had heard about our medicine. We treated him for dysentery, and he went away. But from that moment we knew we had to accept the challenge. Finally we set out with some of our Indian workers and scaled the heights. The people fled from us in terror until suddenly this man came running toward us, crying, 'Why, it's the doctor!' The people returned. We gave them medicine and told them the good news of the Gospel. They begged us to come back and tell them more. But, as to Isaiah in his vision, God must be saying, 'Whom shall I send and who will go for us?' "

Evie felt faint with excitement. "Here I am!" she responded silently. "Send me!"

Later the young missionary came to the Harris house for tea. She longed to talk with him, ask him questions, tell him her plans. But something in his abounding male vitality, the black vigour of his thick wiry hair and big moustache, the dark intensity of his eyes, like glowing magnets, repelled her. To her embarrassment he seemed to be staring at her. She shrank back into the shadows, leaving her sisters to pass the plates of cakes and sandwiches.

5

FROM THAT DAY there was no further hesitation. The time had come. She must tell Father. It was the most rending experience of her life, far worse than the dismaying revelation on shipboard. She saw him age before her eyes.

"So—you say you want to be a missionary. You—really mean this, Daughter?"

"I really mean it, Father."

He sat down, heavily, as if his feet found the weight of him too much to bear.

"But—you're over thirty years old!"

"I know. It's taken me a long time to be sure. Now I know. It's what I was meant to do."

"But—my darling, *why*?"

"Because it's God's leading, Father. I want to serve him where I'm needed most."

"But—surely there are enough heathen right here in London! You don't need to go halfway around the world to find them! Haven't I always encouraged you in your work among the poor, supplied you with plenty of money for your charities? Haven't I—given you a nice comfy home, where you have every comfort—" He did not finish, but she knew what baffled helplessness lay behind the stricken eyes, unspoken. *Haven't I worked all these years, often beyond my strength, to keep you safe and happy here under my roof, and yet one by one all my daughters are leaving? Five gone already, Stella about to be married, and now you! Oh, I know I've brought you up to support missions, to pray and urge workers to go. But not you, not you!*

She stood before him, the embodiment of his dream for his daughters, beautiful, immaculate, well fed, presumably saved from every peril of time or eternity, and watched his dream slowly crumble. With a little cry she knelt beside him.

"But I don't want comfort, Father. There are plenty of Christians to work here in London. I want to go where there's no one to tell people about the love of Christ. Please, Father, please try to understand."

He understood—too well. It was his own stern creed of obedience to a higher Will that she was determined to follow. In this, as in other attributes, she was more like him than his other daughters. Still, he was unwilling to yield.

"I'm sending you to a doctor," he temporised. "If he advises that life in the tropics would be detrimental to your health, then I can't possibly give my consent."

His obvious hope proved unfounded. Evie was not nearly so fragile as the inhibiting female styles and manners seemed to indicate. She passed the test with flying colours. Perhaps Father also had been doing some deep soul-searching. He finally yielded to what he agreed must be God's leading. But he insisted on one means of self-gratification. He would be responsible for her full support on the mission field.

Mother was not so hard to persuade. She had never attempted to dictate the course of her children's lives. And her faith and devotion were profound. One whose Huguenot forebears had willingly swallowed ground glass rather than deny their Protestant convictions, would scarcely balk at the hazards of India's snakes and jungle fevers.

"Bless you, my dear. Of course if you have the call, you must go. I've seen this coming for years. I believe you are a true child of God."

The last obstacle fell when the Mission Board accepted her application. In order to take every precaution possible, she attempted to enroll in a course in homeopathy conducted for outgoing missionaries. At first Dr. Neatby, the instructor, refused her, thinking she was attempting to gain information without going abroad. When he discovered that she was planning to leave for India that same year, he was apologetic and cooperative.

"Come to the class by all means," he urged. "And feel free to watch me in the operating theatre as often as you like."

Events moved swiftly. Passage was booked on a ship to Bombay. To Father's relief she would not be sailing alone. A widow, Mrs. Elnaugh, was also going out as a missionary.

Poor Father! Not one more daughter was he to lose but two. Just before she sailed there was another wedding in the family, for Richard Robbins was marrying Stella, not so brilliant as his dead Rosa, but sweet and lovely in both person and disposition, a "perfect little star".

Evie, the beauty of the family, almost outshone the bride. The last time I'll be wearing plumes and silks and frills? she asked herself with the faintest tinge of regret, for she had always loved pretty clothes. Nonsense! She was not entering a nunnery. Though topee and cottons would undoubtedly take precedence in India, there would still be furloughs. While rejoicing in Stella's glowing happiness, she did feel genuine regret. This was a fulfilment that she would probably never have. For a moment she felt a fierce thrust of envy—but only for a moment. Husband, children, domesticity . . . they were treasures you were glad to resign when you had found the pearl of great price.

But, as it happened, it was not the last occasion for silks and frills. At the farewell party given her at the church she wore her usual festive finery, including a large lacy hat.

"She looks more like an actress than a missionary," someone was heard to remark with more amusement than censure.

It was the first time she had ever spoken at length in public, and words came haltingly. Her text was, "Let not him that girdeth on his armour boast as him that taketh it off". She told of going out on the Yorkshire moors to paint and watch the sun rise. "But for me this is an even brighter sunrise," she ended simply, "the beginning of a new day of service for my Master."

She had no idea how hard it would be to leave. It was she, not Mother, who shed bitter tears when she said goodbye to her at home. Mother was not well, and five years were a long time. It was a little easier leaving Father, with all the excitement of relatives and friends at the boat. She could not know, of course, that she would never see him again.

Two

"I will lift up mine eyes unto the hills. . ."

Psalm 121:1

1

INDIA! FOR SO many years remote and strange, it was suddenly as intimately real as the hills and glens of Hampstead Heath— more so, for now it was England, its fogs and cool rains and pale suns, that was remote and strange. *This* was reality: dust shimmering gold but stiffening hair and clogging pores; smells both pungent and sweet—jasmine, sweat, sandalwood, spices, urine, cow dung smoke; cacophony of sounds—clatter of carts, wails of hawkers, pounding of drums, raucous cawing of crows; colours so sharp and clear they made her eyes smart and her artist's fingers itch; *people*. An excursion through the streets of Madras in a ricksha or on foot through the choking traffic of a bazaar made Piccadilly at rush hour seem like an orderly assembly of high churchmen.

It was almost like coming home, with Mr. and Mrs. Booth meeting her in Madras, taking her to the big, high-ceilinged mission bungalow where Olive Elliott, long her beloved model and idol, welcomed her like a sister. She responded to the new environment like a racehorse to the starting gun. Life up to now had been an impatient marking of time. She was a new person.

She could hardly wait for the new business of living to begin. All these human masses to be saved from ignorance, disease, hunger, spiritual darkness, and so few to do it! But she had to wait. Before entering paradise, it seemed, a new missionary must endure the purgatory fires of language study.

It was Miss Boscomb's school and Mademoiselle all over again, complete with the impending horror of examinations. Only Tamil was to French as calculus is to arithmetic. Beside its intricacies of number and gender the irregular mazes of *avoir* and *aller* and *être* had been child's play. Mr. Booth was a kind but rigid disciplinarian. He roused the new recruits even before the crows began their pre-dawn serenade. John Pillai, the *munshi* who was their teacher, was fully as hard a taskmaster as Mademoiselle, if less intimidating. One of his crafty techniques was passing from one bungalow to another where his students were sweating over conjugations and declensions and taunting different ones with their slow progress, reporting other newcomers' quick understanding and early glibness in the language.

"*Ayoh*! *Pavum*, a pity if you could not the first examination take on time! But I fear—" The skull-capped head moved sideward in that peculiar motion which looked negative but turned out to be affirmative—"*amma*, yes, I fear—"

As tension mounted, so did the heat. Mr. Booth was wise to rouse them before dawn when the temperature might be low in the nineties. By noon it would have soared into the hundreds. If one rested perspiring hands on the table while studying, little pools would form beneath them. The reed tatties at the doors, sprayed with water by the coolies, dried almost as soon as the hot breeze touched them. Clothes, especially the long-sleeved, full-skirted varieties in vogue for Europeans, became steaming compresses. Palm-leaf fans and swaying punkahs merely redistributed the heat. During siesta even breathing made one sweat, and the mosquito net cages into which one crawled at night were like smothering cocoons.

But, thanks to the guidance of the Booths, Evie slowly adjusted to both the strenuous study and the climate. With Olive and her Bible women she made occasional visits to *zenana* homes in the city, contacts which made her all the more impatient to be at work. Yet, even more unsettling was the presence of young Jesse Brand.

She had not expected to find him in Madras. His previous appointment had been in Sendamangalam, a town several hundred miles to the south-west. He was here in Madras to take over the work of Mr. Booth, who was soon to go on furlough. Meanwhile, he was taking courses in medicine in Madras University, in preparation for the full medical course which he hoped to take later in England. Not until after his return to India had he learned of his qualification for matriculation.

Repelling? Frightening in his dark intensity? How could she ever have thought him so! The dark eyes twinkled. Beneath the vigorous moustache the lips could flash the most appealing smile. And when the group met at the dinner table he was invariably the life of the party.

"I thought you'd be coming," he told her one day. "I could see it in your face the day I spoke in your chapel, the way it lit up when I talked about the hill people. I could tell you were hearing the call. Then when I told more about the work in your father's house, I felt I was talking straight to you."

"Yes—oh, yes!" So that was why he had seemed to stare at her. She told him then, eagerly, what she and Mrs. Elnaugh had been discussing. Why couldn't they, two women, go and work in the hills? They could live together and go into the villages and teach the children and help the women find better ways of living and perhaps slowly win them to Christ . . . She stopped, embarrassed, fearing from his quizzical expression that he might be laughing at her. Presumptuous, of course, for a brand new missionary to dream of facing such a challenge!

But he was not laughing. His dark eyes turned luminous and keenly appraising. Yes, it might indeed be possible. But it would take more strength of body and spirit than most women possessed, and a willingness to live in stark simplicity. No luxuries or furbelows on the hills! (Evie flushed. Was he remembering the flowered hat, the frilled dress?) And—the eyes twinkled—it would take a good working knowledge of Tamil.

Tamil! It was her Nemesis. She despaired of conquering its elementals, much less of speaking it fluently. Jesse had been a brilliant Tamil student. After five years in India he could speak the language like a native, not just book Tamil, but the vernacular. Listening to one of his eloquent and earnest sermons, of which she could not understand a word, she felt even more despairing.

"You'll learn," he comforted, "not from books but by using it, as I did. When I went to Sendamangalam in 1909 I *had* to learn. We opened a dispensary. Soon we were crowded every day. Try to do medical work without an interpreter, and you *have* to learn the language! But you make plenty of mistakes. One day a woman came to the dispensary and asked for medicine for a sore throat. Her throat looked perfectly all right. 'Are you sure it's a sore throat?' I persisted. She replied in a flood of Tamil. I was sure I'd heard the words 'sore throat' over and over. I mixed some medicine. She seemed unwilling to drink it but finally did. Afterwards I learned that the sore throat belonged to her baby at home."

Evie's fascination for the hills soon forged a bond between herself and Jesse. He assisted with her language study. He confided to her his hopes, that after returning from England a fully fledged doctor he might be appointed full-time to the mountains of Salem District. They discovered other communities of interest. In his love of nature, concern for all living things, joyous and unwavering dedication, Jesse was amazingly like her father. Not until she overheard a certain conversation—by accident, or had they intended her to hear?—did she realise how deeply her emotions had become involved. She learned from words exchanged between

Mrs. Booth and Olive Elliott that Jesse was engaged to a young woman in England who was deeply committed to the cause of missions, that his marriage was contemplated for the near future—in fact, that he had even sent her the silk for her wedding dress!

Evie fled to her room. Not daring to fling herself on the bed for fear that someone might find her, she shut herself in the cement cubicle of a bathroom, poured water from the earthen jug into a basin, and with shaking hands sloshed it over her face. Tepid though it was, it felt cool against her hot cheeks. Oh, again she had played the fool! Only this time it wasn't her pride that was hurt. Realisation had come suddenly, blindingly, with the words she had overheard. She had let herself fall hopelessly in love with Jesse Brand, and he belonged to another. He would go back to England and return here with his bride, and she would not, could not, face the prospect. She would give up being a missionary, go home . . . Of course, she would do no such thing. She had not come to India to seek her own happiness. Her life belonged, not to Jesse Brand, or to any other human being, but to Another.

In the following days she felt like the sere earth growing ever more parched in the mounting heat. Dust thickened. Grass became a hard brown crust. Leaves either fell or were coated with grey film. Yet out of this death flowers and trees burst into the most glorious bloom. Sprays of pink cassia shaded from pale peach to bright coral. Silvery-white cork blossoms, delicately tinted with rose or yellow, drooped like bells from every branchlet. The *gul mohrs* became bowers of crimson and orange. Laburnums were rich with streaming gold. The jacarandas made one's breath catch with their heavenly blue-mauve clusters. And in the gardens jasmine and roses of every hue and waxy yellow blooms of allamanda vied with the pinks and Chinese reds of huge hibiscus. Try as she would, she could not capture the magic of colour with her brush.

"Let me be like that, Lord," she prayed, "flowering best when life seems most dry and dead."

2

It was a relief to escape to Coonoor in the Nilgiri Hills. Here, several thousand feet above the burning plains, it was heavenly cool, and the vistas of blue-green-purple mountains were balm to a jaded spirit. Again she could take deep breaths, tramp steep narrow paths until her legs ached and she was ready for refreshing sleep. She could even snatch a few minutes to paint a glorious sunset. Best of all, she could find her own quiet place for solitude and prayer on what seemed the threshold of heaven.

"This is where I belong," she avowed with thanksgiving and hope, "not down there on the plains, but up here where there's room to stretch and breathe."

There was language study here, too, for new missionaries of many denominations came to the hills for study during the hot season. Evie lived in a boarding house run by a Miss Stubbs, a kind competent person who provided motherly hospitality. Both the welcome coolness and a more relaxed and less demanding *munshi* made conquest of the hard subject seem more attainable. But it was neither of these factors which suddenly made every day a bright and shining harbinger of hope. It was the letters from Jesse Brand.

At first they seemed just friendly and impersonal, filled with news of the Mission and his work as Mr. Booth's substitute. In spite of his heavy schedule, which included being mission treasurer, he was finding time for his beloved reading. He had found a fascinating book on electronics, which he was alternating with Gibbon's *Roman Empire* and Wesley's *Journal*. His plans were changing. So strongly did he feel the call of the hills that he had decided to give up further medical study. If the mission board agreed, he would begin work there as soon as the Booths returned from furlough.

The letters did not remain impersonal. Phrases of intimacy soon crept in. Would she please have her picture taken and send it to him? There followed terms of endearment. *My darling . . . precious one . . .* She would read the words with flaming cheeks, then rush to her secret place of communion to give incredulous thanks. The world became almost too beautiful to bear. He loved her, he wanted her to become his wife. Their letters sped back and forth full of promises, plans, sweet commitments, all the wonder and ecstasy of new-discovered love.

There would be difficulties. Mission boards were rigid in their rulings. And there was the girl back in England. But Mrs. Booth had said she was not strong physically and might find it difficult to be a missionary's wife, especially in the wildness of southern India's mountains! When Mrs. Elnaugh was obliged to return home in September because of illness, so that it would have been impossible for Evie to work in the hills alone, she was more than ever humble and grateful. How wonderful the ways of God! He could take the failure of human plans and turn them into greater blessings.

Then came near disaster. An epidemic of typhoid swept over Coonoor. There was panic among Miss Stubb's guests. Some threatened to leave if more cases developed. Dependent on this seasonal patronage, Miss Stubbs kept anxious watch over her charges, wondering who the next victim might be.

"It's I," feared Evie as the tell-tale symptoms of fever and headache became apparent. Stubbornly she kept on as usual, shading her eyes with her hand when her throbbing head made lessons almost impossible. Suspicious, Miss Stubbs persuaded her to see a doctor, but surprisingly he found no evidence of fever. "She's just nervous," was his cheerful verdict. It was arranged that she should go to Brooklands, a big holiday house for missionaries, for a period of rest. But once there, she grew steadily worse. When it was discovered that her temperature was 102° she was bundled off to the Coonoor Government Hospital, where she was put in a bare room with an inefficient nurse who snored so loudly that it made sleep impossible. But she was so sick that nothing really mattered, even the daily letters from Jesse which she could neither read nor answer. For days she wandered in a limbo of fever and suffering, indifferent to life or death . . . until suddenly a familiar voice drew her back to reality. Her beloved Olive had come from Madras to nurse her.

Slowly then she struggled up out of the shadows. Life again became precious, worth fighting for. But the starvation diet prescribed for typhoid patients had left her so weak that she was unable even to sit up. Olive had to read her Jesse's daily letters and write answers at her dictation. They became as close as sisters. For the first time she was able to share the intimate confidences of a woman in love.

Jesse's letters were filled with exciting news. In March of that year, 1912, he had been appointed to Vazhavanthi, the mountain site where he planned to establish his mission, forty miles from the nearest railway, ten from the nearest village bazaar. In all the range of hills there was not a single road, shop, police station, artisan, or trader.

"And the thought of going so far away doesn't frighten you?" probed Olive, remembering the daintily dressed and beflowered committee member back in London.

"Oh—no!" Evie's thin face glowed. "All those people, at least 20,000 Jesse says, who have never heard the Gospel! I would gladly have gone alone, but—with Jesse! Where could one get closer to heaven?"

Back in Madras in the beginning of 1913, painfully thin but with an enhanced delicacy of beauty (or so Jesse Brand thought), she plunged into language study with desperate urgency. It was a triumphant milestone passed when, visiting the *zenanas* with Olive, she could stumblingly tell the story of the lost sheep in Tamil. Already Jesse was on the hills, camping in a mud and thatch hut built by him and Mr. Morling. His medical training was helping him meet the wary and suspicious people. So thrilled was his first dental patient with the ease with which Jesse had relieved him of an aching tooth, that he searched successfully for two more offending candidates for extraction!

While Evie struggled with Tamil idioms and soaring heat in Madras, Jesse laid the foundations for their married life on the hills. The framing of their simple house was done in Sendamangalam, the sections of teakwood carried up the tortuous paths on the heads of coolies. Six Indian carpenters were hired on the plains to assist in the building, but before the walls were boarded in, the floor laid, or the roof of bamboo and thatch set on its supports of jungle wood trusses, four of the six, fearful of the deadly fever haunting those "mountains of death", deserted. Another soon followed. The one remaining was only a boy, but he worked with a will, and for ten days or more he and Jesse plied hammer and saw together.

In June at Kotagiri Evie took her examination in Tamil conducted by the South Indian Missionary Association. In spite of the bracing coolness of the hill station, a blessed contrast to the 110 degree temperature of Madras, she endured the two-day ordeal with hot discomfort and sweating fingers. The mission board was strict. Consent to her marriage and hill assignment might well be reconsidered if she proved too stupid to talk to a villager in his own language. Of course she did not hope to pass "with distinction", as Jesse had done. If only she could just pass! One by one she struggled through the assignments—vernacular into English, English into vernacular, grammar, reading, conversation . . . Four days later came the verdict. She tore open the envelope with trembling fingers. She had received 373 marks out of a possible 600, 300 being necessary. She had passed!

3

SHE FIRST SAW the Kolli mountains in August when she went for her wedding to Sendamangalam. There they were, the substance of all her dreams and hopes, dark purple against the rising sun, a pale misty blue line at midday, at sunset a

45

splendour of golds and crimsons which was surely the threshold of heaven.

The wedding was a real *tamasha*, a festive Indian occasion. Evie was amazed and humbled by the crowds of people showing their love and appreciation of Jesse's work, especially for his tireless service during recent epidemics of bubonic plague and cholera. The little chapel swarmed with grateful patients. She was so weighed down with garlands that more than one load had to be removed to make way for another. After a late wedding breakfast with a cake served by the Morlings, she and Jesse set off for their new home in the mountains. They wanted no other honeymoon. The first five miles to the foot of the hills they rode in a *jutka*, a small reed-canopied wagon drawn by a pony.

"I've hired two *dholies*," Jesse told his bride with satisfaction, "so we'll have a real wedding procession."

But as the cart lumbered over the rough roads and at last reached the bottom of the hills, a strange silence greeted them. The *dholies* were there, yes, two rough hammocks of canvas fastened in a rectangle of bamboo poles lashed together with ropes. But where were the crowds of coolies to carry them and their baggage? An anxious Sahib hurried up to Jesse. "So sorry. Everything was ready as we agreed. But you will have to delay a little. They have all gone off to hunt a wild pig!"

Jesse was very much upset. He had wanted everything to be just right. "Sit here in the shade of this big tree," he told Evie. "It's the gathering place for all the hill coolies. I'll try to find them."

Leaving his bride to guard the baggage, he set off into the bushes in one direction while the Sahib went in another. They could find only four in addition to those needed for the baggage. It was nearly four o'clock when they were ready to start. Monsoon clouds were gathering, thunder rumbling. Jesse looked anxiously at his bride. "We could still go back and start up tomorrow."

Evie stoutly refused. The *dholi* was placed flat on the ground, and she sat on it, feet firm against the front crosspiece of bamboo, upraised knees tented by her white wedding dress. Grunting, the coolies lifted the unwieldy frame, fitted their shoulders into the angles of the poles, and jogged away, anxious to get as far as possible up the steep path before dark, anticipating also the coolness of the higher elevations. Their smooth brown bodies, clad only in loin cloths, were soon glistening with sweat. Tensed by the unaccustomed rolling motion, hands clutching the bamboo sides for security, Evie felt her white dress wilting, the neatly parted hair under its confining ribbon becoming more and more stringy and sodden. It was a relief to feel the first gentle drops of rain against her hot arms and cheeks.

"We're climbing fast now," Jesse assured her. "You'll soon find it more comfortable."

Comfortable? She clutched the poles harder as the coolies started up a rocky slope, twisting and grinding her between them as they tried to walk tandem on the narrow path; relaxed with relief at the top, then stared aghast at an equally steep path leading down on the other side.

"Isn't it wonderful, darling!" exclaimed the exuberant Jesse, breathing deeply of the rapidly clarifying mountain air.

"Wonderful," she echoed faintly.

Trying hard to relax, she yielded herself to the proven skill of the coolies, tilting forwards or backwards or to the side with instinctive counter-balance, even becoming indifferent to the thorns clutching at her dress. After all, what use for a wedding gown on the top of a mountain? Then the heavens opened in a drenching deluge. The *dholi*, laced with stout canvas, became a tub, the torn dress a sodden tangle.

"Are you all right?" Jesse asked anxiously.

"Fine," she replied. "I was needing a bath." She tried to control her shivering. Nobody had suggested that she might need warm clothes. It had been so hot on the plains that she had thought the wedding dress would be enough. Finally, when the rain showed no sign of abating, she left the *dholi* and walked along the path beside Jesse, his hand guiding her firmly over the rough narrow trail. Sometimes the long rank grass of the jungle tangled about her feet. Thorns pulled at her skirt. The low branches of overhanging trees reached down clammy hands, slapping her cheeks and blinding her eyes. But she pushed on. It was dark long before they reached their destination. Finally the ups and down levelled off. There was a smell of green grass and cultivated earth and—could it be fruit blossoms? When she put her foot down, it sank deep into mud and water.

"Almost there," Jesse said. "Here we are at the rice fields." The caravan stopped and he shouted. There was no moon, even though the rain had ceased, and they seemed enclosed in a vast sheath of darkness. It was impossible to go on, for the narrow path between the flooded rice fields was invisible in the gloom. Jesse shouted at the top of his voice the name of a hill man, and the sound echoed strangely around the hilltops. Silence. Again he shouted, and presently on the slope the other side of the valley a twinkling light appeared, came flickering down the hillside and across the wetlands where they stood waiting. Taking her arm, Jesse tried to guide her along the high narrow raised pathways

47

which edged the rice fields. Soon she would become as adept at the technique as an athlete on a tightrope, but now her feet slipped often into the muddy ooze. Then there was firm ground beneath her feet. In the wake of the little hurricane lantern she moved steadily up a hill, the arm of her new husband firm about her shoulders. Shivering, wet to the skin, she walked towards the dark rectangle of a doorway.

"Life is not going to be easy," she thought with candid appraisal. "It's good all this happened. I may as well know it now."

But she had not come here for an easy time. She had come for love of God, and of these hill people, and of the man whose strong arms were now lifting and carrying her over the threshold.

Three

"They came to the Delectable Mountain."

Pilgrim's Progress, **Part I**

1

TRUST AND TRIUMPH

JESSE HAD SEEN the words on a motto during the days when she had been so desperately sick in the Nilgiris, and they had lifted him from despondency to hope. He had had them engraved inside her wedding ring. Now Evelyn Brand fashioned the letters with eucalyptus leaves, fastened them on a board, varnished the whole, and hung it on the wall of their new house. It would become the guiding theme of her life for the next sixty years.

If love could crown the trust with triumph, she had it in abundance: for the vigorous young enthusiast who shared her commitment to these clear clean mountains whose heavenly colours she was constantly trying to capture with paint and brushes; especially for the people living in the villages of round mud and thatch huts scattered in clusters for miles around. Surely if one loved them enough, they could be made to understand and accept quickly the message of divine love.

On their wedding night Jesse had given her a notebook, its pages blank. "Evie's and my Prayer Book" he had inscribed as its title. They would write in it each day the things they were most thankful for, their deepest longings, the answers to their prayers. The first few pages expressed all the joyous hopes of their new sweet fellowship.

"28th August 1913. Thanksgiving for God's word and promises . . . Petition for God's blessing on our married life, especially that others may learn of Jesus by our words and actions . . ."

"29th August. Thanksgiving for having been called to this great and wonderful work . . ."

"2nd September. Praise for this first week together of married life, for the fuller insight it has given us of His will . . ."

She could hardly wait to get started on the camping trips which they had long been planning.

"Not yet." The more practical Jesse was firm. First the house must be made tight for the winds and rains of the monsoons. As yet only the framework and outer walls and roof were finished. Immediately he began lining the walls with match-boarding.

It was a small, simple house. The hill people would have been misled by any display of wealth or luxury. But Jesse had built with an almost uncanny knowledge of possible hazards. It sat two feet off the ground on sturdy stone posts, which the ubiquitous white ants could not penetrate. If they did manage to climb up beside the stone, at the top they would find inverted plates of metal, like frying pans—in fact, they *were* frying pans—which were sure deterrents. The wooden steps were set away from the door for the same reason. In such features it was a little like an Australian country house, built on stone posts to cope with similar hazards. Evie tried to curb her impatience by painting water-colours of her new home.

Then one day as she sat on the hill slope she heard bells, soft and tinkling like her own wedding bells, and she followed the sound to a nearby field, where she found a little cowherd tending his herd. He was pitifully thin and ragged. Sitting beside him on the grass, she tried to talk to him in her stumbling Tamil, telling him the story of Jesus. Eyes wide, he struggled to understand. Day after day they met on the hillside and became friends. Worried over his thin little body and lack of clothing, for it could be cold on the hills at night, she gave him a small blanket. Finally she was able to teach him a little prayer in Tamil: "Forgive my sins, Lord, and make me your child." Then all at once he disappeared. His family, who lived in the nearby village, had sent him away because he had inherited some land and they wanted to take it. It would be weeks before she saw him again. He had been brought back to his village, dying of pneumonia, so that his land could be assured to his uncle. She would lean over him in the rough shed where he lay, shocked and pitying. Did he remember the words she had taught him? *Amma*, yes. "Forgive—sins," he whispered the Tamil words, gasping for breath. "Make me—your child, Lord." As long as she lived, the sound of a soft tinkling bell would make her remember and almost bring tears to her eyes. Their first little convert, she called him. It was well she could not know that six long years would pass before they could claim another.

Once the walls were tight, even though the house was far from finished, they began their work, walking to nearby villages, riding on horseback to those farther away. In some, which Jesse and Mr. Morling had visited, they were received eagerly, Jesse's skills with medicines and astonishing words having already gone before him. In others more distant the people fled at their coming, and though they were soon accorded a wary welcome, they were allowed to enter no farther into homes than the stone verandas.

Soon they were able to start camping, spending ten days or more in one area. "Now," Jesse exulted, "we can really get to know the people, live among them." Hopes were high. Everywhere they went crowds gathered and listened gladly, hungrily it seemed, to the story of the loving Swami who had gone about helping and healing people and wanted them to become his followers—a far cry from their devil-swamis who inhabited queer-shaped stones, dead trees, darkness, caves, the tiny little shrines which were nothing but a few iron spikes stuck in the ground or a lump of stone covered with red stain and oil. For the hill people were Animists, their world teeming with frightening deities who must be placated with spells and incantations and libations of the blood of pigs.

Camping on the Kollis was a curious procedure. No tents, no camp cots, no vehicles for travelling. They took only the barest necessities. A box strung on a bamboo pole and carried by two men contained all the food—tinned meat and fish, tinned milk and butter, a little bag of flour, a tin of coffee, plenty of rice. They travelled in a long procession—a dozen or so coolies, each with a burden on his head, perhaps a roll of blankets, and in his hands other articles, such as a kettle or lantern or frying pan. Then came the mare, a sorry beast but the best Jesse had been able to buy, led by the Indian cook with all the pride of a wild-beast-showman revelling in the stares of amazed villagers, most of whom had never seen a horse. Next came the Indian preacher, Daniel, whom Jesse had brought up from the plains. Last came Jesse on foot and Evie, mounted on an equally nondescript specimen of horseflesh.

"Please send me a lady's sidesaddle," she wrote Winifred Booth in Madras.

"But, my dear," replied the missionary's wife, who knew that Evie was expecting a child, "surely you shouldn't be riding horseback over those wild hills!"

Evie chuckled. Mrs. Booth should see her noble steed, also the man following the beast with an empty kerosene can on which he had to drum to move the decrepit animal to a walking pace!

Their first camp was at Kulivalavu, an incredibly beautiful valley overhung by great purple cliffs. There was a small forest bungalow built by the government for the use of Forest Conservation, one side of the house levelled by wind and rain but with a single room intact. They stayed there five days, visiting villages, preaching and tending the sick. One man was so impressed that he boldly rubbed off the ritual ash from his forehead. They moved on through thick forests and undulating valleys, camping in field sheds and empty grain huts. While Jesse treated the sick, Evie would gather the women about her and try to teach them. So accustomed was she now to their manner of dress—simple headdress fastened at the neck, white cloth wrapped above the breast and falling to the feet—that her own dress of cotton challis seemed almost as strange to her as to them.

People listened, yes, but that was all. With each camp the first high hopes gave way to disappointment and frustration. "Never," they had been warned, "will a Kolli hill man break caste and follow your way. It has never happened, and it never will."

2

THEIR SON WAS born on 17th July, 1914 at Ootacamond, another of the hill stations in the Nilgiris, over a hundred miles from the Kollis, Jesse pacing up and down in the garden outside. There was no doctor, but Miss Butcher, head of the nursing home, was very capable. They named the baby Paul Wilson Brand. Long before his birth they had dedicated him to God's service. They did so once more before Jesse rushed back to the Kollis to prepare the house for his increased family.

Changes had to be made. The beautiful thick thatch roof was not only a breeding place for rats, snakes, and other vermin but also a dangerous fire hazard, as the hill people often came for medical help at night with their flaming torches of tightly bunched straw. One flying spark, and the little wooden house would have exploded into flame. He replaced the thatch with corrugated iron, noisy as a kettledrum in the monsoons but far safer. The plain board shutters, letting in drenching clouds of mist when opened and shutting out light when closed, must be changed for plain glass casements. And they needed a weather-tight bathroom of corrugated iron instead of the present one of interlaced twigs lined with bamboo sticks. A fire could then be made on the stone floor so that, returning drenched at night in the monsoons, they could dry themselves before going to bed. Jesse completed most of the work before returning for Evie and the baby.

For the new mother it was a gruelling trip. Down to the plains by carriage, rail to the nearest railway station, then thirty miles by bullock cart to the out-of-the-way town of Sendamangalam. They left the station at midnight. In spite of Jesse's efforts to make her comfortable, the jolting of the springless cart was torture. They had to stop for a time until her pain lessened, as always in such an exigency resorting to prayer. Pain was not the only torment. The night was pitch black. There had been robbers about. Once a light was flashed into the cart, and they were warned by a friendly stranger not to go on. But Jesse was not easily intimidated. It was midday before they found comfort and safety in the Morlings' bungalow at Sendamangalam. A day's rest, then a bullock cart again to the foot of the mountains, and a *dholi* up the rough steep mountain trail, rocking and bouncing the new mother and child like an uneasy cradle.

Blessed to be home again! The daily notations in the notebook were all of jubilant thanksgiving. *Stottherum*, praise! This, her favourite Tamil word, was on Evie's lips a hundred times a day.

The baby accomplished what months of words and deeds had failed to do. At last the hill women accepted her as one of themselves. She had delivered a man-child, a mark of divine favour. Their common motherhood surmounted differences of dress, culture, colour. They crowded around the baby, admiring, fondling, mirthfully comparing his white skin with the darkness of their own offspring. Many came long distances to watch her nurse him, for they had been told that foreign babies would feed only from a bottle. Teaching, even in her imperfect Tamil, was easier with the baby in her arms.

"See! Water boil over fire, not make baby sick. Put to sleep under net, cloth with holes. *Kosu*, mosquito, not good. Fever make hot. *Pavum*, bad!"

And as he grew little Paul developed his own techniques of appeal, adjusting to the hill life with the zest of a healthy young mountain goat. The delight of the women knew no bounds when his first spoken word sounded like the Tamil *Akka*, big sister. He loved the camping trips. In those early days camp shelters were usually grain huts and field sheds, thatched and doorless, and he came to associate all thatch with such joyous camping expeditions. "Comp, comp!" he would crow at first sight of a roof of overhanging straw.

Evie's love and concern for the hill women became agonised yearning. They needed so much more than clean water and mosquito nets! She saw the terrified eyes of a mother creeping to

55

make offerings at the hideous little shrines of the smallpox goddess; the desperation of a young wife whose husband had sold her for a good price; the tragedy of a mature girl married to a mere child and forced to bear children to him by any man available.

"I heard you had a marriage here today," she said once to a villager. "Where is the bridegroom?" He pointed to a child, perhaps two years old, in his arms. "And where is the bride?"

A young woman sat in the doorway. "There she is."

On another occasion a proud father came to Jesse from the nearby village. "My son has a little child born."

"How can that be?" asked Jesse. "Your son is just a little cowherd."

"That is true, but he married a big girl. We brought a man into the house for her, and she has borne my son's first child."

Once, it was said, the hill people had had a high standard of monogamy, but family life had degenerated, due largely to the need for agricultural workers. More sons had been needed to till the fields, and to procure them the old customs had been set aside. If a man had much land, he would take more than one wife. He might marry his little son to a grown girl so she might come and work on his farm. Then for her the family would take a *vaisi*, a "kept man", so that he also could work the land. So the evil had spread and venereal disease had become rife.

It was the women who suffered most, and Evelyn's heart bled for them. How they needed the transforming power of Christ and his saving Gospel! Yet months lengthened into years, and still they made no convert.

3

Six years! They began with such hope and expectation, for the people listened so eagerly! It was the *poosaris*, priests, who thwarted every trend of the hill people to become Christian.

One of the most powerful of these was their near neighbour. At first, when Jesse had been building the house, this *poosari* had been his friend, letting him live for months in his shed, waiting on him, bringing him water and firewood when his helper fell ill with fever. Then slowly he came to understand the reason for the missionary's presence. He saw crowds coming for medical treatment, some remaining for days. He heard the teaching, noted the intense interest of the listeners. He was a popular priest, much in demand all over the Kolli Hills for his service in swami-worship, in treating sickness, in conducting rituals against devil possession, all of which commanded high fees. And when he discovered what belief in the Yesu-swami would do to his people, demanding their rejection of the old gods and eventually depriving him of his prerogatives, he began subtly but with deadly purpose to undermine their work.

They planned to open a school. The people were eager. One man loaned a field shed. The date of opening was decided. The people were asked to send their children. The great day arrived. Jesse took a little boy's hand, and they set out for the shed. They found it empty. No amount of persuasion could bring the children. Patients were lured away. Prospective converts were warned of the anger of Nachi, Pidari, Karuppan, or one of the other deities. And indeed misfortune often did visit the enquirer. His cattle died, his wife disappeared, or some strange malady attacked him or his relatives. Asked permission by a tribesman to worship the Christian God, the *poosari* would promise to consult the swamis. After much chanting and swaying the answer would come.

"Yes. Worship this Yesu-swami if you choose, but you must worship the other swamis also."

However, he could not discredit Jesse's increasing fame as a "doctor". The white man's seeming miracles of healing were bruited far and wide. One early case challenged all his skill. A man was hurrying through the jungle with his young wife in the late afternoon when a bear rushed out of the woods and attacked the woman. Running to her rescue, the man was felled by the bear, his leg laid open with a blow from the beast's claw, his arm broken, wrist dislocated, and scalp torn from ear to ear. He would have been killed had not his wife, a frail, timid-looking girl approaching motherhood, come to his rescue. With no weapon, not even a stick, she pushed at the beast until it ran off into the woods.

Evie nearly fainted with horror when the man was brought to them the next day. But Jesse calmly faced the challenge. For hours he stitched away carefully, gently drawing the torn scalp together over the shining skull. The leg wound had become badly infected through the long exposure. The patient had to remain nearby for further treatment. What an opportunity to tell him again and again the story of Jesus! But as yet they had no place for an in-patient to stay. Helpfully the *poosari* volunteered the use of his grain shed, so near their compound. Helpfully? No, for immediately the attitude of the patient changed. He listened to

57

the Gospel talks with indifference, then with obvious fear. Whenever Jesse talked of religion, he simulated pain and began to groan. He averted his face from pictures of the life of Christ. The *poosari* had so frightened him that he feared he would be bewitched. But he recovered, and Jesse's reputation as a doctor was still further enhanced. People began coming, not only from all over the hills, but even from the plains.

The *poosari* grew desperate. He turned his own little grain shed close by into a "hospital" where he could give competition, enticing patients with threats and promises. For a few rupees he would make a small ring of cow dung and plants over which he would intone his *mantrams* and work his spells, invoking evil spirits to cast out demons of sickness or wreak vengeance on those who visited the foreign usurper. In the little notebook for praise and prayer he was often included in their petitions.

"Praise for help in surgical cases (two cysts taken out successfully and one difficult tooth extraction)..."

"Prayer for the *poosari* and for all who oppose our work..."

"Praise for our deepening love . . . For the lovely scenery surrounding our home . . . for news of a horse . . . For Evie's progress in Tamil . . . For a weather-tight house in all this rain and wind . . . For chicken house completed . . . For eggs, milk, butter, and all that we need for body and soul..."

"Prayer for medicine to take effect on rheumatic girl . . . for recovering of the cow . . . for more vigorous faith and triumphant lives..."

"Lord, convert *poosari*, or remove him from spoiling Thy word!"

The *poosari* might prevent his people from accepting the white man's religion—and did—but not the white man's medicines. In one year the Brands treated 1500 patients. Though he had had only a year's training in tropical medicine, Jesse's success in treating ailments was phenomenal. Wherever he went he took his bag of simple medicines and instruments, which were constantly in demand, especially his forceps for extracting teeth. To the hill people he seemed a miracle worker. His magic could banish the *kirumi poochie*, small thread worm, and the *naga poochie*, big round worm, which caused such agony in the bowels. His pills eased the torture of malaria, prime curse of their Mountains of Death. He could wind up a yard-long guinea worm bit by bit, an inch or so each day, so it would not cause an abscess, and if they did what he told them, kept their feet out of water and cleaned up their wells, they could banish guinea worm altogether.

Evie also had had her year of training and, though she favoured the homeopathic methods rather than the more generally accepted types of treatment, the two worked in perfect harmony. Indeed, Jesse sometimes turned some of his most hopeless cases over to her, having found that her simpler drugless treatments, plus the sheer persistence of her intense faith and will power, often succeeded where more conventional methods failed.

To Evie the unfolding revelations of her beloved husband were a constant marvel. Builder, doctor, teacher, preacher, naturalist, agriculturist, industrial promoter, scholar—his talents and interests were legion. One day in his rare spare time he might be reading a book on relativity, another on electronics, alternating them with Carlyle's *French Revolution* or Bunyan's *Grace Abounding*.

"He is not only a saint," she acknowledged humbly, wondering how he could have chosen a simple soul like herself, "but a genius."

An absent-minded genius at times, she had to admit. Once he had been reading aloud to her an interesting book by a Frenchman named Fabre dealing with the power of instinct in animal life. Jesse had been fascinated by the author's experiments to discover the extent of animal reason, and had even performed some himself. They had finished a chapter on the burying beetles and one on processional caterpillars and had just arrived at one on bluebottles. At morning prayers they were accustomed to have a prayer list, with names of workers, departments of work, patients, relatives as their concerns.

"How far have we got on our prayer list this morning?" asked Evie as they were sitting at *chota*.

Intent on his coffee and private thoughts, Jesse replied absently, "As far as the bluebottles, dear." Then, leaning back in his chair, he roared with laughter.

All of Jesse's talents, even his prodigious sense of humour, were dedicated to God and these people he had come to serve. Having learned the building trade during his youth in England, he taught the hill men how to build and gave many of them employment as new buildings were erected on the compound. After the thatched roofs of some of their huts caused disastrous fires, he introduced tile making. As time went by he planted orange trees and sugar cane and helped people in nearby villages to market them. He raised poultry and sheep, teaching better methods of growing the staple village crops, rice and ragi and millet and castor oil plants and lentils and coriander. He established outposts in a half-dozen centres scattered over the hills, camping out at each one in turn and setting up clinics and agricultural projects, as well as endlessly proclaiming the good news of the Gospel. In spite of the *poosari's* opposition schools were established.

"Our scholars number fifty all told," he was able to write in 1916, when the third school was opened.

Doctor, agriculturist, teacher. For all these services the hill men became Jesse's devoted slaves. His help they accepted gladly, but not his religion. Years passed, and still not a single convert. Yet faith never wavered. "Thanks," wrote Jesse in the notebook, "that although the people all gather together and decide not to have Christ, He will have them."

4

WHEN THE MORLINGS went on furlough for a year in 1916, the Brands were obliged to leave the hills and take over the work in Sendamangalam. The war had long since limited the mission board's funds, and no other workers were available. It was heartbreaking, like turning back towards Egypt with the Promised Land in sight. But the year on the plains brought blessings as well as frustrations. Jesse set up a medical unit on the compound and was able to treat hundreds of victims of the "eye fly" epidemic, a painful infection caused by a tiny gnat which attacks the eye area. Evie and little Paul fell victim to it also, enduring months of suffering.

Near the end of the year the Brands' beautiful baby, Connie, was born. It was well that they were on the plains. Jesse, who had not escaped the plague of the Mountains of Death, was sick with malaria. It was a difficult breach birth, and without the attendance of Miss Butcher, who had helped to deliver Paul, the precious new life might well have been lost. The notebook abounded in outpourings of praise.

Heavenly to be back once more on the hills! Yet even their bracing air could not restore Evie's strength. Fortunately they were able to go on holiday that year to Kodaikanal, a hill station 7,000 feet above sea level. Or was it so fortunate? On the long and dangerous journey Evie wondered. They had to cross the Cauvery River in a *jutka*, one of the high flat canopied carts drawn by ponies. The river was in flood. As the swirling waters rose higher and higher on the unsteady wheels, creeping towards the floor where they sat, she prayed desperately that they might be spared. When little Paul began to cry she tried to stifle her fear in comforting him. But even at three Paul Brand's least concern was his own safety.

"Oh, what shall we do," he wailed, "the horses will be drowned!"

Kodaikanal was a paradise worth even this trial by water. Still weak and running a low fever, Evie consulted a skilled woman physician, Dr. Innes, who, fearing tuberculosis, prescribed rest and rich nourishment. Alarmed, Jesse fed her on six eggs and a large measure of milk each day, and she quickly responded. But the healing of Kodai was as much spiritual as physical. There was Dr. Ida Scudder, the radiantly beautiful and dedicated founder of the Vellore hospital, now in this year 1917 ready to launch her daring project of a medical school for Indian women. There was beauty to make one's eyes burn and one's fingers itch—a sapphire lake, incredible vistas of earth and sky, paths winding along the very edge of heaven. And gardens! Longing to make her beloved Kollis bloom with the same luxuriance, Evie took back cuttings of rose trees, passion fruit seeds, plantings of red cactus and wild orchids and the Easter lilies that grew wild over the hillsides. They grew and thrived, keeping pace with baby Connie and Evie's own returning strength. Soon the camping had begun again with the eager listeners, the hope, the *poosari's* subtle opposition, the disappointment.

It was easy to understand the reluctance of even the most heedful listener to become Christian. It meant not only giving up the old familiar worship, which he might be prepared to do, but breaking caste. If young, he would be denied a wife and family. He must literally leave mother, father, sister, brother, and go out alone into a new and strange world.

Six years! It was 1919. They were due to be sent home on furlough. But—should they go? They discussed the matter in an agony of indecision.

"If we take the children now," wondered Evie, "could we bring them out again?" The thought of leaving them in England, even with her loving family, was like a knife thrust. But before another furlough was due Paul at least would require education which they could not supply in India.

"Would the board let *us* return here?" probed Jesse. "They will think our work has been hopeless. What do we have to show the home churches but disappointment? They expect converts, members on a church roll." His voice held an edge of bitterness. "How could they understand that in spite of everything we are bringing new life to these people?"

The decision was made. They asked that their furlough be

postponed for at least a year, and the request was granted. Not until long afterwards did Evie learn what her father had said when the news reached him. "Then I shall never see them."

It was 1919. In the wake of the great war came the influenza epidemic, penetrating even to the remote mountains of southern India. It came in the wet season, when disease was most rampant. Cholera, smallpox, dengue—with such familiar demons the villagers knew how to cope. The afflicted ones left home and lodged in their grain huts. A man who had had the disease would consent, with good pay, to take them food and drink, but there was no attempt at nursing or treatment. If he found the patient dead, he would drag the body into the jungle and leave it. Jesse had learned long since to carefully choose certain paths and avoid others. But this strange new demon! There was no escape. Even the foreign doctors had no drugs to combat it. The villagers fled from it in panic, leaving the smitten ones to die. Left alone, they succumbed to the disease with no one to feed them or even bring a drink of water.

Regardless of their own safety Jesse and Evie left the children in the care of their Christian helpers from the plains and were constantly in the villages, doing what they could to help the sick. They made rice gruel by the gallon, feeding it to the sufferers whose tortured bodies were shrunken from lack of fluids. The *poosari*, so active in combating other demons, gave no help. So frightened was he of the infection that he would not leave his home even to help with the burials. The epidemic had almost passed when someone came with the news.

"Have you heard? The *poosari* and his wife are both sick with this terrible demon!"

Jesse himself was ill with malarial fever. Evie went alone to the priest's house. She found his wife in the middle of the yard, clinging to a string cot, struggling for breath. The *poosari* lay on the mud veranda of his swami hut, panting. Both were close to death. On the veranda of their house, crying, lay unfed their nine month old baby. Evie offered the *poosari* gruel, but he was too weak to do more than taste it. "You—must take—our children —our baby," he gasped. "Don't give them to—my people. Please—"

Evie ran back home, her feet flying on the path. She hurried into the bedroom where Jesse lay tortured by alternating fever and chills. She was so excited she could hardly speak. "We're— going to have—another baby!" she blurted, then managed more calmly to explain what had happened.

Sick though he was, Jesse rose immediately and went to the *poosari's* house. The priest had really meant what he said. "I—

give you my lands and—my children." He managed to mouth the words. "Been good—servant to—swamis. Now they—desert me. Curse them! Only one—helping is servant of—Yesu-swami. He must be—true God—"

"You must send the baby to me, and your son must come willingly," Jesse insisted. "Otherwise I cannot take them." He wanted to risk no chance of being accused later of taking the children home against their father's wishes. At the *poosari's* request he signed a paper promising to look after the boy and to legally adopt the baby. He returned home, radiant.

"I think," he told Paul and Connie, "you are going to have a new little sister."

But—would the priest send them? Would the boy be willing to come after all the stories he had heard about the foreigners? Evie stood at the edge of the garden with the excited children, hoping, fearing. Then they saw him coming through the gap in the hills, a forlorn little figure with a small bundle in his arms. When he came closer they could see the tears running down his cheeks.

"Don't be afraid," Evie comforted him. "We'll take good care of her. And you can come every day and watch me bathing and feeding her."

Slowly he relinquished the bundle into Evie's arms.

The baby was little more than a skeleton, racked with dysentery. Evie washed her, cut her matted hair, dressed her in one of Connie's baby dresses, placed her in a little bamboo basket. The next Sunday Evie stood in the makeshift chapel holding the baby in her arms while Jesse consecrated their new little daughter to the Lord. They named her Ruth, for had she not left her own kindred to join the people of the true God? It was at Christmas time that she came, fittingly, for she was indeed a gift of new life in the form of a little child.

Was the door opening at last? At least it stood ajar. For the *poosari* had died with the name Yesu-swami on his lips, and in the camps the hill people flocked to watch the baby Ruth being bathed, fed, clothed, and tenderly nursed by her new mother. A different sort of swami it must be, they said among themselves, who told his *poosari* to care for a helpless little orphan instead of leaving it to die!

5

SUDDENLY THE DOOR seemed to be flung open. One day
Selvanathan, their teacher from the plains who also managed the
new government post office, came rushing to the house. He stood
perplexed on the doorstep scanning an envelope in his hand. "Sir,"
he said, "what can this mean? 'Stephen Kangani.' A Christian
name on the Kollis, but there are no Christians here among the
hill men."

Excitedly Jesse searched his map for the address, Puliampetty, a
village in a remote corner of the hills. Hastily an expedition was
arranged. Arriving at the village, he found it easy to spot the man
Stephen among the scantily dressed hill men, a stately figure in
his long white *vesthi*. For twenty years, he explained, he had
worked in Ceylon, promoted to the post of Kangani (overseer) of
a tea plantation. He had come here to retire.

"Yes," he admitted, "I was a member of the church there. But
how can I be a Christian here? If you will only come and build
a school and send us a teacher, then I will gladly join with you
and bring this whole village with me."

Evie read the joyous news in Jesse's radiant face. At last the
long-awaited miracle had happened. Plans were made. They
would build a small school-chapel at Puliampetty. It would
become their first Christian out-station. Excitedly they prepared
for a long camping expedition.

They pitched their two tents under spreading banyans between
two villages in full view of the building site and close to several
tiny temples, also to a great bundle of iron rods, swami Karuppan's
tokens of evil power. The people were worried, they discovered,
for fear the "dark ones" would resent their presence. Stephen
Kangani sent Selvanathan secretly with a message, "Please! Go
to the kitchen and see what the boy is using for his grate!"
Entering the little enclosure of reeds, Evie gasped. Three of these
sacred rods were happily doing duty supporting the kettle and
saucepans! Knowing the strictness of Indian law about sacrilege,
she hastily removed the offending utensils and spent the next
hour rubbing mud on the blackened rods to restore their usual
appearance.

One day when Jesse returned from a trip to headquarters, to
Evie's delight he brought two boys with him. One was Aaron,
Ruth's brother, who was slowly conquering his fears of the
foreigners. The other was Sevi, whose father was both headman

of the hills and munsiff, a government official who tried minor cases. In his village of Koilur Sevi had listened spellbound to the Christian preaching, and he had run away to join his new friends. From Puliampetty also came an orphan boy whom they named Moses, first for treatment of a chronic face ulcer, which he soon became convinced that only the Christian swami could heal. His grandfather, knowing he had no parents to care for him, was glad for him to remain in their care. Now Evie had three boys beside her own Paul to mother.

One day she sat in the tent talking with Sevi, his slim straight little figure silhouetted against the light as he stood in the tent entrance. "I believe you've grown taller since you came to us—" she began, then stopped, for suddenly as if by magic he had disappeared. Turning to the opposite end of the open tent, she saw the tall imposing figure of the munsiff.

"Where is my son?" he demanded.

Evie hesitated. "Why—I don't know," she said truthfully. "He was here a minute ago. I guess if you want him, you will have to find him."

Impulsively Evie kept talking, hoping to give the boy time to hide, for she knew how unhappy he was in his home life. The munsiff and his men searched the camping ground thoroughly, but in vain. Finally he went away. That evening after the search party had gone, Sevi came sliding down a tall tree in a neighbouring forest, from which he had watched the search with trembling glee.

"I'm sorry, Sevi," pronounced Jesse, "but we can't keep you. Your father is your legal guardian. We can't go against his wishes."

Paul, who loved Sevi, lay under his mosquito net crying. "His father will punish him," he sobbed. "Don't make him go."

"He can't," Sevi assured him. "I'll just keep running away, and I'll keep coming back."

Knowing this to be true, for the boy had often run away from beatings at the hand of his drunken father, Jesse made no further protest. Sevi remained.

The six weeks in the camp at Puliampetty were some of the happiest Evie had known. Except for a terrifying episode when Paul, always as fearless and adventurous as a young squirrel, managed to hang himself in a noose of banyan tendrils, happily with no worse consequences than a brief blackout and a severe pain in the neck, the days passed in utter joy. Her artist's soul feasted on beauty, for it was a place where mountains and plains, earth and heaven, seemed to meet. Also it was the hour before dawn, when all their hopes were to be realised. True, though

65

Stephen Kangani came to prayers each day, he seemed reluctant to be fully identified with them.

"But when the day comes," Selvanathan, who had been teaching him, assured, "he will be ready."

The day came. The building was finished. A great celebration was planned. Lantern slides would be shown with a new machine bought in Madras. The people seemed full of anticipation. Working with Jesse on the building, the men had come to love and trust him. The women had become Evie's devoted friends. Then ... "Look!" said Jesse suddenly.

They were sitting at their midday meal in the tent with both sides open. In full view was a small temple for the worship of Mariammal, one of the chief goddesses of the hills. About it a crowd was gathering, obviously making preparations for a festival. "But—they can't!" gasped Evie. "Not today!" She stared in sudden horror. "Look! Isn't that—Stephen among them?"

Jesse sprang up, his food untouched, and left the tent. When he returned his eyes were bleak, his voice strained. "It seems our celebration coincides with one of their Swami festivals. Unfortunate, but—they'll come to us when evening comes. They can't resist the lantern slides. You'll see."

Night came, bringing a roar of drums and an orgy of wild, drunken dancing. But no celebration in the new building, no lantern slides. The machine from Madras failed to work. Silently they stood and watched the whirling, swaying figures silhouetted against the flames of a great bonfire, the white-clad figure of Stephen Kangani, wildest participant of all, in their midst.

Blighted hope, yes. Heartbreak. But not despair. The building was there. Children would be taught in it. Sometime it would be a house of worship.

Breaking camp, they moved on through wild country, over streams filled with great boulders. Once a huge snake crossed their path, and their frolicking little dog Rover, always the family protector, was on it with a flying tackle. Instantly he was enmeshed in its deadly tightening coils.

"*Ayoh!*" cried Paul in an agony of terror. "He'll be killed!" He would have rushed to the rescue if someone had not held him forcibly back. Somehow with sticks and stones the men managed to kill the reptile and disengage its coils, and the caravan went on leaving it faintly wriggling, its chastened victim trotting meekly at Jesse's heels.

They camped near other villages. Selari, deep in the jungle . .
Never had they been so eagerly received. The head man of the village was so moved by Jesse's preaching that he with others sat up late into the night to hear more of the Gospel. It looked as if

the whole village might become Christian. "Come tomorrow," they were told, "and we will give you our final word."

Hopefully they returned, to find the village empty and silent. Wandering through the empty spaces between the mud thatched huts, at last they saw the men squatted in a group about their *poosari*, who was excitedly talking. The head man greeted them with respect but obvious lack of interest. After they left, they discovered later, he arranged a festival for their demon-swamis and had a small new temple built, to atone for his brief aberration. They could almost have quoted the admonitions of the priest.

"Accept this Yesu-swami of the foreigners? No. Your priest and elders forbid it. Do you want to be banished from caste and all its privileges? Take their medicines, yes. Listen to them and treat them well, but join them—*never*!"

Kurungunadu . . . the same story. On to Puthuvallavu. They set up their tents in the corner of a field under a sheltering tree. A place of promise it seemed from the beginning. Evie even found a hollow tree nearby with room for a prayer space inside. "The Lord your God went before you," she read the first morning, "to search out a place to pitch your tents in." Surely a sign of coming blessing! And here at last after six long years the seeds so tenderly planted and tended began to bear fruit. Among the patients who came crowding to the tents was a mother who had dedicated her little son's hair to the swami-god. Neglect from birth had resulted in dirty hopeless tangles, aswarm with lice, and a painfully septic scalp.

"I'm sorry," said Evie in her fumbling Tamil which five year old Paul patiently tried to correct. "Cannot dress head or medicines give till hair I cut off."

"*Illai*, no!" Terrified the woman clutched the poor mite to her breast. But as Evie gently talked, explained about the more loving swami, refused to help until the head was cleaned, mother love slowly conquered fear. In the field, where the parasites could not possibly get back to the tents, Evie carefully cut away the filthy hair, gently washed and medicated the pustuled scalp, and wrapped the tiny head in a cap of bandages.

It was a wonderful camp. During the six weeks they treated over a thousand patients. Land was given for a school, a tree donated and sawed for the roof, the building completed. And then came a hill man who later took the name of Solomon. First he dared to brave the threats of his *poosari* and become their water carrier. Then boldly he announced that he was leaving the old ways and following the Yesu-swami. He was put to severe tests. His wife was taken away from him, but he managed to bring her back. He suffered jibes, threats, ostracism, expulsion from

67

caste. Some time later Jesse and Evie were called to his village for the premature birth of his baby. Both his wife and the baby died. "*Ayoh*! You see?" jeered his neighbours. "Did we not tell you what would happen if you joined their way?" But Solomon did not waver. His father joined him in avowing his faith. The door had finally swung open. From that time on the Christian community on the Kollis slowly began to grow.

6

BUILDER, DOCTOR, TEACHER, preacher, naturalist, agriculturist . . . father. It was in this latter capacity that Jesse Brand excelled. His amazing knowledge, his insatiable curiosity opened to his children fascinating vistas of worlds great and small. His absences were voids of dullness, his returns rekindlings of excitement. At the first beat of horses' hoofs, the monotonous chanting of coolies, they would be off down the path to meet him, and long before they reached him he would be off his horse and holding out his arms.

"Ho, there, my darlings! What's this? Don't tell me you've grown all this in the few days I've been away! You'll soon be as tall as I am."

Always there would be a story of his adventures, usually about some insect or bird or animal he had seen, perhaps a bear or a tortoise or a trap-door spider, or even something as small as an ant.

"What do you suppose I saw as I rode up the path today? A whole long train of foraging ants, marching in twos and threes. And the strangest thing was that a big light-coloured fly was standing solemnly at the very edge of the line, like a general reviewing his soldiers. So I said to myself, 'I'll just stay and watch to see if I can find out why the big fly waits there.' "

"And did you?" It was usually Paul who did the prompting.

"I surely did. I watched until thousands of ants must have gone past. Suddenly the fly turned round and gave a big spring to where an ant had wandered from the main column and came down with its feet bang on the head of the poor ant. Now that ant was carrying a nice leg of mutton, or rather, a nice leg of grass-hopper home for dinner. When the fly came down with that awful thump it was so scared it put down the leg of grasshopper and opened its strong jaws to bite the fly. But already the fly had picked up the nice leg and flown off laughing to a quiet spot about two feet away . . ."

Jesse was never too busy to stimulate their curiosity.

"How do you suppose those white ants build their towers? Let's watch."

Then he would carefully break open one of the great towers, some as high as four feet, to reveal tunnels and runs, the beautiful intricate compartments with doors and passageways. And once they dug right to the bottom of an ant hill, at least three feet, through combs of eggs and young ants, to find the queen.

"Look at her, see how big she is—at least two inches! As much bigger than an ordinary ant as an elephant is bigger than a dog."

Sometimes Evie wished Jesse would be more strict at discipline. True, he taught them a healthy fear of real hazards, like scorpions and the snakes that lived in a crack between the earthen stove and the wall in a corner of the bathroom. Fortunately they were not cobras, though the family never got close enough to find out if they were poisonous. But Jesse put few limits on the children's freedom. They ran as wild as their darker-skinned playmates, if not in the same state of undress. As Paul grew taller and leaner he climbed higher and higher in the spreading jackfruit trees, the plumper Connie not far behind him. Evie's objection to the lofty jackfruits was not wholly on account of danger. They ejected a sticky sap which played havoc with legs, arms, and clothes.

"Nonsense!" pooh-poohed Jesse. "Be thankful they can run wild, like the young animals they are. Better a broken bone than a pair of cowards or weaklings! Childhood should be a time of freedom and adventure. Besides—"

He did not need to finish. Evie's heart skipped a beat at the unspoken words. *Besides—we won't have them with us long.* She counted each day, each week, each month as if they were priceless pearls slipping through her fingers. Three years . . . then furlough, when they must leave their precious ones in England. It was the price one must pay for the high privilege of service.

The children were as conscious of this commitment to a supreme loyalty almost from babyhood. They shared in the family prayers each night. Weeks of their childhood were spent in camps, listening to Jesse preach, handing out tracts and Gospels, helping Evie display the big rolls of Bible pictures while she told the familiar stories. Once she found them talking earnestly to baby Ruth as she sat in her basket cot, great dark eyes fixed solemnly on their faces.

"We're teaching her, Mummy," explained Paul. "We're telling her she must leave her old *poie swamis* and follow Jesus."

Then there was a day in camp when, after a morning of gruelling activity, Evie had thrown herself on her cot in the tent. She looked up to see the two children regarding her anxiously. "Mummy, the women have all come," said Paul.

"Yes, dears, but I'm too tired to see them right now. Please ask them to wait."

Later she found them surrounded by the group of women holding between them the heavy roll of pictures, so big and long it almost hid their small bodies. Too timid to speak, they were attempting to fill the need in silent witness. Once, when she had tucked them under the mosquito nets at sunset to protect them from the malarial mosquitoes which swarmed at dusk, she heard them talking together.

"We must go all over the world," Paul was enjoining seriously, "in trains and motor cars and jutkas and bullock carts and maybe even aeroplanes, *all* over the world and tell people about Jesus and God's love."

Evie was almost as ingenious a teacher as Jesse, though the three R's were far less intriguing than ants and monkeys and trapdoor spiders and even snakes, especially to Paul. Seated at the round table with sums to do or a composition to write, Connie would perform her work diligently while Paul sat staring out of the window.

"Come," Evie said one day. "I know where you'd like to be."

After that he did his sums high in a tree in the little copse at the left of the house. When he finished he would drop them down to Evie, who sat on the ground below. If they were wrong he had to climb down and get them, reascend, and start again. For years this was his school room. But she taught them more than the three R's or the love of God. On holidays at Kulivalavu, their camping spot wild and high on their own Kollis, far above the malaria, they had the full benefit of her creative genius.

"Look, children, all these rocks—no, not rocks! Birds, animals, ships, trains!"

Great stones lay all around. Helping the children lift them into standing positions, she showed them how to place triangular stones on the standing rocks to look like great birds' heads. Soon they had a big flock of vultures, storks, prehistoric birds like dodos, looking so real that when Rover came on them one day he rushed around barking furiously. They found long rectangular rocks, chipped off pieces of crumbling stone to form wheels, made engines and carriages. Climbing with her to the mountain top to see the sun rise, they would watch her joyously splash watercolours on art paper or, when that ran out, on the backs of old letters and envelopes. They learned that a sunrise could be a thanksgiving feast.

"Oh!" she would cry when the gorgeous colours began to unfurl. "Look what it's doing, look what it's doing! Quick, quick!" Then she would rush to get her paints. And over and over while her swift fingers were trying to capture the glory she would break out in gratitude, *"Stottherum, stottherum!* Oh, praise the Lord!"

By 1920 they were responsible for the feeding, clothing, and education of four children in addition to their own two—Ruth and her brother Kongan, whom they named Aaron; Raman, the boy of sixteen from Puliampetty with the chronic skin disease, whom they named Moses; and Sevi, who had run away from his father the munsiff and hidden in the camp at Puliampetty. After this his father had tacitly agreed to let Sevi remain with the foreigners and go to school. But though willing to have his son educated by the missionaries, he did not want him to become Christian. Living together in one small room on the compound, the three boys were often in conflict. Raman would lose his temper and throw his sandal at Sevi, who would promptly pick it up and apply it vigorously to Raman's head.

"They must go to boarding school," Jesse decided.

Arrangements were made for them to attend the Brethren School for Boys two hundred miles from the foot of the hills. Moses and Aaron had no parental ties to prevent their going. Sevi's father gave his consent, and when the Brands went to Madras for the church conference in 1920, the three boys accompanied them as far as the plains. As the boys raced down the hill, in passing they struck some swami bells hanging from a bush and dedicated to the hill gods. This time they rang with joy to God, a peal of sound that seemed a last farewell to their old faith. Though in deference to his father's wishes Sevi had never confessed the Christian faith, they knew that he was in secret a believer. In the school he took the name of James.

The work kept growing. New teachers came from the plains. A station was opened at Kurungunadi, making five in all. With the gift of thirty pounds from a church in St. John's Wood a chapel was begun at Vazhavanthi. Instead of paying exorbitant rates to entice artisans from the plains, Jesse used hill men whom he trained himself to perform the building operations. Soon there were a dozen or more young men learning to be sawyers and carpenters. The last sheet of corrugated iron was laid at dusk on Christmas Eve, and on Christmas morning the opening service was held with all the Christians on the Kolli Hills, mission

71

workers, converts and their families, about forty all told, in attendance.

"In this place will I give peace," was Jesse's sermon topic, the same text from which he had preached his first sermon in Tamil in Madras just thirteen years before.

The years passed slowly, swiftly leaving their footprints in Evie's diary.

"9th July. Bitter and sweet. So our lives balance up and down. Those who have never been missionaries can little guess the crises of hope and disappointment we pass through."

"31st October. Although Sevi is lost and although David has gone and Stephen refuses to come to prayer, and David is bad tempered and would not join us in prayer for peace, yet will I rejoice in the Lord."

"18th December. Tomorrow will be Connie's fifth birthday. I'm glad she's kept four so long. Such an exquisite treasure!"

"23rd July. I feel sick, indescribably weak and low. Everything tires me, and I know I'm just where a sea voyage home might do wonders, but we've decided not to go, and God must do it."

"17th September. My heart has been filled with sorrow and shame at the thought of the unworthiness of our workers. Their hateful money grabbing . . . But a look into one's own heart does good. We have never had need of money. We have all we can desire, and their means how limited!"

"16th November. Beside me lies a little plant in embryo, but it will never be the tree it should have been. My little Paul's eager fingers have broken open the seed and revealed the long delicate little leaves, stem, root and all. Now it will never grow. God help us not be too eager to tear open his secrets. They will grow."

They had not been too eager, and the seeds had taken root and grown, if not into a tree, at least into a few healthy shrubs. There were preachers and teachers for a half dozen stations. Villagers had been taught carpentry and weaving. Guinea worm had been practically abolished. A strong but healthy settlement was growing at Vazhavanthi, since those who wished to become Christians were unable to stay in their villages.

But the decision to remain another year meant tragedy for Evie. They were sitting at the dinner table when the cable came. Her heart beat hard as she tore it open. It could tell so many things. A death! A new baby? Hearing her gasp and noticing her pallor, Jesse rushed around the table to her. "It's Father," she moaned. "He's gone." *If only we had taken our furlough when we planned*! Details came in a later letter. The superintendent of a Sunday School made up of several hundred children, Father had been standing on the platform speaking when suddenly he had swayed. Brother Charlie had caught him. He had never regained consciousness.

It was 1923. They had been ten years on the hills. At last it seemed possible to leave for a year—too late. Mr. and Mrs. Watts, another missionary couple, would come from the plains to fill their place. The children were old enough, Paul nearly nine, Connie six, to be left to attend school in England. Resolutely Evie tried not to look beyond the twelve short months of reprieve.

"We're going home," she told the children with a fine display of gaiety.

They looked bewildered, shocked. "But this is home, Mummy."

"Yes, yes, so it is." Her heart lurched. *And may you keep remembering it, my darlings*!

They were leaving the compound for the last time when Paul suddenly remembered. "But—who's going to lay the mats for the chapel service when I'm gone?" he called out anxiously to his father.

Jesse smiled down into the small worried face. "Yes, yes, son, we must arrange that," he agreed reassuringly.

Determinedly Evie resolved to make the journey a happy, not a sad one. At last she and Jesse were going home together on their first furlough. Fortunately she could not know that it would also be their last.

7

WAS IT ENGLAND that had changed, or she herself? It seemed almost as strange to her as to the children, wide-eyed at a new world of steamers, tall buildings, hordes of people with white skins like their own; chafing at the confinement of house-lined streets, rooms cluttered with furniture, good clothes that must be worn every day, not just on Sundays, and shoes. Especially shoes! Not mere encumbrances, as on a trip to the mission station in Madras. Permanent, inescapable liabilities.

Evie could sympathise with them, for at first she too felt stifled. It was not just the chilling absence of beloved Father that rendered her old world so constrictingly cold. The tall narrow house, enclosed within its brick walls and tight-shut gates, even its beloved garden at the rear, seemed cramped and suffocating. She stared in amazement at the polished furniture, the once treasured trinkets, the cabinets of fragile heirlooms, the priceless specimens of Martin Ware, the loaded table with its damask and silver and crystal, all of which she had once considered so important. What would her hill people think if they could see her now? Remembering the poverty of their little thatched huts, the meagre contents of their rice bowls, she felt a gnawing sense of shame and guilt. She might have been a visiting stranger instead of a homecoming sister and daughter.

Not so the children. They took the new environment in their stride, unawed and intensely curious. Within hours they were sliding down the long polished balustrade which ran, continuously curving, the full depth of the house, increasing momentum at a terrific speed, narrowly missing the alabaster statue standing on its pedestal at the foot. Hustled outdoors, they contented themselves for awhile with sliding down the flat sides of the twelve steps leading to the front door and climbing up and down the high iron gate which opened on the street. But these were tame sports for confirmed tree climbers. The lamp posts lining the street offered temporary substitutes. Hanging from the high crosspieces upside down by their knees, they grinned engagingly into the startled faces of passersby. They did not mean to be naughty. Even on their first Sunday with Jesse's relatives in Guildford when they preceded their horrified aunts down the aisle of the church carrying their shoes in their hands, they were merely following acceptable and devout Indian custom.

Evie herself did not escape some gentle chiding. "My dear, your clothes! That sort of style went out ten years ago! We must get a dressmaker . . ."

She yielded to her sisters' concern about her appearance—to a point. But on one thing she was firm. No frills, no flounces, no furbelows. One plain best dress for speaking engagements, the rest simple cottons such as could be worn later on the hills. Sitting in the big ornate church on wooden pews (strange after the bare little chapel with its mats laid on the floor!), she watched the silken finery, the big flowered hats of the worshippers and was appalled. Had she really looked like that once, been so concerned over her appearance?

She worried lest the children's heads be turned by all the gifts and luxuries showered on them by doting relatives. Her supreme wish was that they grow up honest and unselfish. A trip with sister Eunice on one of her charity expeditions, Evie decided, might provide exercise in generosity. "Connie," she said, "we are going to visit some poor children. What about taking one of your dollies to them?"

Connie had three, all very precious, one a present from a passenger on the steamer. Her eyes filled with tears. "Mummy, they wouldn't know how to put them to bed and feed them."

"All right, dear." Generosity could not be forced. "Why don't you just carry a doll with you?"

They reached a house, climbed the wooden stairs and knocked at the door of a room. Inside was a group of pathetically pale sickly children with their poor mother. Connie and Paul were allowed to present the parcels of groceries and cooked food. Connie sidled up to her mother. "Mummy, may I give them my dollie?" As she presented the doll to the eager children, her lovely face glowed. "Mummy," she enthused later, "did you see them clap their hands when I gave them my dollie?"

"You needn't worry," remarked Eunice sagely. "Your children may have faults, but selfishness will never be one of them."

If there was spoiling, it would not be done by Eunice. Always meticulous, keen of mind and with a primness of manner which belied an innate kindliness, she had stepped easily into the shoes of her father as manager of the household, ruling it with an even more rigid and efficient hand. Though her younger sister Hope, more emotional and sensitive, presumably shared this responsibility and both paid dutiful deference to their invalid mother as head of the family, it was Eunice who made all major decisions and implemented them. She made them now. It was natural that, having willingly undertaken the upbringing of these two uninhibited young creatures from the jungle, she should attempt at once to absorb them, kindly but firmly, into the regimen to which they must finally adjust.

"There is a very good school, a Miss Chataway's, within walking distance. We had better enroll the children at once." . . . "I shall expect Master Paul to render a strict account of his income, yes, even though it is but two pence a week." . . . "Yes, of course you must wear gloves, Connie, when you go to church."

Knowing what it must cost her sisters to have their placid life invaded by young whirlwinds who set priceless alabaster statues swaying, probed curious fingers into mahogany cabinets, slid down the carpeted stairs on tin serving trays ("But, Mummy, it's silly to care about old chairs and carpets!") Evie tried to be understanding. But she often felt as torn between two worlds as did the children. She was glad that Jesse, away much of the time on preaching tours, was spared most of the pains of adjustment.

Fortunately there were two realms in the house removed from all tensions. One was the basement breakfast room, which became

75

tacitly recognised as the children's playroom. Here, except for the two maids and the cook Cissie, who presided over the adjoining kitchen, pantry, larder, and cellars, they were comparatively free to exercise their ebullient energy. The maids Dora and Caroline, although strongly disapproving of certain activities, like swinging on the curtains, were remarkably lenient and understanding. In lieu of high trees to climb the children devised other sports. One was to get completely around the room, filled with old polished mahogany furniture, without once touching the floor. Another diversion was taking out the shelves of the food lift, squeezing themselves in, and pulling themselves up and down by the ropes and pulleys.

And high up on the third floor was the domain of "Grandma", a haven of peace. Though Evie's mother was an invalid of over eighty, there was nothing senile about her. Her pink cheeks were unshrivelled, her voice strong and coherent. The hour after tea when Evie took the children to visit her was one of joy and relaxation. The children adored their grandmother. Seated in her armchair, usually in a purple velvet gown, snow-white ringlets framing her little lace cap, face shining, she would talk to them of Christ, recite whole chapters of the Bible, give them prizes for learning and repeating scripture texts, tell them stories of her Huguenot ancestors in France, especially of the one who had been tortured to death for his faith by being forced to drink powdered glass.

The year was blessing . . . and it was torture. Everywhere the message was well received. Evie went often with Jesse on his preaching missions. Over and over she told the story of the little cowherd, who had died with the name of the true God on his lips; of the *poosari* and their little adopted daughter Ruth; of Sevi-James, who had dared leave his powerful father. Generous giving assured increased work among the hill people. Jesse's people arranged for a big camp meeting at Guildford, one of the great blessings of which was the commitment to service of Ruth, Evie's brother Bertie's oldest daughter.

"I want to be a missionary," she told her delighted aunt.

But as the sands of the year ran low the constant dread of parting turned into agony. To leave her children, even in capable and loving hands, for five or six whole years! Why, Paul would be almost a man, and Connie, her precious golden-haired treasure, now scarcely out of babyhood . . .

"I can't do it," she blurted suddenly to Jesse about a month before they were due to sail. "Paul, yes. He's old enough to stand the separation, and he must have his schooling now. But Connie, my little darling . . . Jess, I must take her."

76

Jesse's face reflected the pain in her own, but he shook his head. "I know. But, my dear, it would be cruel to separate them." Then, looking into her ravaged eyes, he relented. "Very well. Why not take Connie apart and ask her if she would rather go back with us?"

Evie thankfully grasped at the thread of hope. Connie regarded her gravely. "Can Paul come too, Mummy?"

"No, darling. Paul must stay here and go to school."

The child shook her head. "Oh, not without Paul, Mummy. Not without my Paul."

The last of the sands ran out quickly. They were leaving early the next morning soon after the children started school. That night Paul and Connie recited the five Tamil texts which they had learned and which they would repeat every Sunday morning at breakfast for the next six years. Evie had painted other texts in English, beautifully illustrated, and hung them beside their beds. "I will be a father unto you." . . . "As one whom a mother comforteth, so will I comfort you." . . .

The day came. The school principal had prepared a little contest with prizes. Evie's sister Minnie had sent special toys. The family knelt and prayed together. Then Paul and Connie hugged their parents tightly, seized their school satchels, and ran down the steps. Evie stood by the gate looking after them, eyes so blurred with tears she could scarcely see the waving of their hands before they ran around the corner.

"As I stood watching them," she confessed later, "something just died in me."

8

He that loveth father or mother more than me is not worthy of me; and he that loveth son or daughter more than me . . .

It was the hardest test of loyalty she had ever had to face. At first she thought she could not do it. She must stop at the first port, take the next steamer back, bring the children back with them to India. Then one February night when they were on the *SS Leicestershire* in the Mediterranean there came a terrible storm. Though they shut the outer and inner doors and both windows of their state room, the waves washed over the deck with such force that their floor was soon swimming in water. The ship tossed so violently that they wondered if they would escape alive.

"I'm glad," Evie told Jesse, "that the children aren't with us. They would be so frightened." With the coming of calm and sunlight on dazzling blue she became conscious of an assuring "Peace, be still."

It was March, just a month after sailing from England, that they looked across the last *nunjay*, valley, and saw the little settlement at Vazhavanthi, its iron roofs gleaming ruby-red in the sunlight. A crowd of eager people came to meet them. Led by a man blowing on a long curly trumpet, they were taken to a reception room of boughs and branches, laden with flower garlands, honoured with gifts and speeches.

"*Stottherum, stottherum*!" For the first time since leaving the children Evie gave voice to full and joyous praise. This was where they belonged. They had come home.

Of course there were constant reminders. The little house with its three rooms, built tandem like a train of cars, seemed indescribably empty. Everything conjured visions of a bright golden head or a little lean figure, volatile as quicksilver—the small single beds in the two corners where bright eyes had peered through the mosquito nettings; the tree where Paul had climbed for his lessons; the passion fruit hedge into which Jesse had thrown two squealing, bouncing little bodies; the mats which Paul had laid each Sunday on the floor of the chapel; the rose bush which, to Evie's dismay, Connie had denuded of both buds and blossoms to bring cheer to a mother sick with fever. ("But, Mummy, aren't you glad I picked them for you?" "Yes, darling, of course I am.")

But—*stottherum*!—her arms were not empty of children. Jesse had collected promises of money in England for a girls' home and set out at once to build it. Little Ruth, who had been placed in a boarding school in Salem while they were away, came back to them, still tiny but sweet and sturdy. Word soon went out over the hills that here was a haven for unwanted children. It was the practice to marry children of ten or twelve. Then a man might take a kept woman to help on his farm, and the child wife might be told, "*Vendam*", not wanted. Several of these little discarded wives came running to them for food and shelter.

"There's a small girl in the shed at the foot of the compound," a worker told them one day. "She does not speak but will not go away." Evie brought the sickly child to the house, treated her for worm infection. Morose and quiet but refusing to go away, she became one of the family. One day some women from her village peered through the window and saw the child sitting with Evie.

"There she is! Give her to us," they demanded. Knowing that she must not kidnap children, Evie invited them to come in. Crowding into the house, they scolded, coaxed, threatened, but the child refused to leave. Finally they seized the roll of hair which unmarried girls wore on the front of their heads and dragged her away, screaming. She ran away again, this time to the mission house in Sendamangalam. Later Jesse saw her sleeping on the veranda there. "Is this something of yours?" he was asked teasingly. To Evie's delight when he returned the little one was with him. They named her Nesamoni, Jewel of Love.

Another baby had been left to die on the village dust heap. Her mother had died in childbirth, and the father was too ill to care for a seven day old child. The school peon came secretly to Evie. "There's a baby girl there crying," he confided. "It will die there." "Bring it quietly to me," said Evie. As she held the tiny scrap in her arms, she saw that her arms and legs were bruised where she had beaten them against the rough winnowing fan on which she had lain. It took weeks of loving care before it was certain she would live. They named her Samathanam, Peace.

Others came who did not live. Evie would wrap them in a little piece of white cloth and carry them to the place where Jesse had dug a small grave. While he prayed she would stoop and lay the tiny body in its resting place. She loved them all. Though they could not fill the void left by her own children, they brought a happiness which only the saving of human life can bring. Indeed, she and Jesse called one of the babies Bakkyam, Happiness. It was in 1925 when Jesse wrote to the children about her coming.

This week a lovely thing happened. Remember the old *Poosari* at Kirangadu? Very old, first man to have a tooth out. One day last week he appeared and asked Mama if she would take an orphan baby. Mama could not believe her ears, so she brought the man to me. He had a girl baby about a year old whose parents had both died, and he wanted us to take it. We told him to bring it along the next morning. He turned up with a lad carrying the baby, pretty, with large dark eyes. We cut off its swami hair and have named it Bakkyam. In our seventh year on the Kollis a *poosari* brought us Ruth. Now in our second seven years another *poosari* brings another little girl baby.

She was suffering from convulsions. For two hours Evie held the struggling mite in hot water, pouring cold water over her head, until the terrible jerking fits subsided. For a long time she nursed her in the bungalow until she was strong enough to be trusted to those in care of the Girls' Home.

"Mama has a new baby," wrote Jesse again that same year. "A poor woman was brought to our little hospital last week suffering from pneumonia and died. Her husband brought a tiny baby, one month old, and gave it to Mama. We have named it Devakirabai, meaning 'Grace of God'."

Such scraps of human cast-offs, literally from earth's refuse heaps, worth saving? Jewel of love . . . Peace . . . Happiness . . . Grace of God. Evie envisaged them all as they would, or at least might be some day, Christian women, wives, mothers.

Of course, the children who came under their care were not all girls. Camping in the village of Alathurnadu, on the lower slopes of the Kollis, Evie saw a little boy, a wild sorry scrap of humanity, running around with a coconut shell begging for a bit of rice. Even at a distance she could see that his small body was covered with running sores. She managed to catch him and treat the infection—once. Terrified of her, he would not come back. When she tried to coax him to return for further treatments, he would dart away into the forest. She knew why. She had heard the stories people were telling about the visitors, that they made a practice of eating little children.

"He's in the veranda there," someone told her. Quickly she went and sat nearby where he could not escape. Knowing that his people had turned him out and that he must have treatment in order to live, they took the child with them when they returned home. But he had a brother, and one day he appeared. "You're not going to take my brother!" he defied them.

Evie was indignant. "How dare you talk like that? You didn't even feed him!" But they had to let him go. Later they were in the same village at a harvest festival. "*Ammah*," someone said to her, "there's your little boy."

This time he did not run away and when they took him home, no one appeared to protest. What joy to bathe him, give him a clean little shirt, nurse him back to health! They named him Enoch and, as soon as he was well, installed him in the boys' small hostel and began his education.

Until the Girls' Home was finished in 1925 Evie cared for the babies in her own home. The new building was worth waiting for. Jesse's brick-burning experiments had proved a success, and the inner walls were smoother than those of undressed stone used heretofore. All the timber used was cut by Kolli men trained in the mission Industrial School and framed and fixed by young carpenters trained there.

The Home grew . . . five . . . ten . . . fifteen girls. At one time its numbers increased to twenty, with ages ranging from infancy to adolescence. The girls were given an elementary education by a Tamil teacher from the plains. Many of them became Christians. Often when they became old enough marriages were arranged for them with Christian young men.

"The first sound every day in the Settlement, as dawn is breaking," wrote Jesse in one of his reports, "is a song of praise from the girls in the Home. And the last sound at night, when the noise of the day's work has died down and darkness has fallen, is the sound of the teacher's voice in the Girls' Home, giving them their evening Bible lesson."

He was not satisfied with elementary education. The girls, as well as the boys, must learn practical skills—gardening, mat making, weaving. A hand loom was built, and the older girls were taught to weave the plain clothes worn on the Kollis. It was hoped that in time all the Christian women on the mountains would learn to weave their own garments. Jesse planted two acres with mulberry bushes and bought silk worms. The bushes flourished. But—would the leaves hold out until the worms were ready to spin? When they finally began to spin, all hands were summoned to transfer them to the big trays of plaited split-bamboo where they could build their beautiful new nests. The girls learned to reel silk. First a big double handful of the cocoons was put into hot water and boiled for five minutes. Then the reeler sat down by the big pot in which the cocoons were floating and dabbed them with a bunch of twigs. The silk filaments became entangled in the twigs, and the girls pulled and shook and jerked until the rough outside waste silk was stripped from the cocoons and was ready for reeling. After the tangled mass of waste was cut off the reeler lifted single filaments from a dozen or more cocoons, to form a single very fine silken thread. This was passed through a hole in an iron plate and connected with a spinney which was turned by one of the girls. The silk could then be reeled as fast as a girl could turn. When about three hundred yards had been reeled off, the cocoons were finished, and just before this happened, the reeler had to "throw", with a deft movement of the hand, a number of fresh silken filaments on to the quickly moving thread as it passed through the hole. There was an adhesive property in the silk as it emerged from the hot water which caused the "thrown" filaments to stick to the moving thread, and so new cocoons were drawn into the circle of revolving, bobbing cocoons which were yielding up their silken treasure. Thanks to a qualified demonstrator loaned by the government, the girls became surprisingly adept at the work. Soon there were several pound weights of the nice shiny hanks of pure silk, for which Jesse tried to find a market on the plains.

But it was in building that he took greatest delight. Soon after their return from England work was started on a new bungalow, one made of stone which would be more resistant to storms and cold and heat—also to the ubiquitous ants, snakes, and other pests. However, the project might well have ended in tragedy. One day he was up on the scaffolding examining the stonework of the nine-foot wall. There was a row of new stones placed on its edge ready for mortar. Suddenly the scaffolding gave way. As he fell he grabbed at one of the newly laid stones. Instead of supporting him it came tumbling down as he fell to the floor below. Fortunate that he had on his good strong topee, for *bang*! came the stone, all forty pounds of it, on his head! He was not seriously hurt, only a few scratches and bruises.

"But if I had had on my other topee," he wrote the children, "it would have injured my head, and if there had been no topee at all, I expect it would have made quite a dent!"

By March of 1926 they were able to move the office into one room of the new house, waiting for a suitable tree to be cut, sawed into planks, dried, and made into the ceiling of another room. So nice to be in a well-ventilated room away from sun and heat!

Jesse's labours were legion. In the carpenter's shed, built with corrugated sheets, he taught boys the skills of carpentry and masonry. In time they were able to construct furniture, make repairs, supply doors and windows for the mission buildings. He hired other men to work in his rice fields, his orange orchards; promoted the culture of sugarcane. He taught the villagers new methods of growing their own staple crops and helped them market their products. He maintained supervision of the schools in all parts of the Kollis. And of course his medical services were in constant demand. No sooner had he arrived after furlough than people began crowding to the dispensary. One of the first to come was a man with a badly decayed tooth.

"I have been waiting for you to come and pull that one out for the last six months," said the patient, gratefully eyeing his erstwhile source of pain.

The coming of Dr. Samuel, a Syrian Christian from the ancient church in Travancore, was a miracle of good fortune. It was a tribute to the value of the Brands' work by the government, which paid his salary. On the way to his new post Dr. Samuel heard evil reports of the land where he was going. Expecting to be able to purchase most commodities there, he was surprised to find no shop or bazaar on the Kollis, to learn that even such necessities as meat, eggs, flour, and rice must be purchased by a hired servant living ten miles away at Sendamangalam and carried to the hills on the heads of coolies. But to their relief he was not discouraged. He seemed the very man they had been praying for.

Soon after the doctor's arrival Jesse himself became one of his patients. An ardent and fearless rider, he kept urging his colleague to use a horse for his frequent trips into the out-stations. Dr. Samuel's reluctance to mount was hardly relieved by the sight of Jesse returning one day covered with mud and slime from head to foot. His horse had slipped off one of the narrow raised paths separating fields where the rice shoots grew in water and had sunk deep into the ooze. But Jesse cheerfully persisted in his urging.

"See, it's easy!" he prodded. "Watch me." Springing on his horse, he dashed down the path toward the fields, not realising that a great stump was hidden in the cut-down bushes. Even Evie, inside the house, heard the crash, then shouts as crowds ran to the scene from all over the compound. Fortunately the horse had stopped soon after the rider fell, or Jesse might have been dragged to his death. His leg was broken just below the knee. For weeks he was confined to cast and crutches, but happily the healing left only an insignificant limp.

"The slight curve in my leg fits the horse nicely!" he wrote to Paul, always quick to extract humour from even the soberest of circumstances.

His weekly letters to the children were masterpieces. He wrote with the same creative zest and love of life with which he preached. They were happy composites of news, nature notes, anecdotes, and tender if sometimes stringent advice.

"The report that came this week, Paul, was a disappointing one. I don't mind low marks in some subjects, because you were away from school on account of sickness. But what I object to is a remark like 'could do better if he tried'." . . .

"You remember Aaron? I want you to pray for him. He has been baptised, but we feel he is not living in touch with God." . . .

"We have been watching the building of a marvellous house. The architect and engineer is a large hornet. The house is suspended from the under side of a rafter in our veranda. It is shaped precisely like an Indian water-pot, with a long narrow neck." . . .

"Do you remember the kaveru harvest? Kaveru is the grain that looks like a human hand stretched upwards and the fingers folded together. Each separate head has to be cut off by hand." . . .

"Here on the Kollis we could not use a car if we had one . . . If I were twenty years younger and thinking of coming to the hills, I would learn to fly!"

"Mother was bitten by a snake about three feet long. She did not cry out or make a fuss, though we did not know if it was poisonous. She let me tie it up tightly with a piece of cloth and put medicine on it, and was smiling all the time. Then we killed the snake. You know that poisonous snakes have two long front teeth in front of the mouth, with little grooves for the poison to flow through. This one was not poisonous, thank God!" . . .

"I took Mama to that terrible peak that I told you of some months ago. Climbed to the very point and looked over the abyss. Mama lay down flat and just crawled to the edge of the stone that hung over the precipice, while I held on to her skirts to keep the wind from carrying her over. It made us shudder. And there on the bare rock face opposite we saw a troop of big apes, not monkeys, and they were climbing along by the tiniest cracks in the rock, while below them was nothing but a sheer drop into the black void." . . .

"Ruth is standing at my elbow watching the typewriter. She is a dainty, pretty girl, but she does not grow very big. Aaron was with us for Christmas. He has grown into a fine tall boy and could beat all at the high jump."

A fine tall boy! Evie read the words with a lurch of the heart. On one wall of the little wooden house were two series of short horizontal lines, like the rungs of a ladder, with dates beside each line. They were marked with two initials, P. and C. Sometimes her fingers touched the last date with a caressing motion. 1923. How high on the wall would the new rungs be placed if the two bonny heads were here to push the ruler and pencil up the wall to their utmost stretch, heels, of course, firmly on the floor?

Still more poignant reminders were the camping trips to Kulivalavu, so reminiscent of past holidays. Each time she climbed to the rocks behind the forest bungalow. There were the stone trains and birds just where the children had left them, so real that the little dog Rover still barked at them. One year she found that storms had blown off a few wheels from the trains, the funnel off an engine, and the beaks off some of the birds. Carefully she replaced them.

On more than one such holiday her beloved friend Olive shared her wanderings on the heights at Kulivalavu. After the sudden death of his first wife Mr. Morling, left with two little boys, had been completely helpless. There had seemed just one solution. He must marry again. There had been reports to make in which both Morling and Olive were involved. The Brands had invited them to go on holiday with them. Then Evie, often the matchmaker for the young hill Christians, had gently helped bring about the desired denouement. Olive had not wanted to be married. Her work with the *zenana* women had been her first and only passion. But, always selfless, her loyalty to the good of the mission prevailed. She had married Mr. Morling. Though it was not a love match, in time they became deeply devoted and united in their work together. After their marriage they had often spent a holiday on the hills with Evie and Jesse.

"This morning," Jesse wrote the children on one such occasion, "Mama and Mrs. Morling went up to the rocks behind the bungalow where you used to build trains and make birds and animals with the stones, and they had a little service together." Yet even Olive's companionship could not fill the void left by merry childish voices and small running feet.

Not that there was ever a dearth of children to care for. In every camping place, every school, as well as in the Girls' Home, she found the sick to be tended, the unloved to be caressed, the destitute to be clothed. At Christmas time every child was fitted with a warm garment. One year there were not enough coats to go around. There were so many wee people in the Gundunni school that, by the time all were fitted out with coats, there were but few small ones left for Avarankadu. Finally there was just one, too small even for the tiniest scholar. Many little hands had seized it to try it on, but it just would not fit. At Avarankadu Evie and the Bible woman Gnanamoni set to work cutting down the long sleeves of the bigger coats to suit the small scholars. The children went away happy, though they were odd little figures in the long coats with big short sleeves.

The next day was Sunday, and after the service Evie went outside with the teacher and his wife to find a tall man standing by the door, a weak, pale baby in his arms. Her heart leaped hopefully. Could this be the little orphan they had been told about and for whom they had been praying and longing? For a year and a half no child had been given them. At the Girls' prayer meeting someone had suggested that they should ask for at least one child to be given them before the year ended. With great earnestness they had prayed, but now the year was nearly gone, and no child had come.

"Is your baby well?" enquired Evie, not daring to ask why he had come. Then—Oh, the joy of having the child quietly handed to her, of clasping the sweet mite in her arms, of cutting away its unkempt hair and giving it a nice warm bath! But—where to find clothes in that far-off station for such a tiny thing? Of course! The wee coat that would not fit! It was just right. Coincidence? She did not think so. Surely God had planned this answer to prayer just before Christmas! They named the baby Rhoda.

But even these satisfactions could not fill the void left by Paul and Connie. Perhaps it was the absence of their children that so tightened the bond between Evie and Jesse. So completely had they become one that during even brief separations she felt only partially alive. They could not always travel to distant stations together. When the doctor accompanied Jesse Evie had to remain at Vazhavanthi to carry on the medical work. And then there were the terrible weeks when he was away on the plains.

"A few days with him somewhere on the hills is not so bad," she wrote once during one of these long preaching tours, "but when no letter comes and he is four days away— !"

When letters finally came, they helped assuage the loneliness. Jesse was an incurable romantic. "Darling," one of them ended, "I love you and long for the time when I shall return to you. It is three weeks tomorrow since we parted. I reckon that we shall be together within another three weeks. Perhaps in a fortnight . . . I kiss your sweet lips, my own girl. Your husband, Jesse."

His return made up for all the waiting. One year he and Mr. Morling were invited to preach at the huge Syrian Church convention held on a dry river bed in Travancore, for four days preaching to an eager congregation of some two thousand Christians. His absence seemed interminable.

> Jess came up the hills on the horse I sent down for him [she wrote to the children]. We watched and watched till the sun had nearly set and I began to wonder however I should feel if darkness fell. Then at last to my 'coo-ees' a faint sound came in answer, and then we saw a distant mounted figure and rushed down to the rice fields to meet him. But even then we could not reach him for the horse refused to cross the muddy stretch, and I had to flounder about seeking a way over . . . Well, I've got my own dear Jess back again, and I feel like having a prayer meeting every day!

The next year, 1928, she was able to go to the convention with him. It was a memorable experience, sitting in the great *pandal* with hundreds of people, all dressed in white, all radiant of face and rejoicing in the faith that St. Thomas was supposed to have brought to India nearly two thousand years ago. Then there was the journey home in a houseboat down the Pamba river, by the lagoons and backwaters of Travancore, beautiful as a dream, followed by the train trip through the western ghauts.

"Mother nearly frantic," Jesse wrote the children, "because she could not paint both sides at once!" . . . "The people were so glad to see us back, and we rejoiced to find all well, including some 30,000 young silkworms that had hatched out during our absence."

The work was becoming more and more demanding. By now Jesse was preaching in some ninety hamlets surrounding the six stations. During one year he gave nearly 4,000 sermons to over 25,000 people. By 1927 medical service had been given to more than 25,000. Medicine, agriculture, silk industry, education, weaving, carpentering—yes, and banking, civil rights, even law. The missionary's task was like his Master's. He had come that men might have life and have it more abundantly. He spent hours reading law that he might better understand the rights of the hill people who were constantly being victimised by the landowners and money lenders "downstairs" on the plains. Shocked to find farmers burdened with debts and ruinous interest, thirty to thirty-five per cent per annum, he organised a cooperative society, funded through money borrowed on bond from the Salem Bank, so that the farmers need not pay such exorbitant interest to the lenders.

Such crowds of people to see me today [he wrote the children in August, 1927]. A group of cooperative society members to whom I have just issued loans from the Salem Bank totalling fifty pounds. This same society only last week finished paying back the money they had previously borrowed, and I was able to shew their old bond, cancelled, to the other missionaries. It reminded me of the passage in the 2nd of Ephesians (I think it is) about Christ taking the torn fragments of our bond (of sin) and nailing it to his cross.

That same year Jesse persuaded the government to build thirty miles of bridle paths on the Kolli Hills. The poor people had been paying the road tax for many years, and he reckoned that during the past thirty years not less than two thousand pounds had been taken from their pockets—that is, if they had had pockets! Yet not a yard of road had been made. He was also able to persuade the district board to hire hill people to do the work. He himself supervised much of the road building.

One day in 1928 a crowd of farmers came to the house in fear and consternation. Four hundred of them had been given notice to quit their lands, some of which they had been cultivating for generations. Would the *Dhori* not come with them and plead with the collector? The *Dhori* would.

Gathering together the victimised farmers, Jesse descended with them to the plains and, accompanied by Mr. Morling, led the procession through the streets of Namakal to the office of the Collector, the highest district official. Never, confessed Mr. Morling later, had he felt so self-conscious as when marching through the main road of this populous town with a motley crowd of three or four hundred simply clad hill men. Not so Jesse. These were his people. He was as proud to be their champion as was Joshua leading his desert riff-raff into the Promised Land.

"What's all this *tamasha* coming?" demanded the Collector in amazement. Finding his compound stormed, he speedily gave the leader of the threatening army an audience.

Jesse explained. "These people have all their lands mortgaged to merchants here on the plains. None have lands of their own. Their crops, bananas, grains, all have to be brought down. They are so heavily in debt that they get no benefit themselves from all their labour. Now, as a crowning injustice, they have been ordered to leave the lands they have cultivated for generations."

The Collector was amazed. Unjust certainly, he agreed. After the interview Jesse stood on the steps of the office and told his clients that no man need leave his land unless he received higher orders. There was every possibility of the dispute being settled in their favour. It was. It was decreed that no plainsman should hold land on the hills unless he himself tilled it.

A Joshua? Yes. And often a Judge also.

Three brothers were quarrelling [Jesse once wrote the children] about the division of their property, so I arranged for them to first make three equal divisions of all their land and trees, etc., not saying who was to have each portion. Then when all had agreed that the property was equally divided, they were to put three pieces of paper in a bag, marked No. 1, No. 2, and No. 3. Then a little child was to come and pick out of the bag the slip of paper that came first to hand. That portion was to be the eldest brother's. The next slip was to be the younger's, and the last the youngest's. I hope they will not quarrel any more.

Occasionally Jesse became an arbiter in marital problems. For instance, there was Malayan, one of the *tapal* (post) men who had been employed as a runner in the early days before the post office, sent down to the plains to collect and deliver mail and bring up supplies. With others he had helped also in the rice fields and

88

attended the Bible class. He lived in a poor village at a distance and longed to join the Christian community at Vazhavanthi, but his wife was too bound by caste customs. At that time those who wished to become Christians were usually cast out by their fellow-villagers. "I'll bring my wife," Malayan kept promising. Then one noonday they saw a tiny group wending its way across the field, slowly, so slowly, Malayan urging on his wife with her baby. They were given a great welcome.

Soon, however, their Hindu relatives arrived, coaxing them to return, then, when this was to no avail, cursing them in the name of their gods. Evie, who had been called away, returned to find poor Malayan sitting on the ground, his little son stiff in his arms with a convulsion. The result of their cursing, crowed the relatives. But the fit passed, and Malayan remained true to his faith. He wanted to be baptised and take the name of Paul. But first his marital status must be legalised. He could not marry the woman he called his wife because she had once been married to a small boy, though she had never lived with him. Jesse wrote to lawyers in Madras. No, they replied, there was no divorce in Hinduism. Poor Malayan! Attending a baptism, he was even more grieved to see another man take the name of Paul. But all ended well. On holiday in the Nilgiris Jesse met a Christian High Court judge. Hill people, said the judge, had a code of their own which permitted the divorce of cast-off wives. The husband merely had to declare in public (or put his thumb mark to a statement on paper), "*Vendam* (not wanted)". It might be necessary to refund the marriage fees. They returned to the hills, jubilant. Malayan's marriage was regularised, and, as no two boys at that time took the same baptismal name, Malayan became Stephen.

It had been seven years before they made their first convert. Now more than another seven years had passed. Still the number who had dared acknowledge Yesu-swami as their Lord and Master was pitifully small, but it was growing. At last one of their fondest dreams was being fulfilled. For years Jesse had been training young hill men to become Christian workers. Now six of them had been accepted as members of the mission staff, to be sent out as teachers and preachers into their own hill villages . . . Solomon, Jacob and his wife Manomani, Aaron, Moses, James. It was the first glimpse of the goal towards which they had laboured : the evangelisation of the Kolli Hills by Kolli Christians.

But Jesse had far bigger dreams. One day in 1928 Evie stood with him on a high crest at Puliampetty. Behind them, bare rock sheer and steep, the Kollis reared their last thousand feet out of green skirting forests to the skyline. Below, the plains shimmered in a golden haze. And on the horizon, ranged in stark grandeur, were four other mountain ranges, as remote and mysterious as the Kollis had once seemed.

"Beautiful," murmured Evie. "Oh *stottherum, stottherum,* praise!" Seating herself, she drew paints and brush and a scrap of paper from her knapsack and, with fingers almost trembling in their haste, began to paint.

Jesse did not sit down. Hands plunged in his pockets, dark eyes kindling, he stood brooding, restless, gaze sweeping from one remote crest to another.

"Kollis, Pachais, Kalryans . . ." he repeated softly.

"Yes," said Evie, her fingers trying vainly to capture their beauty. She well remembered the story about the three ranges which had become inhabited when the armies had swept down from the north, forcing many of the southern plainsmen to seek refuge in the hills. According to legend three brothers quarrelled and fought each other with knives. Coming to the Cauvery river they washed their blood-stained weapons, then, like Abraham and Lot, decided to separate. The oldest chose the larger hills of the range, the Kalryans, the middle one the Pachais; the youngest came here to the Kollis.

Jesse too was remembering the legend. "In Christ," he said musingly, "they might become one again. We must go to them." His voice quickened, rose to vibrant intensity. "And not only the Pachais and Kalryans. The Peria Malai also, and the Chitteris! All five of them. You hear, Evie? Before we die we must go to all five ranges and take the saving message of the Christ!"

Evie's fingers became still. She looked up into his face. Was it sacrilege to compare it with that other which had also been transfigured on a mountaintop?

"Yes," she said eagerly. The word held all the solemnity of a vow.

9

SOON AFTERWARDS THEY made a long trek to the Pachais (green mountains), about five miles from the eastern side of the Kollis, travelling on horseback, crossing the plains between the two ranges, staying in the forest bungalow and taking the long zig-zag mule path up the mountain. They took some of the young Kolli Christians with them, including James, to give their witness to the people. The people of the Pachais traced their origin from the elder of two brothers, children of a younger brother having gone to the Kollis. Thus the two tribes were related and called each other *Anna* and *Tambi*, elder and younger brother, but the Pachai people were not allowed to enter Kolli houses because they practised tattooing, a custom offensive to the Kolli swamis.

As they travelled over these new hills they were surprised at the extent of forests. There were no large open areas as on the Kollis. The lower hills were covered with bamboo clumps, always a sign of fever. There was much sandalwood. Narrow footpaths ran in all directions with a fine disregard for steep grades, bogs, streams. Instead of being walled in, as on the Kollis, the villages were surrounded by extensive bamboo fences, the people living in the middle, surrounded by their cattle and pigs, an arrangement doubtless diminishing the loss by wild beasts, but adding to the variety of village smells!

When they entered the first village the people lurked behind their houses or peeped out through cracks in their doors. At last some of the Kolli Hills Christians began to sing hill tunes so curious to strangers but familiar to the tribes. Swiftly there came a change. The villagers drew near and listened to the Gospel story. As they went from village to village, they were struck by the effect produced by the testimony of the people's fellow-castemen from the Kollis. Eyes were riveted on each one that spoke.

Not until their second camp, in a northern portion of the hills, did the people wake to the fact that they had brought medicines. Then they were thronged from morning to night. Numbers came to have teeth extracted. They found many cases of enlarged spleen and other malarial complications. They treated 115 cases in one day. Medicines were exhausted, but it was hard to send people away. When the time came to depart crowds still surrounded them, clamouring for medicines. They kept on doing their best until their baggage coolies could be seen in the distance wending their way towards the plains. Still the poor folk stood pleading. Never would Evie forget that line of fevered and disease-stricken people holding out empty hands!

As they rode through hill villages on their way to the plains, villagers came out in smiling crowds. After a rough scramble down to the plains 2,500 feet below they came to a village of hill people who literally besieged them with demands for medicine. They were able to treat only a few surgical cases before starting on horseback across the plains back to the Kollis. It was a memorable ride. The first four miles were a waste of howling wilderness hemmed in on both sides by spurs of the main range. Then they came to a green and smiling country watered by streams from both Pachais and Kollis—miles of green rice fields with water sparkling among the emerald shoots, then a great lake where fishers were casting their nets and swarms of water fowl were swimming and diving; then into the jungle fringing the foot of the Kollis. They spent that night in a forest rest house at the foot of their own hills, with great pinnacles and towers of gneiss blotting out the western sky. By afternoon they were home again after fifteen days of adventure. But they had left forty villages still unvisited.

"Some day," vowed Jesse, "we must go back there and stay!"

Later they discovered to their dismay that as well as giving his witness to the people James (Sevi) had carefully explained to them that he was the son of the *Nathan*, head chief of the Kollis!

"Oh, James, James," thought Evie when she heard, "how could you sell your heavenly birthright for the pride of the Kolli kingdom!"

Such disappointments were not uncommon, for the new disciples were as human as Peter and Thomas and—yes, as Judas. Not long afterward two of the workers, Jacob and his wife Manomani, left the staff to receive higher wages on a planter's estate in Ceylon. The hill workers began complaining because they were paid less than those from the plains. Jesse promptly equalised the wages, but with this extra expense it seemed necessary to close the station at Chulavandi. No, decided the workers, it must not be so. They held a meeting and agreed to subscribe enough to keep it open. *Stottherum*, praise! Perhaps at last some were beginning to understand the implications of their faith.

Never had the work looked so promising. The Christian community had grown to fifty. In 1928 medical attendance numbered over 12,000, 3,000 of them malarial cases, more than 600 minor operations. There were nine schools on the hills, two taught by hill Christians. The mission farm was producing sufficient food grains for the whole community. The carpenter shop, employing four young hill men, was providing furniture for all the schools and constructing the woodwork for an enlarged chapel. The silk industry was thriving. A store in the centre of the compound, with a rat-proof grain shed adjoining it, provided foodstuffs and cloth for both community and outsiders. The bridle paths which Jesse had secured from the government and helped build served the whole range with a network of communication.

The Brands were due for a furlough in 1929, but, as had happened before, another missionary family seemed to need it more than they did, and they agreed to postpone it for a year.

"It will pass quickly," Jesse assured cheerfully. "A year is a short time. And who knows? This one may bring the greatest blessings of all!"

A year short? To Evie it seemed interminable. In a year a boy could grow into a man, a beautiful carefree golden-haired child into a sober young woman. With Jesse gone for nearly two months on a mission tour with Mr. Morling of the churches of South India, she felt indescribably alone. It frightened her sometimes because she knew her dependence, her weakness without him. Jesse knew it, too. "Never leave Evelyn alone," he had secretly begged Mr. Morling when, some months before, he had been so severely ill with paratyphoid that his fellow missionary and his wife Olive had been called up from the plains.

Jesse came back from the long mission tour more tired than she had ever seen him. They should go to the Nilgiris for a rest, she told him. But he would not agree, and she did not insist. Very well, then they must "stay put" for a time, no long trips. Never had he been so full of hope, so glad to be back in his beloved hills.

"How I love it all," he exclaimed with a glow of enthusiasm, "the red earth, the grey rocks, the green fields, the lofty hills, all these works of God—how I love them!"

His letters to the children that spring abounded in the joys of living.

He wrote to Paul in May: I was glad to hear of your long walk with Norman to Northwood. I wonder whether you make observations of nature on these jaunts. Yesterday when I was riding over the wind-swept hilltops around Kulivalavu, I could not help thinking of an old hymn that begins, "Heaven above is deeper blue, flowers with purer beauty glow". When I am alone on these long rides, I just love the sweet smelling world, the dear brown earth, the lichen on the rocks, the heaps of dead brown leaves drifted like snow in the hollows. God means us to delight in his world. Just observe. Remember. Compare. And be always looking to God with thankfulness and worship for having placed you in such a delightful corner of the universe as Planet Earth.

Already they were making plans for the coming furlough. "We think that the first week in March will be the probable time of our setting sail. That will land us home about the end of March, in time for your Easter holidays."

The Mountains of Death were no respecters of persons. For fifteen years both Evie and Jesse had struggled with frequent onslaughts of the Kollis' worst demon, malaria. But seldom had

93

they let it interfere with any task they considered important. It was so this spring. Jesse's diary recorded such aberrations as he might have mentioned changes in weather.

May 17. Fever 102 . . . May 23. Dr. not back from leave. No quinine! . . . May 30. Putting pump down well . . . May 31. Preparation for monthly meetings. Began reaping paddy. Fever 101.5 . . . June 1. Fever 104 . . . June 2. Monthly meetings. Got up with 100 but fever went off as day went on. Preached on Matt. 4: 19 . . . June 4. Reaping paddy . . . June 5. Pulled down end wall of chapel and brought wall of addition to floor level all around . . . June 8. Started to Moonoor, but Dobbin lost a shoe at Yelligrar, and I had to return . . . June 9. Preached on "Arise, shine, for your light is come".

As usual, he could joke about such things as fever.

My darling girlie [he wrote Connie on June 10]. Cannot write a long letter this week, 'cos a rise of temp. is just coming on. These attacks of fever are very amusing. They give one due warning by unmistakable signs and symptoms of their approach, so one can make preparation by giving directions to workmen and getting urgent letters written, etc. Do you remember the "snake stage" when you want to wriggle like a snake? Really, that is the most unpleasant part of the attack. When the heat comes on, I generally sing Tamil lyrics or compose sermons. Do you remember how you and Paul used to sit on my back in the ague stage? I suppose you have grown so big nowadays that to sit on my back would squash me flat! Heaps of love from Your own Daddy.

It was the last letter he would ever write her. On Tuesday, June 11, Jesse made his usual rounds with Dr. Samuel, visiting each house to see if there might be standing water or any uncleanness which would encourage malaria. Immediately after this Jesse himself complained of fever. His temperature rose to 106. A few days before, one of the teachers had been suddenly attacked by a strange malady which was later discovered to be blackwater fever, an illness almost unknown in southern India. They had given him injections and reduced his temperature with cold water baths. He had subsequently recovered. Fearing Jesse's symptoms were similar, Evie and Dr. Samuel applied the same treatments, and the following day his temperature was down to 100. Still Evie was not satisfied. She sent a message to the Morlings, asking them to telegraph for Miss Savage, a nurse on the Nilgiris, and to bring a doctor from the plains. Olive left Namakal at once and arrived at Vazhavanthi on Thursday. The doctor came soon after. Never having seen a case of blackwater fever, he applied conventional remedies for malaria and sat chattering while Jesse, who seemed to be rallying, listened with quiet resignation.

"It will be all right," Olive assured Evie. "He's going to get well."

False hope. For the next torturing days and nights Evie listened to her beloved calling for water which he could not retain, watched his eyes glaze, his flesh turn dry and yellowed, his blood slowly drain away. If only I had taken him to the Nilgiris! she blamed herself, guilt almost outweighing weariness and despair. Dr. Innes would have known what to do, given him blood transfusions. If he dies, I will have killed him!

All day long the people stood outside, looking in the windows, weeping, expressing their grief volubly yet not with the violent wailing so characteristic of their race. It was a subdued, private grief, too deep for extravagant effusion. "He is our father and mother! If he goes, who will protect us? What shall we do—oh, what shall we do!" But when the end came, on the evening of Saturday 15th June, just as sun was setting, such a wailing went up that it must have reached the very portals of heaven. It was the people who mourned. Evie was too dazed, too broken even to weep.

But there were things to be done, words to be said, and she did and said them. "We will bury him as we have buried others, our teachers, our children. No coffin, just a simple bamboo mat." . . . "Yes, come and look at him, all of you who loved him. But he is not here. He has gone to be with his Lord." . . . "Lord, if by his death more people can be saved than through his life, let it even be so!"

From all over the hills they came, those whom he had healed and taught, whose lands he had restored, whose souls and bodies he had struggled to save. Men to whom grave digging was the repulsive task of the lowest outcastes willingly prepared the *dhori's* resting place; those who would never enter the place of a funeral because of death's defilement came crowding into the chapel that Sunday morning to listen to Mr. Morling's service. Though four men had been appointed to carry the body to the hillside grave, men walked in a thick line on either side, and those who could not put a shoulder under because there was no room stretched out their hands to touch the wood, feeling they must do something. Christians and Hindus, all were united in common grief. "*Deva Pitha!*" they sang as they moved in sad yet triumphant procession. "The Lord is my shepherd." At the last minute Solomon, one of the workers in a distant station, came dashing up to the grave, wailing for "my father".

"Do not weep," Olive tried to comfort Evie. "Try to think of his blessed homecoming."

Not weep? A useless plea. Her eyes were empty and dry as the Indian river beds before the monsoon.

Though Jesse was buried exactly as other members of the community, simply, nothing separating his body from the earth he so loved, his mountain friends insisted on providing a fitting memorial. Stone masons, fearing the dread fever, could not be persuaded to come to the hills. After futile attempts to make a headstone, first by fashioning a ferro-concrete slab, then by chipping one out of solid rock, they almost gave up the idea as impossible. However, finally a giant stone was hauled for about half a mile over fields and across swamps by thirty-two of the hill men, who spent three and a half days bringing it to the site, using ropes, poles, rollers, crowbars, and any other implements they could find. Words would later be cut on the smooth square panel:

Jesse Mann Brand, 1885–1929
In the year 1907 he came to India and
in the year 1913 he settled on the
KOLLI HILLS
On the 15th of June (2nd of the Tamil month Ani), he
delivered up his life to the Lord on behalf of the people
of these hills.
'O death, where is thy victory? Thanks be to God, which
giveth us the victory through our Lord Jesus Christ.'

Four

"Though I walk through the valley. . .
thou art with me. . . ."

Psalm 23:4

1

THE SECOND CABLE followed closely on the first, which had apprised the families in England of Jesse Brand's sudden death. "Cannot one of you come?" it begged in starkly simple desperation.

Ruth Harris, Bertie's oldest daughter, was in her fourth year of medical study. Her father met her as she returned home from college on the Wednesday after Jesse's death. "Your aunt has wired for someone to go to her," he said.

The girl nodded. "Of course. She should not be alone. Who is going?"

"We don't know yet. No one seems able to—unless—"

She sensed the troubled implication in his voice. Surely, she thought with dismay, one of the other nieces could fill this need, one free from all except home duties! But it soon developed that all had reasonable excuses. Very well. She must go. She made the decision reluctantly but cheerfully, satisfied that the need constituted a call from God.

"But—your studies," objected her father, knowing how anxious she was to complete them and begin her work as a well-qualified missionary. "Should you interrupt them? It might mean a whole year's delay."

"If this is God's will," said Ruth confidently, "He will see to that."

On Saturday she was on a ship *en route* to India.

The cable announcing her coming was for Evelyn the first glimmer of light amid bleak desolation. At least she was not left completely alone. She must go home, of course. The mission board expected her to leave at once, in accordance with strict mission policy, but in her stunned bewilderment she saw only one goal clearly. She must continue the work on the mountains until other leaders were appointed. Stubbornly, blindly, she clung to this purpose as one shipwrecked clings to a bit of driftwood. She must save the work for which Jesse had given his life. The board had never given it more than halfhearted support. Even Mr. Morling believed that work on the plains was more important. She would wait here for months, if need be, until another appointment was made. Yet *how*! How could she bear it without Jesse?

She was a machine, automatic and mindless, driven to action by some invisible force, a puppet manipulated by strings in remote impersonal hands. Even the words she spoke or wrote seemed to come from other lips and fingers . . . except when sudden realisation broke through despair and bewilderment and she tried to give expression to the terrible aloneness, the groping after a faith and assurance she kept glibly proclaiming but could not feel. She could not paint. The world had lost all colour, and brushes were soft, made to create beauty. But words were stark and poignant, like knife thrusts. They could be a better catharsis than tears. She found a bitter release in writing poetry.

> We were only one
> So when the sun shone,
> Shone on us,
> It shone on one.
>
> And when the rain came
> It was just the same
> It rained on one
> It fell on one.
>
> When He withheld from us
> 'Twas ever thus,
> We were but one
> To feel the miss
> Of any bliss
> Under the sun.
>
> Then came the storm
> The cold and bitter weather.
> It hurt us not,
> For we were one together.
>
> When He took him away
> Nothing was left
> But a heart bereft
> With no one to share
> No one to care.

No, He who took him is here,
No one by my side
But He is my guide.

Trying vainly to compensate for Jesse's absence, also to drown her own despair, she plunged into feverish activity, visiting the stations, holding clinics, inspecting schools, giving Gospel talks, holding prayer meetings, settling quarrels, paying the workers, keeping the accounts, superintending the Girls' Home, the little community store, yes, even the woodworking shed, where the young carpenters were making furniture for the new chapel addition. She had done all these things alone, joyously, when Jesse had been away on the plains. Now there was no joy. Dutifully she prayed, sang hymns, repeated the divine promises, talked of the more perfect life to which the beloved *dhori* had gone. But the word *stottherum* was not on her lips.

Suddenly she had lost all fear. Always before she had been timid about riding Jesse's horse, a spirited animal capable of erratic speeding. Now she chose that horse in preference to her own gentle mount. What difference now if she did have an accident, even one resulting in death? Much easier to die than face the future! Besides, she needed the more efficient means of travel for all she must do. She felt driven, compelled to carry on the work as nearly as possible the way Jesse would have done.

There was a distant village that he had visited just before his death. "Honey Village", they had called it. He had camped there overnight, found the people interested, and promised that he would come back. She had to keep his promise. But the village was far distant, on one of the most difficult and stony mountain trails. At one point the path led straight over sheer outcroppings of rock, with a sharp drop at one side. It had always terrified her, even with Jesse. Now she must travel it alone. As she approached the spot most dreaded, memory smote her.

"I've found a new way to travel," Jesse had said just before his last sickness, "so we don't need to pass over those terrible rocks."

She could almost hear his voice. Not since his going had she felt so alone and desolate. *Now he will never be able to tell me!* So overcome was she with grief that she scarcely noticed that the horse, *his* horse, had turned from the path at right angles and entered into the jungle bushes. Jolted into awareness, she did not turn him back but gave him full rein. Amazed, scarcely breathing in her wonder and excitement, she let him carry her through the forest, over a little stream, and finally by a circuitous but much easier path, lead her straight into the village which was her destination. How? He had been there only once before, but he had gone unerringly, as if he felt a strong sure hand on the reins.

" 'I will lead the blind in a way they know not,' " she thought in humble gratitude. " 'I will lead them in paths they have not known.' " For the first time she felt an easing of the terrible loneliness.

Ruth Harris arrived near the end of July, and Evelyn went down to the plains to meet her. The sight of the familiar face, the embrace of the strong comforting arms, released emotions which had been locked in frozen numbness. For the first time Evelyn Brand was able to weep, unrestrainedly.

Ruth, young, competent, dedicated, immediately became a tower of strength. Determined herself to become a missionary to India, she was preconditioned by a love of the country and its people. Undaunted by the "mountains of death" with their hazards and discomforts—heat, dust, winds, snakes, worms, malaria, rocky trails, frightening declivities—she took everything in her stride. Evelyn was still living in the little wooden house, only the office having been removed to the new building, and she found bitter solace in sharing each beloved feature with this first visiting member of her family.

"See—his desk, where he wrote all his sermons, just as he left it, the Bible still open at his last text." . . . "Jesse built the two little wooden beds, with the bars across, such a clever builder" . . . "I remember when we named those two little shelves on the wall of the dining room. See? One says 'God first', the other 'Emmanuel' " . . .

Ruth entered into the work with zest and skill, her medical knowledge supplementing Evelyn's canny know-how and experience with tropical disease. Together they rode all over the hills visiting the eight out-stations, Evelyn on Jesse's horse, Ruth on Evie's, which was fortunately more tractable since it was Ruth's first experience in the saddle. Now that tears were released they flowed easily. Wherever they went Evelyn would start to cry, and the people would wipe her tears away, weeping with her, as was their custom, loudly and copiously.

Ruth was not spared the discomforts. Though it was not the monsoon season, she had more than one taste of mountain rains. One day when they were trekking into villages from a little forest bungalow, where they had left overnight equipment, thunder clouds rolled up suddenly and a fierce storm burst upon them. Frightened, the horses speeded into a wild run, and it was all they could do to control them. When they arrived at the bungalow they were drenched. They had brought night gear but no changes of clothing. The roof of corrugated iron leaked badly, but they managed to drag their cots to a dry section of the floor. They got into bed by the light of their hurricane lantern, and dried their soaked clothes piece by piece above it. Several times on camping trips they crawled into drenched beds. To Evie these were obviously common occurrences, to be treated with unconcern, even humour.

"Oh, how jolly!" she exclaimed once, settling herself on a rough plank, the earth floor soaking wet all around.

It was her hill children, Ruth soon discovered, who were "Mother Brand's" chief concern. Each morning early she hurried down the little path under big jackfruit trees and over a small grassy patch to the Girls' Home, and in every village they visited she followed up cases of babies or young children who she felt were being mistreated or neglected. One disturbed her especially. Day after day she visited the house where a small child was kept and, watched her being slowly starved and going blind.

"Her relatives don't want her," Evie scolded. "Still they refuse to let her go."

Finally in her concern she became reckless, took the child up, and bore her away to the bungalow, where, in spite of careful and tender nursing, she died.

To Evie's great relief a couple was found to take over the work. The Throwers, who had barely started their furlough in England, agreed to return at once to India. It was soon after Jesse's death that Mrs. Thrower came on the words in her daily reading. "Moses my servant is dead. Therefore arise . . ." It seemed like divine leading. Knowing what the sacrifice must mean to a young couple just returned home, Evie sent up a prayer of thanksgiving.

Now she became more unrelaxing in labour, especially for the young inmates of the Girls' Home. The new missionaries could not possibly know their backgrounds and problems as she did, or the mountain customs which could so jeopardise their futures. There were eight or nine girls who were old enough to be married. She must find good husbands for them before her departure, preferably Christians. She was keeping her accounts in the bungalow when one of the young workers on the compound entered. Approaching her desk, he stood silently, fumbling awkwardly at the loose folds of his *dhoti*.

"I know what he has come for," Evelyn said in a low English aside to Ruth. "He wants a bride." Without looking up, she kept busily engaged with her accounts. When the silence continued she added, "I'm not going to help him out. If he wants a bride, he must get up his courage to ask for her."

He might have stood there for hours, saying nothing, if she had not finally taken pity on him. She looked up smiling. "What do you want?" she enquired in Tamil.

Still silence. She returned to her accounts. No use. Resigning herself to the inevitable, she repeated the question. "*Ayoh*! What do you want?"

"A girl," he muttered finally.

She knew the one he wanted, Kulanthi. It would be a good marriage. Evie talked with the girl and found her willing. Soon after in the chapel the wedding was solemnised by Mr. Morling. It was one of many such marriages she arranged during the last weeks of her stay on the Kollis. The Throwers were to arrive early in October, and passage for Evelyn and Ruth was engaged on the steamer *Mantua* sailing from Bombay on the 12th.

The last days were not all times of sadness. In her report to the mission board Evie was able to cite many reasons for thanksgiving.

How much confirmation and proof there was of His unfailing love and mercy to us and the hill people in those last meetings! Firstly, at the Harvest Thanksgiving when we had to acknowledge a better ingathering of crops than we feared owing to the dry seasons, and all brought their offerings. Then Mr. Morling came, and we opened the new wing of the chapel, the foundations of which our dear one had laid but five months before. Very lovingly did Mr. Morling unveil the memorial slab erected by the workers and hill people in his memory.

And in addition to more weddings there was a baptism. How Jesse had rejoiced over his first convert to be baptised, clearing away the reeds from the stream that wound through the meadow at the bottom of the hill where the cows grazed! Always baptisms had been occasions of thanksgiving—even the time when Jesse, still standing in the stream after baptising Sevi-James, had seen a large snake poking its head up out of the water just where the immersion had taken place!

She heard some of the children whispering to each other. They were sure that "Papa", as they had always called him, was watching.

2

ALWAYS ON A sea voyage Evelyn had had someone to guide, protect, manage the details of travel. This time it was Ruth Harris. Efficient, cheerful, practical, she attended to the baggage, the cabin accommodation, the tips. Healthily robust, she nursed her aunt through the agonies of seasickness. Released from healing activity, Evelyn had time now to immerse herself in grief. No rushing with her paints on this voyage to capture the emeralds of Egyptian palms, the snow-capped wonder which was Etna, the incredible blues of the Mediterranean. During all the long month she withdrew into a sort of netherland, suspended between past and future.

"Just think!" Ruth tried to wake her out of introspection. "You'll be seeing the children within days . . . hours. Aren't you excited? How long has it been, six whole years?"

Six years, yes. The children. But it was only the brisk stimulus of the Channel and the sight of Dover's white cliffs that roused the mother in her to anticipation. Yet when the ship docked at Tilbury it was Ruth who hurried first down the gangplank, Evelyn who followed almost reluctantly in her shadow.

"There they are!" a familiar voice shouted.

The family had come down by the boat train from London and was there waiting, waving, shouting. While Ruth rushed about, kissing, shaking hands, Evelyn's eyes sought frantically for two small figures. Would she know them? Suddenly she was enveloped in a warm embrace.

"Mother!" The words were smothered in sobs. "Mother, mother, darling!"

They clung to each other, weeping together. Thankfully Evelyn kissed the wet cheeks, smoothed back a stray lock of golden hair, felt her starved arms filled again. Older, of course, taller, less chubby, but the same Connie. Then her eyes went searching again, scanning the faces.

"See, there he is, Mother! There's Paul!"

Evelyn stared. Not—not that slender young man standing so aloof and dignified, a stranger yet with features incredibly like— With a little cry she went towards him, arms outstretched, tears running down her cheeks. She had to reach up to kiss him, and he stood rigid, unbending. She could not help seeing the dismay in his eyes, feeling the cold restraint of his returning kiss. Of course. Six years was a long time, especially to a boy of fifteen. She probably looked as strange to him as he did to her.

Later, years later, Paul Brand would disclose his reactions to that meeting. Riding down on the boat train, he had been almost sick with excitement. He had tried to picture Mother as he had last seen her, tall, graceful, full of fun and laughter, vibrant as the bits of quicksilver he had once spilled from a broken thermometer. And then there had come trailing down the gangplank in the wake of cheerful, competent Cousin Ruth–a little, incredibly little, shrunken old lady! This is Mother, he had had to tell himself over and over, trying to make himself believe it. This is my beautiful, tall, graceful, sparkling Mother! It had not occurred to him then that she had found it even more difficult to convince herself that "this is my son".

Like all the Harrises, Evelyn had never been one to keep thoughts and emotions to herself. It was a relief now to let the long-dammed-up streams of her grief overflow. With the host of sympathetic brothers, sisters, nieces, nephews, and, of course, her own two children, she shared all her hopelessness and frustration. All the light had gone out of her life, she kept asserting. She could never be the same again. She and Jesse had been absolutely one, and now her life was worth nothing. Her usefulness was ended. Only Paul listened with reservations, his aching sympathy tempered by shrewd insight. It was his father's death which had done this to his mother. It was wrong for anyone to love another so much, to be so dependent on any one person. He would never, never let this happen to him.

In good time both mother and son adjusted to the new relationship, and in her children, especially in Paul, Evelyn Brand found the focus of a slowly awakening purpose. If her usefulness was ended, then she must make Jesse and his dreams come alive in his son. Of course Paul would follow in his father's footsteps. No need to arouse his sensitivities to the mountains of southern India and their needs. The Kollis were as near to his daily experience as Hampstead Heath, Aaron and Ruth and James and Moses as real as his English schoolmates. Jesse had seen to that. His weekly letters through the five years were masterpieces of humour, adventure, nature notes, inspiration, lively description. The children had read, reread, treasured them, typed quantities of his nature notes into a booklet full of fascinating stories with intriguing titles: "A Fight with a Leopard", "A Tigress and a Motor Car", "The Spider, the Wasp, and the Frog", "A Bullock with Bad Manners", "*Pambu, Pambu* ! (Snake, Snake !)," "Who Steals the Rice?" Some were gems of perceptive truth, like "A Sermon in an Insect". Evelyn reread it with brimming eyes.

. . . . .

In my sermon this morning I told about a wonderful poochi I had seen in the rice fields. The people call it the "monkey insect" because it is so clever. It lives right inside the slime and mud of the rice fields, and yet it is never dirty. When I first discovered it I did not see the insect, but only noticed a heaving of the slime at a certain spot. I stooped down and said to myself: "I wonder what is making the mud heave like that? There must be something alive underneath." Sure enough, as I watched the spot, suddenly up popped a head and a bright little eye. When it saw me move it drew back and buried itself again. This taught me to be quite still next time. The next minute it popped its head out again, watched a little while, and then came right out of the mud as clean as a new pin. It was about one and a half inches long and moved quickly about. Soon it dived down beneath the slime and came up in another place. As it came out of the mud I looked closely at it, and it seemed to be moving in a big air bubble so that the filth did not actually touch it. That is what Jesus means when He says, "Abide in Me".

We can move about in the world with sin all around us and not be made dirty if we abide in Him. That does not mean that we are to be prigs or Pharisees, or to hold ourselves aloof from others, or to be proud, or not to mix in their games. No! Jesus wants His followers to be the sunniest and happiest of people . . .

She was weeping so hard she could not finish. Oh, Jesse, Jesse! You had so much to give and I so little! Why couldn't I have been the one to go? Why, *Why* . . . !

Paul was in his last year at University College School. His mother's presence was a delight and a stimulus—also at times an irritant. Unlike Connie, he had not always applied himself to his studies, as his father's letters had often noted. Now Evelyn saw that he did. There was no concentrating on science, which he liked, at the expense of geography, which he hated, or skipping through lessons to slip off surreptitiously to his scientific experiments or his carpenter's bench in the basement. Pranks also were more prone to discovery, such as climbing up one of the square corner posts of the school's main building and scratching his initials on the second stratum from the top, perhaps forty feet above ground. The aunts had winked at all such escapades, probably because they did not know about them. His mother had a nose for detection.

Then, too, there was the question of his future. This was the year when plans must be made. It was expected, of course, that he would become a missionary like his father. Though he had never actually made the decision, he had vaguely taken it for granted, like growing up to be a man. Now his mother kept depicting the needs of "India's millions", especially those of the tens of thousands on the mountains, in as glowing colours as she had once painted its sunsets. "Remember that high crest, son, at Puliampetty? Your father and I stood there and looked out at the five ranges. 'All of them,' he said, 'we must win all of them for Christ!'" But Paul found the prospect of filling his father's shoes appalling. As if he could!

Evelyn tried hard not to dictate, but she was not the kind of person to keep silent. "You can stay on at school, you know, dear, and take your higher certificate, then go on to college. You have the offer . . ."

Paul shook his head determinedly. He had had enough of that kind of school.

She tried again. "Your father, dear, always wanted to be a doctor. Did you know that he started a course in medicine at Madras University and that he almost returned home to go to medical school here in England? I know he would be pleased if you—"

"*No*!" This time the negative was explosive. Paul had seen his father at work in India and been repelled. Blood and pus! If there was one thing he was sure of, it was that he did not want to be a doctor!

One Sunday a lay preacher came to speak in the church in St. John's Wood. Though a builder by trade, he was known to many as Pastor Warwick. He was a gifted and practical speaker, using homely illustrations from his own experience. When he drew a carpenter's rule from his pocket, Evelyn felt her eyes fill. Just so Jesse, also the loving craftsman, had used the same tool to teach his boys spiritual truths as well as carpentering. She could actually hear his voice.

"See this line, son? Looks straight, doesn't it? But let's put the rule to it. Ah, see how crooked it really was? Like us. We always need to keep the Golden Rule handy, and apply it to everything we do."

Conscious of a quick-drawn breath beside her, she stole a glance at her son's rapt face. Was he remembering, too? She was sure of it when, after the sermon, he whispered, "He's more like Daddy than any other man I've ever seen!"

Of course the visiting preacher came to dinner at the Harrises'. He took time to talk with Paul. "Like tools, boy?"

"Oh, yes, sir! I have a small bench in the basement."

"Use it?"

"I've made a few things."

"Let's see them."

Flushed with pride and embarrassment, Paul took the visitor downstairs and showed him things he had made. Evelyn could not resist following. Paul exhibited a canoe, some intricate apartments he had made for his pet white mice, an aviary. Mr. Warwick was heartily approving. "Good. Like your father. He had a feeling for wood and tools."

Later that afternoon Paul managed to get his mother aside. "I like that man," he confided. "I—I wouldn't mind learning to be a builder myself."

Evelyn Brand's eyes lighted, almost with their old sparkle. She took occasion later to approach Pastor Warwick. "My son is going to be a missionary like his father," she told him, "but if he does he should learn to be a builder, since in the mountains of India we have to build our own houses. His building experience was of inestimable value to my husband Jesse. Would you take Paul into your business and teach him?"

It was settled. When Paul would leave the University College School in December, 1930, he was to become a building apprentice. Meanwhile Evelyn also was making plans. During the year she had been attending more and more meetings in churches around London and telling of the work on the Kollis. She knew now that she herself must go back. Her commitment as a missionary had been to God, not to man, certainly not to one man. She might be less than half a person, but what she was had been committed to her Lord. She was a broken vessel, yes. She would never be whole again. But slowly time was piecing together the fragments. Even a battered, mended pitcher could be a conveyor of living water.

She asked the mission board to return her to the Kolli malai. They refused. It was not sound policy, they had found, to appoint a previous worker to a post under new superiors. It made for tensions. But the importunate widow of the parables was the perfect prototype of Evelyn Brand. Her arguments were caustic and persuasive. Jesse had created the Kolli mission, and she had helped him. Without them it would not exist. They had built most of its assets with their own hands and—she might have added but did not—with their own money. Since she had received a small income from her father's estate after his death, she and Jesse had taken no salary from the board and, not wanting to have more than other mission workers, they had used from her income only enough for the barest necessities, investing all the rest in the work. The board knew this without her telling them, but by subtle innuendoes she made sure they remembered. They finally agreed that she might return to the Kollis, at least for one term.

She sailed in the autumn of 1930, weak, fearful, intolerably lonely, yet struggling desperately to keep contact with the Companion-Presence more real and satisfying than the one she had lost. And somehow she found words to help her gain the necessary strength.

> And must I now go on alone with You,
> And is there no one near to hold my hand?
> And no one who can really understand?
> "I'll do it all for You."
> But there'll be silence round me all the time,
> Silence which even You with all your infinite resource
> Cannot break through.
> "Silence to hear My voice, that's all,
> And I have planned it all for you.
> You have been speaking all the time,
> You would not listen, now no other choice
> But to sit still and hear My voice."
> Speak, Lord, thy servant waits to hear
> Thy gentle whisper, strong and clear.

3

"*Santhosham*, happiness! The *doraisani* has come back! Our mother has come home!"

From all over the Kollis they came, loading her with garlands, bringing gifts of eggs, fruit, handfuls of rice and ragi from their meagre stores, little earthen pots of ghi or clabbered milk or chutney, spices, dearly purchased sweets, bits of treasured finery. Hindus came as well as Christians. They would have knelt, as performing *puja*, worship, if she had let them. She might have been one of the mother goddesses to whom they brought offerings, except that they came in love instead of fear.

Home. Yes, in spite of the desolate sense of loss, she had come home. Good that the new stone house was occupied by the Throwers and that the little wooden house was empty, waiting for her occupancy! Empty? Yes, indescribably so, yet full of memories. She went through the three small rooms built tandem, as Paul had said, like a train of cars, touching familiar objects:

the desk in Jesse's study where he had made his reports and written his sermons; the round table in the middle room where they had eaten, studied, joked, prayed, first four, then two, now one; the little built-in beds which Jesse had made of rosewood, a bar across so little children could not fall out, between them the tall chest which Paul had been sure was "twelve feet high"; the ladder-like marks on the wall.

There was balm as well as sadness in this impact of the familiar. The small empty beds held promises along with memories. The children had merely outgrown them. Sometime they would be coming back to join her in this work so dear to all three of them. "But where are they? Why don't they come now?" the people kept demanding. She tried to make them understand that, like their own boys and girls sent to school on the plains, Paul and Connie must spend years preparing themselves for God's work, learning to teach, perhaps to build and grow better crops and heal. Here also, in spite of the emptiness and silence, Jesse seemed nearer than at any other time since his going.

There were times when memory brought actual physical pain, as when, soon after her arrival back in India, she spent an hour in the post office "downstairs", redeeming 660 rupees worth of cash certificates. How well she remembered being in Jesse's office and discussing if they should put that bit of money into certificates! 1931, when they should mature? If she had known then that she would have to go alone to redeem them! "Come and look, dear," he had said so often when reckoning the accounts. "Maybe you will want to know some day all about it." She had laughed indulgently. "Oh, no, I'm older than you. I'll get to go first."

"Daddy seemed so near," she wrote the children as she sat in a stalled bus beside the road, "and yet I felt sad for it seemed like giving a little bit of the old life away. When I meekly and thankfully took the money, it was with a big ache in my heart for him and those gorgeous days when I laughed and said I'd never need to do the accounts."

The small beds in the house were not often empty. When not away on camping trips much of her work during this term on the Kollis was with children. She was given charge of the hostel, which had been started long ago with Ruth and one or two other little girls. Numbers were constantly increasing. A girl might run away from an unhappy home, sure of finding a haven at the mission compound, and if she was sick or undernourished Evie would keep her close by for a time to give constant nursing. A baby somewhere on the hills might be pronounced *aharthu*, unlucky, and, hearing it was discarded or neglected, Evie would persuade its parents to let her take it. Then she would bring it home and care for it with mother-tenderness until she dared trust it to the matron and older girls in the hostel. This work with children was her greatest joy during these years of lonely adjustment, partly assuaging the constant hunger for her own. Her letters to Paul and Connie abounded in such satisfactions.

Such cute things, sweet babies clinging round your legs when you go in. Just had a romp with them in the moonlight. Not the tinies. They are all lying on the floor calling to me from their wee blankets. . . .

Con Precious, you'd have loved it. I just revelled in it. Mrs. Thrower is away on camp and Matron wanted to go for a village trip with the girls. So I said, "Let me have the babies." Oh, I did enjoy a Sunday romp, with them marching up and down the veranda shouting "Joy, joy, joy!" Then from all sides compound children came running till we were twenty playing at "Joy, joy, joy". Well, if David danced before the ark we ought to be able to jump about on Sunday with babies. . . .

Do hope my little boy the little beggar will get better. He is Enoch, but I don't want him to be "he was not, for God took him"! Such a dear quiet little boy. He has pneumonia . . . Anbu's baby sick. Little Enoch a bit better. Morning: Have just carried little Enoch over here. So many flies and no comfort there. . . .

It died, poor little girlie! But God let me clean it up and make it comfy before it went. So I am thankful and know it is better so, as it would have been a little blind creature . . .

"Babies are all sitting around me. How I love them!"

There was solace, too, in just being once more in the mountains, able to climb higher and higher.

"My little angel girl," she once wrote Connie. "Oh, I've just come down from my high Sunday perch on the rocks. I put my things in a heap, Bible, etc. including stockings and shoes and went a bit higher for a walk. Then forgot which way I'd come and where to find my stuff. You can guess I had a Mauvais Moment, looked here and there, a perfect tangle of bushes and rocks. Well, I'm down again and did find them. But I pictured going on barefoot into the night."

Not that she would have minded going barefoot except for the shock such breach of dignity might cause her fellow missionaries. She loved contact with the earth, even its dirtiest and most repelling features. There was a piece of land down near the garden, a sort of bog which she and Jesse had always coveted. ("You know, Con, I love a bog dearly!") It now became possible for her to own it. Of course she would turn it over to the mission, as she and Jesse had done with other land they had been able to buy. She pictured the garden she would make of it, thanks to the precious water. ("Oh, Con, if you were here, we'd plan it together —a pool with water lilies. You say it's a dream? Well, the pool is yet to be dug but the water is there all right. Can't you see it? A little blue kingfisher to eat the goldfish that eat the mosquitoes, a sort of delightful vicious circle, and I can bring plants down from Ooty, God willing. I think He means me to have it, and I'll prepare it for you.")

But the gardeners were needed for more practical duties, and two years later her garden was still a dream. Yet in time she was writing, "I have blue lotuses out. They are sweet in my dream garden. I thought they were all perishing as the pool dried up. But the flowers had dropped seeds and a whole bevy of new wee leaves came, and now the rain has come the pool is full of leaves and now two new flowers."

She fed her hunger on beauty. One July day, after bringing back cuttings from her holiday in Kodai, she climbed far above the compound to some high rocky hills which were a favourite haunt. In her hands were some small roots of rock orchids. She wandered around trying to find oozing rocks. At last her eye fell on a tiny pool as large as a sheet of writing paper, the wee home of some frogs and mosses. Ah, a spring! Delighted, she stuck her orchids into the crevices of the rocks. It was Paul's nineteenth birthday.

"Will he and Con someday come and find you," she wondered, "sweet smelling and fair?" As usual, the thought was accompanied by prayer. "Oh, let Thy kingdom come on the Kollis when they have taken root and bloomed. So bloom, little orchids, and let my children find you, if it be His will when they find something much greater."

It was well that she had such high moments, for this five-year term on the Kollis was filled with tensions and frustrations. Though the missionary couples in charge, first the Throwers, then the Champions, were capable and dedicated, they were not Jesse Brand, and of course their methods were their own. It was inevitable that differences of opinion should arise between them and one who for sixteen years had been co-creator, co-manager, co-builder of every enterprise in the beloved complex—one who, moreover, could be neither meek nor silent when she felt a principle was at stake. Even her management of the Girls' Home was subject to policies she did not wholly approve. The new missionaries could not possibly understand the hill customs and culture as she did. They permitted girls to go home on visits, thus subjecting them to influences, both moral and religious, which could jeopardise all the results so carefully achieved in the Home.

It could not have been easy, moreover, for the hard-working and dedicated couple in charge to see their predecessor lauded, garlanded, showered with gifts, sought for advice while they were bypassed, hear her addressed as "mother", "beloved sister", "honoured lady", treated as if her mere presence gave *darshan*, the blessing shed by the proximity of a Hindu holy man or woman.

"Oh, I should not have come back here!" she told herself more than once.

Her happiest times were on camping trips, visiting the six out-stations, assisting the Bible women, going into the surrounding villages, teaching, preaching, healing. It might almost have been in the old days, with Jesse merely away on pressing business. The camps took her over most of the 120 square miles of the Kollis, ranging from five or six miles in distance up to fifteen. Up and down she rode her horse, through forests, through rivers, along the edge of fields, over precarious rock outcroppings, creeping through long tunnels of bruising lantana, skirting dizzying stretches of sheer slopes with breathtaking views, following paths which Jesse had painstakingly laid out long ago. He might almost be riding just ahead around the next corner, or about to call from behind the string of coolies carrying camp supplies . . . "Watch these rocks, Evie, might be snakes in the crevices" . . . "Remember this view of the plains, Evie? The first time you had to stop and paint a picture!"

There was no one to call her "Evie" now, or "Babs" except in letters. "Aunt Evie", yes, for Dr. Ruth Harris was in India. After graduating from the Royal Free Hospital in 1931 she came as a missionary in 1932, spent three months near Madras, then a year at Vellore working with Dr. Flora Innes, then was assigned to medical work in Sendamangalam. They met occasionally either on the plains or on holidays in the mountains. And Evie was "Mother" not only to her adopted daughter, another Ruth, who was making a fine record in school on the plains, but to the hundreds all over the mountains to whom she was "Mother Brand". There were few friends close enough even to call her "Evelyn".

Her letters to Connie were full of the joys and frustrations and disappointments of camping.

"What a bit of luxury! Oh, this lovely river! One can just lie in it and forget the sticky heat. I just go down and pull off my dress and bathe in my petticoat, then take that off and put on my dress. It is soon all dry again . . . You'll love my wee little tent. I manage to get my bed and a row of medicine boxes into it. Good night, my lovely little chum. God knows if we shall some day work together. Your own Mumpsie." . . .

"I came to camp early, leaving word for my mail to be brought . . . My boy has arrived. I left him to bring my mail. He's brought himself and no mail. Wretch!" . . .

"Have been examining the Kurungunadi school. One child told the story of the lost sheep quickly, ending, 'So he brought the lost lamb home and had a feast and ate it up!'" . . .

"Am at Kullivalavu, on our dear rocks. I know someday we'll meet here, my angel girl, even if it's not till Resurrection day. Well, let's hope before." . . .

"January. Just off on camp. The Christmas presents are so useful, Uncle Charlie's lovely little clock, Minnie's lovely wash-stand set. Auntie's basket is never more than three or four days unpacked. And Auntie Stella's medicine box. Ruth was so pleased with her hankies. She is downstairs at school and already in the sixth form although there only a few months. I have bought two Kolli Hills cloths and made them into dresses. Feel need of living the simple life among people and not letting them get the idea that when they become Christians they must discard their cloths and put on grander stuff."...

"Called to see James (Sevi) working in the fields. He has determined to stay with his father. Already his hair is cut Hindu fashion. His old grandmother has got him back and intends to keep him."

Such backsliding of the Christian converts was her greatest sorrow. She struggled endlessly to reclaim them, praying, scolding, admonishing, loving. "Am anxious about dear Aaron. He is getting into trouble." . . . "A frightened face looked in at my door last night. Her husband had not come back, said Pushpam. They had quarrelled. Naughty children! I went about the compound seeking Lazarus and at last found him. Tears stole down his cheeks. He could be a nice boy, but he beats her, and she deserves it." . . . "Have had a time with Naomi. It really does seem that when one is very pleased about anyone that there has to come a time of disappointment. She is so changeable, saying she will run off to the estates, then suddenly deciding to stay with me."

But such sorrow was nothing compared with distress over her own shortcomings. "Am so full of tears! I failed Joseph and Deborah, and when one is at fault things are far harder to bear. Their wee baby was born. I rushed off directly I heard and found her with fever. Should have gone again. She was brought here yesterday with pneumonia and died today. Oh, why didn't I go again !"

Tears over her own failures but often amusement over others' foibles, even of their sins, if one could call ingratitude a sin. "One girl says I've never done a thing for her, when I've kept her two children for the last year in the boarding home! One must keep a happy laughing spirit out here, be amused at it all. Kind of a reminder of what we are like to God. Almost flooding the ground with tears for deliverance and when He gives it we forget to say thank you."

One would have thought that as the years passed the loneliness would have lessened, but instead it seemed to increase.

"Have been back on the Kollis a year now. Have just been pouring milk into a poor girl's mouth, Moses' sister, so ill. How I love you, and when I was alone last night I got the gramophone record and listened. I always say goodbye, precious, in answer to your lovely cheery goodbye."

"How I remember the gorgeous nights after Jesse got home! Difficult to believe two and a half years after that he is really gone. But it is very quiet in this little house, so he must be away. Thank God I've got you two for real comrades !"

"I have just tipped the milk bottle over, and there's no one to say—'Oh dear' !"

"Just lumps of endless love, my darlings. I think I'll die with joy when I see you again."

"Sixteen years old, and I'm not to see you !" she wrote Connie in November, 1932. "Never mind. God has been gracious to you, my own."

She would not be lonely always, of course. In a few years the children would come to join her. Paul was still studying building and liking it, conducting youth work, even preaching, and Connie was enrolled in a Bible college preparing for mission work. Not that Evie ever tried to influence them—she hoped. In all her letters she leaned over backwards in an effort not to dictate. It was God's voice they must listen for, not hers. "Perhaps even before you have finished your training," she wrote Connie, "some call from elsewhere will have come, and oh, I do want you to keep a listening ear to His voice, not your mother's only."

Her own future was uncertain. She knew that she must not return to the Kollis for another term. Tensions did not decrease. The work was too close to her heart to permit meek acquiescence in the face of developments she knew Jesse would not have approved. There was no quarrelling with the couple in charge, yet she could not blame them for wanting the hills as their own.

Evelyn Brand

Early work on the Kollis

A watercolour by Evelyn Brand in the first year on the Kollis, 1913

Paul's childhood home

Jessie and Evelyn Brand, Paul and Connie

Evelyn with her paints

With Dr Ruth Harris, her niece, in the boarding home in 1929

Constantly on horseback, Granny travelled to the most outlying villages

Ruth Harris with the medical van on the plains, 1937

Dangerous trails were a constant hazard

Native hut where Granny Brand ministered

April 1966: Carol Weeber and Granny Brand with two Indian friends

The *dholi*, a principal means of mountain travel

With a group of Christians

Astride the hill pony
that carried her over the
"Mountains of Death"

Granny with two
bamboo sticks,
determined to participate
in every activity

But the closing of one door merely opened others. Those five mountain ranges! "We must take the Gospel to all of them," she and Jesse had vowed together. The vision they had seen so clearly had grown even more vivid with time. "*If thou canst believe, thou shalt see the glory of God.*" The promise had been her steadying strength all through the frustrating years of her work on the plains. Surely the time had come now to take another step toward their *luccu*, goal. Which should it be? The Pachais, which she and Jesse had visited just before his death? The Kalryans? Or perhaps the Peria Malai, *peria* meaning "great", the highest and most forbidding of all the ranges?

The Pachais and Perias were the responsibility of other missions, but no work was done there. "Would you object to my taking a few hill boys on camp to the Pachais?" she asked Mr. Lamb, an official of the mission responsible for those hills. He would. Any such interference might cause friction. But later he reversed his decision. Since no work was being done there and none was contemplated, he felt he could not stand in her way any longer.

She was jubilant. She went camping on the Perias. It was one of the most strenuous trips she had ever taken.

"But God has given me marvellous strength," she wrote. "Miles and miles I walk each day, villages all separated from each other by great seams of hills. Wherever you go you must climb over hills of great height. But the people are ready to hear. There is only one way to live here, build on top, for the hills rise to 4,000 feet. The malaria is deadly in the valleys. How I would like to take two Kolli families and make a wee colony on top of the heights! We would keep ponies . . ."

Her head buzzed with ideas. She even drew plans of the tiny house she would have built with dispensary attached, and sent them to Paul. "Double doors, Paul! Here, the silly way is to put the doors so you can't shut one without opening t'other. One must have space between or you do not dodge the mosquitoes, they being brave enough to pass one door but you're through the next before they've found out where they are!" Yes, and there would be houses for the Kolli Hills families who would accompany her, with mosquito netting across their windows, too, Why not?

But her own mission board frowned on her proposal to go to another range. Mr. Morling, who had been first to explore the Kollis with Jesse and had been their loyal friend, was one of the most adamant. To Evie's dismay and shock he was questioning the value of the work on the Kollis, to say nothing of her proposals to extend it to other ranges. She went to the mission conference in 1934 with both apprehension and stubborn grit.

"The Champions see the need of work here and will not sit on it. Oh, if the Lord will silence certain dear people about it, we might have a quiet conference without my having to get up on my hind legs and defend the work !"

Vain hope ! Once more the Kolli Mountains were, as she wrote Connie, "in the public eye and on the public tongue". "D'you know, Con, I feel like a mother with a baby, and when you see a crowd of people seize it, feel its pulse, shake it a bit, look down its throat and discuss whether it should live or die . . . ! It's also like pulling up a precious plant by its roots to see if it's growing."

The last year of her term was equally indecisive. The Morlings were sweet and friendly, especially her dear friend Olive, but as soon as Evie mentioned another range, Mr. Morling turned hot with protest. At the Conference in Koilpetty in June of 1935 before leaving on furlough the next year she boldly opened the subject once more, "going at it hammer and tongs".

"So far he feels it's impossible," she wrote Connie, "as most things are concerning the Kingdom, because it is God's plan to do the impossible for us and let us see the impossibility first. Great! Look on your difficulties thus, my angel, with a sort of jubilant chuckle and say, 'Another of God's opportunities to lead me on !' How jolly to be absolutely at His disposal !"

4

SHE WENT HOME in April, 1936. The joy of seeing the children again was almost more than she could bear. Children? Paul, twenty-one the last July, straight, keen of eye, toughened by his five years of physical labour in the building trade, was startlingly like his father. And as a further analogous feature, he was talking of growing a moustache ! Connie, beautiful, grave and poised at nineteen, looked at her with Jesse's eyes. Yet in spite of their familiar features they were strangers. She knew their activities, yes. She believed she knew their hopes and thoughts and aspirations, for letters had been frank and revealing. But these adult bodies were hard to associate with personalities she thought she knew. They must get acquainted all over again.

Paul, after finishing his five years in the building trade, had faced momentous decisions. He had applied to the mission board and, to his dismay, been rejected, told that he was not ready. What, not ready? With a public school diploma, a rich religious experience, and all his years of building training! He had supposed they would snap him up. It was missionaries they needed, the board had told him kindly, not technicians. He had been confused and troubled.

Of the two avenues of training open for a missionary, Bible school or a brief course in tropical medicine such as his father had taken, he had rebelled against both. More school? He had had enough of study, and memories of the medical work observed in his childhood still filled him with revulsion. Evie, still in India, had resisted the impulse to advise, resigned herself to trust to God's leading—and wait, the hardest of all disciplines for her impatient nature.

It was the memory of his father which had persuaded him, reluctantly, to take a year's course at Livingstone Medical School, which provided training for future missionaries in tropical medicine. To his amazement he found himself loving both the work and the study.

"My whole attitude towards medical work has changed," he had written his mother in October, 1935. "I used to think diseased people would be rather repulsive *en masse* and that it would be an effort to spend a whole day in hospital with blood and pus and sickness all around. But as we begin to understand more of the causes and cures of these things and are able to help people in pain, the whole thing is taking on a new aspect."

Now, on Evie's return, he was approaching the end of this year at Livingstone, and Connie was finishing her courses at the Ridgelands Bible College. She also had applied for mission service at the age of eighteen and, like Paul, been refused. Evie agreed with the board that she was probably too young, yet her dream of their working together on one of the ranges, even without the support of the board, was still alluring. "You and I," she had written Connie not long before, "would gladly deny ourselves a mission salary, live on little, try to work up here alone. But . . ." There was always the "but". Her children must listen to God's voice, not their mother's. Here also she resigned herself to wait.

When Evie was invited to speak to the students at Ridgelands Connie faced the event with both reluctance and trepidation. Of course it wasn't that she was ashamed of her mother, but—one could never tell what she was going to do or say. Memories still haunted her of five years before when Evie had attended one of her school sports days. Her mother had actually shouted, at the top of her voice, for Connie's school house, a thing that adults never did. Only the girls were supposed to shout. Her clothes also, in spite of the aunts' efforts to bring her up to date, were often of a long-gone vintage. And she was likely to pick a dress which was hopelessly unbecoming merely because its colour, always the important thing, intrigued her. Her speech was uninhibited, her manners unconventional. Connie was not the only one who was sometimes embarrassed.

"Oh, Evie, you can't wear that!" her sister Hope would protest as she donned some shapeless hand-me-down to wear to a missionary meeting where she was the principal speaker. Evie not only could but did. They finally learned to be thankful if, time lacking, she did not don the outmoded garment over the dress she was already wearing.

They found her disregard of the small amenities equally disturbing. When, shivering from the contrast between chill London fogs and India's sweltering humidity, she would slip her hands under the tea cosy to warm them, Eunice would exclaim, "Oh, Evie, you can't do that! The tea will get cold. And besides, it—it just isn't done!"

But, being more loving than proper, they adjusted themselves to the vagaries of this nonconformist sister just as, years before, they had graciously transformed their lives for the sake of Evie's children, two little savages to whom confining walls had been mountains, schoolrooms the treetops, playthings any object under the sun which their curious fingers could find or make.

Connie, being younger, with the adolescent's sensitivity, found adjustment harder. At the beginning of the informal meeting at Ridgelands in one of the college hostels, her heart sank.

"You girls don't mind if I sit on the floor?" Evie enquired with a beaming smile. "We do it in India, you know, and I'm happier that way."

Connie need not have worried. Her mother held the girls spellbound. They clustered about her, hanging on her words. Her radiant smile, her joyous testimony of God's love and a life committed to Christian service stirred them as no formal sermon could have done. They kept her talking long after the hour was over.

Once the strangeness was past Evie exulted in the companionship of her grown-up children. They had a glorious holiday in Scotland together. Wonderful to be back again where there were moutains to climb! She insisted on getting to the top of every one in sight and taking them with her. "Let's get up—somewhere where it's high!" she would rouse them at dawn. Then, in the highest place they could find she would share with them the joyous necessity of mingling prayer with wonder.

In England she always missed the sunshine of the tropics. Even the incredible greens of the spring countryside, vying with the jades and emeralds and beryls of Indian rice fields, could not compensate for the fogs and rains of winter. As on other furloughs she would bundle herself in wraps the moment the sun broke through lowering clouds and venture out to absorb even its feeblest rays. When writing letters or notes for her talks she would find a patch of sunshine, set herself and her typewriter on the floor within it, and follow its progress from window to window around the house. Sunshine and colour and high places—they were as essential to her spirit as were food and drink to her body.

Time was as precious a gift as sunshine, and she used every minute of it. She attended meetings and conferences, telling over and over the stories of work on the mountains. She spent many hours with her mother, now old and weak and needing constant care, giving Eunice and Hope the rest they badly needed. She even took a refresher course in medicine, attending lectures by Sir John Weir, one of the King's doctors, who had been her teacher during her short study at the Missionary School of Medicine. From one of these she came home looking sorely shocked and chastened. She had heard herself referred to as "an elderly woman"!

Early in her furlough she was able to attend Paul's graduation from Livingstone College. She met his closest friend, David Wilmshurst, a quiet, shy, studious young man who had been Paul's academic rival, taking turns with him for top honours in the class. Evie sat through the ceremonies radiant with pride and high hopes.

The future looked rosy. Surely Paul would soon be joining her in India. Already his plans were made to enter a missionary colony in Norwood, Surrey, designed to give missionary trainees not only intensive Bible study and practice in preaching but also practical experience in the crude Spartan life they might be expected to encounter in the jungles of Asia or Africa or South America—yes, and on the mountain ranges of southern India. When he had finished this training the board would surely approve his commission, and—who could tell? Even Mr. Morling might not frown on the appointment to one of the ranges of the son of Jesse Brand!

She looked up to see one of Paul's instructors, Dr. Wigram, sitting beside her.

"What are you going to do about this son of yours?" he asked abruptly.

"What am I—" She stared at him in confusion. "I don't know what you mean."

"You are his mother and a strong-minded one. You have influence with him. What are you going to advise him to do?"

"I don't advise my children," she replied with dignity. "But I know he plans to come out with me to India, soon."

"No!" The doctor was emphatic. "He must not, at least not yet. He loves medicine. He must go on, enter medical school, become a doctor. Remember? I wrote you about it while you were still in India."

"Yes. I remember." Vaguely, she might have added. There had been such a letter, and she must have answered it.

"You wrote back that one of his uncles had once promised to assist financially if he ever decided to take up medicine."

It was true. After Jesse had died, when she had suggested to Paul that he should study to become a doctor, her brother-in-law, Richard Robbins, husband first of Rosa, who had died, then of beloved Stella, had offered to help him.

"Would the offer still hold?" persisted Dr. Wigram.

"Yes," she replied. "I am sure it would."

"And you would not object to his taking the full five year course?"

Evie's head swam. Object—to Jesse's son fulfilling his father's dream? Object—to the postponement, perhaps the defeat, of her own dream of their working together on the mountains? Five years! Perhaps there would be no work on the hills by that time. Perhaps a successful doctor would seek other careers than an obscure missionary post on a remote mountain. She felt torn between two conflicting but worthy goals. There could be only one answer.

"My son is a man," she said. "He will make his own decisions, I trust with God's help."

Paul made his decision. Though sorely tempted by the possibility of further medical study, he could not face its implications. Five more years of study, plus perhaps another two years of missionary training? He would be thirty years old before getting started on his life's work! At that age his father had been working in India for nearly ten years! No. He would proceed as he had planned. He entered the missionary training colony soon after his graduation from Livingstone. Connie also was making her own decisions. After graduating from Ridgelands in that same year of 1936, she decided to take a short medical course, following in her mother's footsteps, at the Missionary School of Medicine, which specialised in the homeopathic type of treatment. Though plans for the future of her children were indefinite, Evie had the satisfaction of knowing that both were committed to missionary service.

If their plans were indefinite, how much more were her own! She returned to India in 1937 like Abraham journeying to the far country, "not knowing whither he went". Of only one thing was she certain. She must not return to the old station on the Kollis. Where, then? To a far out-station on the same range, in the region of Puliampetty, where the board had once talked of sending her, to work alone? To one of the other ranges? It was a forlorn hope, with the mission officials so strong in opposition. But she would get there sometime. She had made a vow with Jesse, and it must be fulfilled.

5

IF ONE HAD to be "downstairs" on the plains, better to be here in Sendamangalam, where Jesse was still remembered with love and awe, where they had made their vows together, and where, best of all, their beloved mountains were in view. This was the way she had first seen them, dark in the morning, full of mystery, but in the sunset glowing with promise. As long as she could be in sight of them she would be content to wait.

The mission board had not yet decided what to do with her. She knew she was a problem to them. They could not send her back to the Kollis. They *would* not send her to one of the ranges, though, like the importunate widow of the parable, she stressed the needs at every opportunity. The success of the widow was at least encouraging. It sometimes paid to make oneself a nuisance.

Though the work here seemed to be marking time, it was a satisfying interlude. Her niece, Dr. Ruth Harris, was at Senda, assigned for medical and evangelistic service. Besides running a busy clinic, she operated a travelling medical van which went regularly on the roads outside the town, ministering to surrounding villages after the manner of "Roadside", the term applied to the peripatetic dispensaries at Vellore. Every two weeks Dr. Ruth went camping with the van in the village of Kakkaveri, treating patients during the day, visiting Christians in their homes in the evening. Evie assisted in all these activities, learning the routine in preparation for Dr. Ruth's impending furlough.

And soon after her arrival she was able to write to Connie from the little wooden house on the Kollis:

This is Saturday and I am really and truly on our dear hills! The girls made a feast for me today, a tea party. They are all so sweet with their babies. I went over just now and saw the precious children all going to bed on the lovely new veranda. It is a nice improvement and all done with money from our dear people, Flo, Mother, Stella, Aunties Eunice and Hope all helping. I've been turning out some of my boxes and finding things I need on the plains, sheets, towels, serviettes, etc., and my dear Tamil Bible and hymn book, so now I'll feel happier going around. Jesse's was too heavy to carry. Shall start marking mine with suitable references to read aloud in street preaching. Oh, it is nice and cool, what a relief for a time! Monday I go down. But I'm glad I have been up and have seen everybody, no, not everybody, of course, not all the out-station people . . .

Painful to close the door of the little house with all its precious possessions, yet comforting to know that they were still there waiting, the desk and table and small beds, even the ladder marks on the wall! It made it seem more believable that some day the children would be coming back. Still she sternly refrained from urging them.

"Still one term for you, angel," she wrote Connie soon after her return. "Let it be a time of waiting on Him. You have the rest of the year before you need think of coming out. Maybe He will show you quite another way. It is possible, as with your mother, one of His servants may ask you to share work with him. I'd love it to be India, but if He called elsewhere you'd follow."

Evie's own future was for the present clearly defined. While Dr. Ruth was on furlough in England studying for her diploma in tropical medicine and hygiene, Evie would carry on her work at Sendamangalam. She was glad of the reprieve. It gave time to plan a strategy for one of the mountain ranges which might seem practical to the board. And the work, combining medical service with village evangelism, was the sort she loved.

"I'm starting out on my own now," she wrote in March, 1937. "I do the dispensary alone. So I'm launched, and if I do look up at the hills—yours and mine—it is with the knowledge that the Lord means me to do this at present."

But in that blistering heat of the plains one could not help a nostalgic longing for the blessed coolness of the uplands. "I've found the one place where there is a bit of draught this baking noontime and spread newspapers on the tiles to get a cooler lie-down, and stick my head against the door where the air, none too cool, comes through. Oh, I wish it would rain! The dust is ghastly!"

It was June when the rain finally came, but, oh, the joy of it! "It's just splashing and dashing, thank God! A real proper rain and I've been out on my little hill praying for my darlings. This is my first Saturday treat, the only day I can get out like this. I watched the clouds in great flocks sweeping up. Before they came too far I was just in time to catch sight of my rainbow colours which are always a pledge to me of His covenant."

Rainbows! Bright colours! How she loved them! One morning out at camp at Kakkaveri she was up before sunrise as usual, sitting on a mass of rock in a field reading her *Daily Light*. "And the Lord went before them," she read, "in a pillar of cloud by day to lead them . . ." As she returned to camp and came to the shed school there over the hills were the Bothais and beyond them the Peria Malai surmounted by a great mass of bright cloud with rainbow colours, a *pillar* upright and fair. With such a promise even the most impatient soul must be willing to wait.

Even on the plains she maintained close contacts with some of her hill people. There was Esther, one of the little wives who had been brought to the Kollis compound terribly mutilated in childbirth. Evie had sent her to Vellore, where Dr. Ida Scudder had operated on her six times before the stitches finally held; then Dr. Innes had trained her in simple nursing. "I love employing her," she had commended. "She always soaps." For a time Esther had worked with Dr. Samuel on the Kollis. Now Evie had her back here in Senda accompanying her on camping trips with the van and on rounds to outlying villages in a *jutka*. There were the boys about whom she was constantly concerned. "Pray for Ezekiel, he has gone back to the hills. Refuses to stay in school." . . . "Pray for dear James at this time of temptation when he has to be in all the arrangements of the great swami festival."

And of course there was her own adopted daughter Ruth. After Evie's return from furlough the girl had been very ill, and she had almost lost her. "My sweet Ruth lying between life and death. Do pray that God may spare her, I don't want to lose her." Evie had lovingly nursed her back to health, then for a time left her in Madras to learn sewing from a kind missionary, Miss Teague. "Am trying to teach Ruth English, but she is too nervous or shy to speak what she does know. But she is a dear child and has made a couple of nice dresses for Dr. Ruth and me. I feel she will be a great help to us in our work on the hills."

The year brought its full measure of joys and sorrows. There were spiritual advantages in living on the plains. She was able to attend an English service where both Dr. E. Stanley Jones and Toyohiko Kagawa spoke, a double blessing. Her brief holiday on the Nilgiris was replete with refreshment and fellowship. News from the children aroused mingled emotions, delight that Connie was taking a strenuous course at the Great Ormond Street Homeopathic Hospital, yet worry lest she was enduring too great a physical strain. Paul, after a year in the Missionary Colony and a bout of influenza which left him doubtful of his divine calling and of his ability to follow in his father's footsteps, suddenly decided to follow Dr. Wigram's advice and pursue a vocation which would at least ensure practical service to humanity, and with the generous assistance of Uncle Dick Robbins he entered the University College Medical School in the autumn of 1937. Evie should have felt only exultation. And yet—five years more to wait!

There were genuine sorrows. Spring brought a cable telling of her mother's death. "I went right away alone to weep and praise for her. Should have liked to see Mummie once more." Nethania was to be sold. "Oh, I wish the aunties need not leave it. Why can't Uncle Bert have it and save it for the family? . . . I hope when they choose a new house it will be with a view to health, high up with long views."

High up. Long views. Her two goals, physical and spiritual. As she studied the mountain ranges she decided that the Peria Malai (big mountains) offered the best possibilities. In January, with Dr. Ruth's return imminent, she planned a camping trip there. Still the importunate widow! To her delight and amazement this time the plea gained a reluctant ear. Yes, Mr. Morling and Mr. Champion would come up while she was in camp and look the situation over.

Joyfully she set out, taking with her three of the hill boys, a horseman Isaac, Joseph, and Mutthai. The beginning was not propitious. The way chosen to go up was the worst she had yet tried. Oh, dear! They would condemn the hills at once if they came up those steep inclines where men would refuse even to carry a *dholi*, much less building materials. Before they came she must find a better way.

They pitched camp in different areas and visited several villages. The people were friendly and receptive. At the last camping spot she began searching for a place suitable to build on in case the board let her come. It was difficult. The hills that might be healthy were covered with lantana, and she scrambled about scratching arms and legs in dense, impossible jungles. These things she must have : a high healthy place above the malarial mosquitoes, a view, water, proximity of a village. No sense in perching oneself high on a hill far from everybody, with no one to preach to or teach or heal, just to keep healthy!

"Oh, I've climbed and climbed today," she wrote Connie in the tent by lantern light, "but just now Joseph shows me a place quite near these tents that seems to fit all our needs. High, clean, healthy. Morling and Champion in all their importance will be here on Wednesday. Oh, I wonder what they'll think!"

She found out. They came. They saw. And she knew by their faces that they, not she, had conquered. Even the easier ascent she had managed to discover did not impress them. They remained unalterably opposed to extending the mission work above the plains. It was understandable. The board considered a hill mission difficult and hazardous, and the results unpredictable. No large Christian community had emerged on the Kollis. Though the Champions had done valiant work there, it was probable that they would want a change after their next furlough, and Evie did not wonder. They had had severe bouts of fever. Moreover, the times were uncertain. Tensions were building in Europe in this year of 1938. Missions were tightening their belts, not expanding. Oh, yes, Evie could understand. As long as they left her here, where the beloved hills were in view and she could slip away to them occasionally, she could be fairly content—for a time. The widow was by no means through importuning.

Then came the blow. A letter from Miss Green, one of the mission board in charge of women's work, broke the news. They had other plans for her.

"Oh, Con," she wrote in a rare burst of despair, "with all my heart longing for the hills they want to pack me away to Madras and then maybe to Tinnevelly, where I have no desire, places that have been worked over and over again, and all those unworked hills waiting!"

For a few wild moments she toyed with the idea of leaving the mission, starting out completely on her own. With the utmost frugality she could manage on the income left by her father. But—no. The children would be coming. She could not subject them to such deprivation and uncertainty. Surely she could leave the sight of her Promised Land and go back into the wilderness for three years or so, until her next furlough. The Children of Israel had done it for forty. She went to Madras.

6

THREE YEARS? By the time her next furlough came, it would have been almost ten years since she left England. For in 1939 Europe erupted into chaos.

They were years of frustration, of impatience, but not wholly of unpleasantness. There were memories here of Jesse also. In this big high-ceilinged bungalow they had renewed their brief acquaintance and fallen in love. His merry laughter still echoed in the dining hall, where they had all sat around the table listening to his jokes. It was in this same familiar bedroom that she had packed her trunk, snatched a brief glimpse of her radiant young face in the mirror before setting out for her wedding in Sendamangalam.

Her assignment in Madras was ministering to the villages in and around the city, with supervision of a group of Bible women. Each afternoon she would set out to visit one or more of them, travelling by ricksha to the stations farthest out, by bus to those in the city. They were not easy trips, especially in the hot season. Madras was low and humid, the temperature often soaring to 110 degrees. Over and over again full buses would pass her by. When she managed to crowd in and find a seat, she was usually wedged in a suffocatingly small space or, if made to stand, rocked and jolted and crushed almost to a pulp. Indians were inveterate travellers, whether in bullock carts, rickshas, *jutkas*, buses, or trains.

She loved travelling by train and always went third class, taking the opportunity to give the Christian message to all willing to listen. Her letters home were full of such experiences. "Lovely but tiring journey, travelled with three Dohnavur girls and we had singing and talk in a third class carriage all among the Indians. Great privilege!" . . . "Been to Conference in the United South Indian Church. Now I am in the train. Had a whole compartment to myself, third. But now a whole crowd of women and children on pilgrimage to Palni temple have come in. I must get a talk with them . . . Well, I've been talking a long time, a sweet girl, several women and children listening. Gave them a Gospel of John . . . Oh, dear, huge cockroaches are running about in the carriage. Good night."

But wedged in a swaying bus there was little chance to exchange more than a *namaskaram*, greeting, or a *salaam*, thank you.

One of her duties was to hold an annual examination for the Bible women on the teaching she had been giving them through the year. It was held in a large room, the pupils sitting far enough apart so they could not see each other's work. After prayer on one occasion they were soon busily at work. Walking quietly about the room, Evie noticed a small piece of paper sticking out beyond one examination paper. The woman was one of the most promising leaders. Walking around to make sure, Evie picked up the slip and enquired, "What is this?" No answer needed. The woman had prepared a crib. Evie at once condemned her before them all and dismissed her from service. The other Bible women were amazed that one who had been so helpful could be dismissed so summarily. She had rendered valuable service in making arrangements for their meals when they had held conferences by the sea. They begged that she might be forgiven.

"No." Evie was adamant. "If a messenger of Christ can stoop to deceive, what is the use of her teaching?"

Had she been too severe, she wondered later, remembering all the scriptural admonitions on forgiveness? But it was not in her nature to condone sin wherever and whenever she found it.

No mountains to lift her vision here in Madras, no high hills to climb. But the mission had built a wooden staircase outside the bungalow leading to the terraced roof. It was her salvation. Here she climbed in the early morning for her devotions. Here she crept up on hot nights with her rolled mattress, spread it out, and slept under the stars. Though nearly sixty when she started the work in Madras, she was still agile enough to be able to roll up her mattress and carry it down when rain suddenly came. Her more serious colleagues did not always approve of her unconventional ways. Perhaps it was a good thing that her time was spent mostly away from their criticism, either in trips to surrounding villages or in camping.

The camping was not wholly in regions around Madras. Though in 1939 she permitted herself a long-coveted visit to Australia to her sister Florrie's family, she was soon making different plans for her holidays. No more weeks of leisure and inspiration with other missionaries at Kodaikanal or Coonoor or Ootacamund when her own five ranges were out there lifting their beckoning crests above the plains! Which should it be? She would have preferred the Pachais, where she had camped with Jesse just before his call home, but Mr. Lamb of another mission now hoped to make them part of his parish. The Peria Malai were frowned on by her mission. Her best opportunity for work seemed to be on the Kalryans, that range settled long ago by the oldest of those three quarrelling brothers.

For about five rupees she hired a little screened hut to be made on the compound in Madras, in sections so it could be easily transported. This she would take with her up the mountains and set up high in an open spot commanding a view. (Even an outhouse must have a view!) At the beginning of each holiday she would take the train from Madras to Atur, where her adopted daughter Ruth and some of the girls she had taught on the Kollis would meet her with a bullock cart. At the foot of the Kalryans they would hire dholis for the ascent, their path winding up and down hillsides, through dry river beds, along the edges of perpendicular slopes, through thickets of rank brown grass and thistles, mounting slowly to an elevation of perhaps four thousand feet.

Occasionally they would pass a village, a brown cluster of huts with steep thatched roofs, many conical in shape, all enclosed in fences of interlaced bamboo and sheltered by palm trees, and the villagers would come streaming out to stare with timid curiosity. There were rare vignettes of beauty, fields of wild lush pink lantana, rugged rolling mountain vistas thickly clothed in jade, skies of clean blue flecked with cloud puffs. Evie's fingers were constantly itching for her paints and brushes.

"*Stottherum, stottherum*!" she cried aloud over and over in fervent praise. Oh, glorious to be up on the mountains again!

These weeks of holiday were sheer paradise—almost. There were suggestions of inferno, as when Santhoshi, preparing their dinner in the little thatched cook house, let the frying oil catch fire, and the whole frail structure went up in flames. Evie would roam over the hills, camping near villages, coaxing the timid women into friendliness, treating gummed eyes and dysentery and festering sores, doling out quinine for malaria and medicine for big and little poochies, winding off guinea worms. This parasite living in the body sometimes appeared through the skin to lay its eggs in water and could be seized by the observer, who was able to wind it off painstakingly an inch at a time to prevent infection in case the long ugly parasite was severed. She instructed in cleanliness and hygiene, showed pictures, played hymns on her gramophone, and of course repeated endlessly the stories of Guru Yesu. All over the mountains she would carry her little portable hut, a tiny shelter enclosed in mosquito netting, sleeping contentedly inside, seeking its meagre protection from monsoon rains, often gathering children about her within it and teaching them to read by the light of a hurricane lantern, then, of course, to pray.

Even the *pukka* shelter in Madras could be less protection from the monsoons than her tiny house. In 1940 there were terrific rains on the plains of South India. One day as she was setting out for church from the Madras bungalow she found water pouring through the door. It lapped over her feet, rose to her ankles, mounted against her shins in steady waves. Hastily retreating to her room, she donned her bathing dress, a blouse and knickers, covered with a little skirt. "Get out, get out!" she heard someone shouting. "It's a flood, you'll be drowned!" As she waded through the living room, water now swirling about her knees, she saw a bookcase, some of its shelves filled with books, others piled high with mission papers. Of course they must be saved from ruin. By the time she had piled both books and papers on top of the case, she was in water to her waist. Chairs, tables, stools, cushions, gadgets, were all bobbing around in a rich muck of unnamable earthy secretions. And the tide was still rising. Efficiently, almost gleefully, for she was always a seeker of new adventure, she started swimming. "This way!" shouted a male voice. Over at a far wall she saw a soldier who had been quartered during these war years with the missionaries. She floundered towards him and, putting out his hand, he pulled her out. Together they clung to the frame of one of the high windows while the water still mounted. It rose to a height of about four feet before subsiding. It was a week before they were able to clear the bungalow of filth.

But the war was a far worse disrupter of emotions than any flood. Though she pursued her usual round of activities, Evie's deepest concerns were far from the steaming city streets, the stifling village huts, the buses crowded to suffocation. In London, starting his clinical work at University College Hospital, Paul was plunged into round-the-clock labour on victims of the blitz, picking bits of glass out of chests, intestines, arms, legs, feet, hands, with bombs exploding all about.

"It's strange," he wrote her soon after Christmas, 1940, "how one gets used to all this. It really does not worry us, and conversation is hardly interrupted by the roar of the planes or the gun crashes that set furniture rattling."

It worried Evie, strained her faith to the utmost. While in body she mouthed scripture, sang hymns, marked examination papers, in spirit she was with Paul sewing mutilated hands, with Connie in Robin's Nest, a home for rescuing children on the verge of crime, with the aunts in Nethania listening to the bombs bursting . . . yes, and with some of her Kolli children in Singapore.

When she heard that a relative of some of the Christian families had enticed them to a Malayan rubber plantation, she knew no rest. Were they in need, in danger from the Japanese? And how could they possibly remain true to their faith without someone to teach them? She had to find out. She must go to them. Irrational, foolhardy, her colleagues pronounced her. Why couldn't she be content with her work in Madras without embroiling herself in affairs which no longer concerned her? She was used to such comments.

She explored the cost and means of getting to Johore, where her people were rumoured to be. On certain days, she found, she could go for half price. She took a month's leave. Finding that it was cheaper to start from Nagapatam than from Madras, she went there by train and was taken in a little boat to the ship, a small craft, but she found the voyage to Malaya entrancing. Given a whole day at Panang, she took her paints, mounted the heights by the funicular rail, and caught gorgeous views of the straits and the opposite coast from the hillside. Though rain was pouring when they reached the top, the beauty was only enhanced when the clouds lifted. She was able to do some swift sketches before returning to the boat.

The cheap trip permitted only five days in Malaya. She landed on a Saturday not knowing a soul, but Mr. Abraham, the health officer, who had been apprised of her coming, met her and took her to his home.

"I've been asked to contact some young men in the Air Force barracks," she told him, "members of our Tinnevelly church."

Mr. Abraham shook his head. They would not let anyone in in war time. But he secured the help of a civil engineer, Mr. Phillips, who took her to the R.A.F. department that same afternoon. "Impossible," she was told, "out of the question." But persistence prevailed. After inspection of her British passport special permission was obtained for her transit to the place where the young Indians were quartered. They were soon crowding eagerly about her. Not only was she able to talk and pray with them there, but the following day they were permitted to visit her for an informal service at Mr. Abraham's.

On Monday she boarded the train to cross the bridge uniting Singapore to Johore. "No European ever goes third class!" her new friends told her in shocked amazement.

"Then I'll be the first to do it," she returned calmly and was rewarded by a happy conversation with native women travelling to market. At the end of the line she discovered with dismay that she was still twenty miles from the Yon Pen Estate. Nothing for it but to take a taxi! It was late in the day when she arrived. Not knowing that there were varying degrees of managers, she drove to the biggest bungalow, and as they went up the drive she saw a man with his family walking towards the house. Accustomed to mission hospitality, she asked if they could put her up for the night.

"Certainly not," was the emphatic reply.

"But I have come all the way from India to find some of my people."

Refusal was even more curt. There was no room for her there. She must leave at once.

Very well. Still in the taxi she set out to find her Kolli people. The rubber estates were miles in extent, and it took much travel and enquiry, but at last she found them. Amazed, weeping with joy, they gathered about her . . . all but the man who had inveigled them away. He was too drunk to appear. What a welcome they gave her! Settling her in an empty room of one of their little houses, they killed a fowl, cooked her a good meal, prepared a hot bath. Afterwards she went from house to house for prayer. They had no Bibles, but she had brought them some. They told her all their troubles, and she comforted them like a mother. The next day the Scottish manager who was their overseer welcomed her cordially, apologising for the way she had been treated. But he was only a subordinate. The manager came that same day and ordered her off the estate, threatening to call the police if she stayed. *Stottherum*, praise, for the few hours they had been given together!

One more duty before her boat sailed. She had been told of a Kollis girl who had run away, unmarried, with a boy. If possible, she must find them. Back to the station . . . another hundred miles up the railway . . . and all in vain. There was no trace of the young couple. She spent the night with a Christian family who could speak not a word of English or Tamil. She had to thank them in signs and that universal language, smiles. She returned to Mr. Abraham's just in time to catch the boat; just in time also to escape the war which was even then sweeping down on Malaya. As the boat steamed up the channel a Japanese plane swooped down nearly touching the deck, trying to discover if they were friend or foe. Except for the officers of the ship she was the only European on board. She arrived back in Nagapatam in June, just twenty-one days after leaving it. It was the time when she was accustomed to come down from the cool paradise of the hills to the sweltering inferno of the plains. As usual, heat seethed, shimmered, crackled, blistering the parched earth, turning dry river beds to molten brass, thrusting prickling barbs into human pores. But this year it was charged with tension. It seemed the precursor of rising storm, not of welcome rain but of skies spilling death-fire.

"Things have been getting so terribly serious," Evie wrote her friend, Miss Nunn, "that one is almost out of breath with the magnitude and horror of it all."

7

THE WAR MOVED closer and closer to southern India. The refusal of Britain to grant even a semblance of independence to a people demanding the right to defend itself had aroused a storm of rebellion. In spite of Gandhi's insistence on non-violence turbulence was rife. Emotions were at the boiling point. Famine, the worst in a hundred years, swept from Bengal through the whole sub-continent. Evie and the other missionaries, sharing with their teachers and village Christians, refused to eat more than one decent meal a day.

In April, 1942 the Japanese bombed Colombo. Not long afterwards, following another huge rain and flood, Madras also was bombed. Yet the danger so close at hand worried Evie far less than that ten thousand miles away. In her imagination it was not Madras but London that lay in the path of each exploding shell. When the time came for her holiday and she was able to escape to the Kalryans, the peace of the hills was almost beyond comprehension. She was there when the letter came from Paul telling of his engagement to a young doctor named Margaret Berry.

"The one thing that is different," he wrote exuberantly, "is that I've got Margaret. It all happened one day when I went over to Northwood to spend an evening with the Berrys. Margaret and I went for a walk and sat on a stile and talked and talked. And then I said, 'Will you?' and she said, 'Yes.' Well, I never have been so really happy before as I was from then on, and still am."

Sitting by the little hurricane lantern in her lonely shelter, Evie read and reread the letter, trying to picture a beloved face she had not seen for more than five years, and another, blue-eyed and young and sweet, which she had never seen. It was not the first time Paul had mentioned this young student doctor who, as her name began with "B", had been paired with him at the laboratory bench in first year chemistry, who had competed with him through the years for top place in the class, but who had only just now become of prime importance in his life.

She wept a little, but whether tears of joy or sadness she could not have told. This was the year she should have gone home on furlough, but for the war. Now her son would be married, perhaps have a son of his own, before she had ever seen his bride. Not that it mattered. *Stottherum*, praise, if he had found a blessedness like hers and Jesse's! Yet . . . what would this do to her dream of their working here on the hills together? Expect two highly trained doctors, even deeply dedicated ones, to devote their lives to a few obscure mountain villages that a mission board considered expendable? Sitting in her lonely hut, the lantern casting such a feeble glow into the surrounding void, she saw the dream retreat slowly into the shadows.

It retreated farther in the months that followed. After his marriage in 1943, his ambition whetted by his doctor father-in-law, Paul studied for his F.R.C.S. (Fellow of the Royal College of Surgeons) and to his amazement passed his first examinations. To Evie the routine of her life in Madras, even the threat of bombs, seemed less real than that lived vicariously with her children. She agonised with Paul, mending the crushed bones and torn flesh of bombed children at Great Ormond Street Hospital, knowing that the worst blazing explosions were close to the Royal Northern where his son Christopher was being born. She yearned over Connie, engaged in a budding romance. David Wilmshurst, Paul's friend at Livingstone and the Colony, now a missionary in Nigeria, had started a correspondence with Connie which had become more and more personal, with the result that they had fallen deeply in love. Vicariously Evie travelled with her to Africa in 1944, saw her married in 1945 to David, rejoiced that she had found fulfilment not only in her lifelong ambition of missionary service but in a partnership as richly satisfying as had been Evie's own. Rejoiced, yes, even though it meant the end of one of her own dreams. Had she not always insisted that her children should listen to God's advice, not hers?

Still, she could not resist a bit of meddling. One day she heard Dr. Robert Cochrane preach in Egmore Wesleyan Chapel in Madras. A world-famous authority on leprosy, he was at present principal of the Christian Medical College and Hospital in Vellore, attempting, as Dr. Ida Scudder had been doing for four years in America, to save the institution from extinction. To raise the college to the graduation level required by the Madras government regulations not only must vast funds be raised but doctors with high qualifications must be secured. As he told of these pressing needs Evie's heart gave a sudden leap. Why not Paul? Dare she suggest such a possibility? Being Evelyn Brand, of course she dared. After the meeting she approached him, albeit a bit timidly.

"Would you be interested," she asked, "in having my son, a graduate of University College Hospital in London, come to Vellore?"

"By no means," Dr. Cochrane replied firmly. "As I said, only the highest qualifications are acceptable. If he hasn't an F.R.C.S., we couldn't even consider him."

"But," Evie shot back triumphantly, "my son has his F.R.C.S."

She saw the keen eyes narrow with obvious interest, but there the brief colloquy ended. Evie was satisfied. If God wanted Paul in India, of course He could arrange it. But there was no harm in giving a little prodding.

There were many satisfactions during these frustrating years, and at least one involved actual meddling. Though her adopted daughter was now living on the Kollis, Evie took her on several of her camping trips to the Kalryans. One day towards evening a young man came striding resolutely towards the small mud and

135

thatch hut which was Evie's headquarters. It was Joseph, one of the hill boys whom she had befriended. At sight of him Ruth uttered a cry of dismay and fled into the house. She was not the only one to flee. His military uniform and swaggering manner, obvious signs of authority, sent the villagers scurrying in terror. Any official-looking person, especially a soldier, boded no good to the oppressed mountain people. Too often he came to *take*— taxes, rents, an unfair share of produce, levies of manpower. Joseph also intended to take, but his business was with Evie, not the frightened villagers. He did not ask, he *demanded* the hand of Ruth in marriage.

"You brought her up," he reminded with a confidence approaching arrogance, "and you paid for my training. So of course you intended us for each other."

"Of course I did nothing of the kind," retorted Evie, conscious of the girl cowering behind her in the hut. "You have not the slightest claim on my daughter."

"No?" The arrogant lips twisted into a defiant smile. "Suppose I tell you that she has promised to marry me?"

"I don't believe you."

With maddening slowness he produced a folded paper. Evie read it with dismay, which it took all her self control not to show. Sure enough, it was a written promise, in Ruth's handwriting.

"She's in the house, I saw her. Let me see her," demanded the young man. He took a determined step forward.

Evie's wisp of a figure seemed suddenly to fill the doorway. "You must go now," she said with a calm authority she did not feel. "We will talk of this together, Ruth and I. You may come back tomorrow."

To her surprise and relief he went. Yes, Ruth confessed miserably, she had promised. He had frightened her into signing the paper. They prayed together much that night. In the morning Joseph returned, and Evie gave him another written statement that she had prepared. "It is true that she has promised, but I am her guardian, and marriage cannot take place without my consent." And, she made it very plain, she did not consent. He went away, but with grudging reluctance, and she knew the matter was not ended.

Sometime later, when on the Kollis, she found Ruth in her brother Aaron's house, and Joseph was there also. The girl's eyes met hers in mute appeal. Quickly Evie came to a decision. "You are going back with me to Madras," she told her firmly.

Still the problem was not solved. "How would you like to become a teacher?" asked Evie after long thought and prayer.

The girl's face lit up, then sobered. "Oh—yes! But—*could* I?"

Evie made application for her, and the training school agreed to take her if she would pay the fees. Ruth was so eager and grateful that she wept. "Oh, Mother, if you will pay, I will *pass!*"

She did. Not long after her accreditation as a teacher a letter came to Evie from Samuel, an Indian fellow-Christian. "Is your daughter still unmarried? If so, there is a Christian man here whom I can recommend to you."

The mission conference was soon to be held in Sendamangalam. Evie wrote and asked the young man to be present and meet them there. She was impressed with John Michael. None of Joseph's swagger or arrogance here! In fact, he was as shy and tongue-tied as Ruth. When Evie left them together to get acquainted, they spoke not a single word! "If you want her, you must ask," Evie told him. Still silence. What to do? The answer was obvious. "Let's pray," she said. Here was a medium in which each felt at home. The young man expressed his desire in no uncertain terms. Later Evie took Ruth for a walk. "Well, my dear, what about it?" "*Ahatum,*" replied the girl, which meant, "Let it be." Her sweet shy face was alight with satisfaction.

The wedding was arranged, and soon Evie was on her way to Tinnevelly to supervise preparations. On the wedding day her little daughter was very shy. Relatives of the groom heaped her with their jewels—all to be returned the next day. Ruth looked very lovely, even though the groom's relatives obviously did not approve of the white dress which Evie had chosen. They would have preferred rose pink, the Indian fashion.

Stottherum! Evie's anxiety for her beloved adopted daughter was over. The little orphan who had come to them so long ago, Poosari's baby and their first triumph after seven long years, had fulfilled all their hopes. The marriage was a good one. She and John Michael would live happily together and render valuable Christian service.

Another great satisfaction was in seeing her niece Dr. Ruth Harris go to work on the Kollis. A couple was stationed there under the mission board, but for some time there had been no medical personnel. Evie knew well that Ruth had no desire to work on the mountains. For twelve years she had been happily employed on the plains. But in 1944 she agreed to spend a short time, until her furlough, in the mission dispensary at Vazhavanthi. Evie was delighted. Just let her stay long enough to learn to love the hill people and see their great need, and surely she would discover that the work there was God's leading! Besides, her being there gave an excuse for Evie to visit the place more often.

As for the work on the other hills, she continued to prod. There were times during the Madras years when there might have been a breakthrough. One official of another mission suggested the possibility of her working on the Pachais. She begged her mission board to let her go, but they were adamant in feeling that a woman should not live on the wild ranges alone. Why had she not severed all connection with the board and started out on her own? Was she afraid of failure, of responsibility, of loneliness? "Ready to halt," she called herself after the character in *Pilgrim's Progress*, based on the verse in Psalm 38 : "For I am ready to halt, and my sorrow is continually before me."

Almost ten years. At least the war was over, and she could take the long-postponed furlough. She returned to England in 1946. If her son Paul, remembering the shock of her ageing after his father's death, dreaded the changes the long absence might have made, he was happily disappointed. She would always be unpredictable. The ten years had not aged her. She had looked the same at fifty-five—wispy body, features pared almost to the bone, short straight grey hair tied back for utility's sake by a ribbon, young probing eyes—and she would look almost the same at eighty-five.

It was a year of momentous events for the family, and Evie exulted in being part of it all. The necessity of the Wilmshursts' temporary return to England on account of David's illness was unfortunate, but it gave Evie a chance to get acquainted with her new son-in-law and be nearby when Connie's baby Jessica was born. Holding the tiny bundle which was an extension of hers and Jesse's love, she relived some of her most precious memories.

"This is a Christmas letter," she had once written Connie during those lonely years on the plains, "and you were a Christmas baby. Those wonderful days when I had you all to myself. I was very weak and lay nearly a fortnight, ten days, to rest, but your head was so soft and gorgeous lying against my breast! I had you there so much to myself that in the long days without you I might know you are mine, my very own."

Evie felt instant spiritual rapport with Paul's beautiful and sensitive wife Margaret and relived his childhood in bouncing two year old Christopher. (If he could only roll and tumble and climb the sticky jackfruits on the slopes of the Kollis!) For the first time she was called "Granny", somewhat to her dismay, a cognomen which was to enjoy a wider and wider application through the rest of her life.

She agonised, but silently, with Paul over the uncertainty of his future. Knowing that all the young doctors who had been involved, like him, in casualty work, would probably be called up for military service, he had applied for a commission in the Army and expected to be called and sent to the Far East. Then suddenly he received a telegram. "There is urgent need for a surgeon to teach at Vellore. Can you come immediately on short term contract? (Signed) Cochrane."

"Cochrane." Evie heard his surprised comments. "Name sounds familiar. I remember Dr. Robert Cochrane, one of our lecturers at Livingstone. But—how did he ever hear of me?"

Still silent, tongue in cheek, Evie waited for further developments. Paul was obviously tempted, but of course it was out of the question.

"Why?" Evie heard Margaret ask quietly.

"Dozens of reasons. For one thing, we're going to have another baby."

"*I'm* going to have another baby," corrected his wife. "And I'll probably have it just the same whether you're in London or the Far East or India."

"It's out of the question," Paul decided. "It wouldn't work out."

"Unless," returned Margaret, "God wants it to."

Evie smiled. This wife her son had chosen was a kindred spirit. She could not have picked better herself. With as much equanimity as she could muster she saw him refuse the offer and settled down to wait. If Robert Cochrane was the man she thought he was . . . He was. Presently a letter arrived which told Paul in substance, "I will meet you under the clock at Victoria Station at such and such a time."

Paul went. A young medico, even one with an F.R.C.S., did not keep men of Dr. Cochrane's reputation waiting under clocks. The principal of Vellore, who had temporarily given up his work as head of a great leprosy santatorium to upgrade the Vellore Medical College, was persuasive, not only with Paul but with the British war department. Paul's commitment to Army service was waived. He agreed to go to Vellore for a trial two years, leaving immediately. He was packing his bags when Margaret entered the Royal Northern Hospital for her confinement and gave birth to a daughter, Jean.

Evie took no credit for Paul's happy departure for India. She had merely been the humblest of agents, a gadfly so to speak, stinging Providence into action which was obviously in accordance with Divine Will. Since she had been playing the role of gadfly with her mission board for years, albeit unsuccessfully, she scarcely considered her little *tête-à-tête* with Dr. Cochrane worth mentioning.

But as the time drew near for the end of her furlough she was faced with problems which demanded far more intervention than the stinging proboscis of a gadfly. The board suggested that she was *getting too old to work.* They wanted her to retire. Too old! They should have gone with her on recent camping trips, lain beside her in the little mosquito net hut through drenching rains, ridden dozens of miles on horseback and in swaying *dholi* over trails that would have blanched the faces of most tenderfoots! At sixty-eight she was far tougher than the young missionaries they were sending out, as a mature stalk of bamboo was tougher than a raw green shoot! Why, she reminded the committee members responsible for the assignment of women, Olive Morling was a year older than she, and after her husband's death Olive had been chosen to remain for a further term to teach Bible women!

Even her own family did not want her to return. India was in crisis. Though Britain had agreed finally to its independence, conflict between the Congress Party and the Moslem League had erupted into bitter violence. Newspapers blazed forth dire headlines: RIOTS SPREAD TO PUNJAB . . . INDIA ON THE BRINK OF CIVIL WAR . . . COMMUNAL CONFLICT SPREADS . . . SLAUGHTER IN COLD BLOOD OF 300 MEN, WOMEN AND CHILDREN.

"You mustn't go, Evie," worried Hope. "It's bad enough your having to cope with all those other horrors—fever, snakes, dysentery, cholera—without getting mixed up in riots and knifings and such things—and at your age!"

"You've already done your part," Eunice, always the sensible one, told her firmly. "The board is right. You're too old to take any more such risks. Spend the rest of your years here with us, in good safe England."

Evie regarded them all with pitying incomprehension. She reminded them that for four years "good safe England" had endured dangers with which India even in its most violent struggles for independence could not possibly compete, that riots in the Punjab were a thousand miles from southern India, that Paul's letters said nothing of conflict raging in the south.

"Never," one of his first letters to Margaret had exulted, "have I seen a more wonderful place with such marvellous people, so utterly dedicated and warmly friendly."

Evie was in the pleasant sitting room of Mrs. Anderson, one of the committee members, when she learned the board's final decision. She was not to return to India. She was to retire. Why, she would wonder later, did the news come as such a blow! Why did she not calmly accept the verdict, sever all connections with the board, return to India on her own and pursue the work she felt called to do? Still "Ready to Halt"? Was it hurt pride that kept her from accepting the decision with dignity? Instead she burst into tears, pleaded. The committee was kind but adamant.

It was the "rules". They could not establish a "precedent". Well —yes, Mrs. Morling had been an exception, but she had already been in India when permitted to remain. Mrs. Brand must see that to appoint a woman sixty-eight years old for a five year term was impossible. It had "never been done".

Through her storm of tears Evie suddenly glimpsed a sliver of rainbow. She was not above using a bit of guile to attain a worthwhile goal.

"Please," she begged, "just send me back for a year. I promise not to make any more trouble. At the end of one year I will retire."

The board was in a quandary. Somehow the usual arguments of "precedent", "rules", "never been done", did not seem to meet the situation. Evelyn Brand *was* precedent. She had been breaking rules, doing things that had never been done, all her life. They remembered that for some years she had been returning her pittance of salary, using her small inheritance from her father to finance her work, buying property in the name of the mission. Reluctantly they yielded to her request.

Through all this heart-breaking experience Connie was Evie's comfort and strengthening support. They suffered together over the disappointment of the board's initial decision, laboured to find possible solutions, rejoiced over the granting of this small reprieve. Only to her daughter did Evie confide her plans for the future, once the final year of service with the mission should be finished, and Connie's understanding and encouragement helped to allay all doubts and fears. After David's recovery she was able to see them all off for Nigeria, David first because they could not get passage together, Connie a bit later with Jessica.

Then Evie herself sailed, saddened only by the secret suspicion that she would never be returning to England. To her sisters' tearful yet hopeful farewells—"Only a year this time, Evie dear!" . . . "We'll be counting every hour!"—she gave only reassuring murmurs. A year, yes. She would serve the board faithfully where-ever they chose to send her for the promised year. And then . . . She and Jesse had set out to take the Gospel to those five ranges. The Kollis had come first. The Kalryans would be next. After that the Pachais. If God gave her time, she would go to all of them. And let nobody try to stop her!

141

Five

"Climb every mountain,
ford every stream. . ."

From *The Sound of Music*

1

EVELYN BRAND RETURNED to India for the last time in January, 1947, not many weeks after her son Paul arrived. Of course he was more than a hundred miles away in Vellore, almost as far by *jutka* and bus and train (and India's inevitable delays) as was London by plane, but it was thrilling just to know that he was here under these same blue tropical skies, able to see the southern cross at night, breathing in this rich familiar fusion of odours— dust, cow dung smoke, jasmine blossoms, spices, people; ears attuned once more to this medley of sound, clatter of bullock carts, nasal wails of hawkers, beating of tom toms, chirrings and pipings and whistlings of minivets and tailor birds and night jars, yes, even the harsh early morning cacophony of crows! She hoped his eyes were revelling like her own in this resurgence of colour which revived her artist's soul like a resurrection—reds and yellows and greens of saris and blouses and turbans, sunlight glinting and flashing on brass pots and gilded domes and silver anklets, oranges and scarlets and pinks and lavenders of flame of the forest trees and cassias and jacarandas and mangoes. In the first joy of return one could almost forget the poverty and ignorance and disease—yes, and the terror and bloodshed accompanying the painful birth of a new nation.

Stottherum! They had sent her, not to Madras again or to Tinnevelly, but here to Sendamangalam. A kind gesture, they had perhaps considered it, letting her end her missionary service in this place so filled with memories of Jesse and their life together. End? They should have known better than to send her within sight of her beloved mountains. Even had her purpose not been crystallised before leaving England, it would have hardened during this year of reprieve into the toughness of steel. Each morning, sitting in her secluded prayer nook, she saw the dark outline of the Kollis waiting against the slow illumination of the sunrise. Each evening she saw them ablaze with sunset glory.

To Evelyn's great joy Dr. Ruth Harris, when she returned from furlough later in the year, offered to return to the Kollis, and the board consented to her appointment there. Her sister Monica, the trained nurse, spent two months there after her arrival from furlough in June, and Ruth, arriving in late summer, found her suffering from an acute attack of malignant malaria. The "mountains of death" were still exercising their evil spells, the days of exorcism through the wholesale use of DDT having not yet arrived. When Monica returned to the plains Ruth remained at Vazhavanthi, to continue the medical work there for the next dozen years. Knowing she was there lifted a great burden from Evelyn's heart. With the Kollis well taken care of, she could concentrate her full energies on her next field of action.

It was a year of waiting, but not this time with impatience. There was too much to do. In addition to her mission work in and around Senda, she must make all her secret plans and preparations. With her Bible woman, Elizabeth, an Indian sister whom she had known for many years, she went camping whenever possible at Kunnur on the Kalryans, staying in the little hut of plastered bamboo and thatch which she had built while in Madras, using the tiny mosquito net shelter for brief visits to the surrounding territory. With its wooden frames which could be hooked together to form four walls and a roof, a door in one of the walls, it made a fairly adequate shelter. One could eat meals, even sleep in it, though it gave no protection from the rain. No matter. She had slept contentedly before now wrapped in a raincoat, with rain pouring, an umbrella hoisted over her head.

Only to a few did Evelyn confide her plans for the future, to Paul, of course, and Connie; to Elizabeth and to her daughter Ruth; to Dr. Ruth Harris and Monica; to Paul's wife Margaret.

The early months of 1947 were troubling ones for Margaret. The black headlines depicting India as a land rocked with turbulence, reeking with bloody communal strife, were in marked contrast with Paul's letters, exuberant with enthusiasm over Vellore and his tremendously challenging work. She was torn between his assurances and her parents' fears and dire warnings. "What's the boy trying to do?" fumed Dr. Berry, her father. "Make us think India is a Utopia when every paper we pick up fairly screams that it's nothing but a bloodbath? Utterly foolish taking two babies into that mess!"

But Margaret's faith in Paul and divine guidance prevailed. She sailed for India with Monica in June, in a crowded ship which steamed through the glaring and oppressive heat of the Indian ocean in the path of the monsoon, arriving in Madras, still bravely gallant, in one of the stickiest and most sweltering seasons. Paul sent his weary and bedraggled family off to the hills for recuperation, and Evelyn was able to join them for a month in the paradise of the Nilgiris. Holiday? She spent most of the days poring over plans for a small house Paul had designed for her, consulting with stone masons and carpenters, ferreting out building materials such as pipes and roofing which could most easily be carried up steep mountain paths on the heads of coolies. No time even to conduct her usual acquisition of shrubs and flowers and other seedlings to take back for planting on the Kollis!

It was a memorable year, that of 1947, one of transition and tumultuous change, a year of new birth.

New birth for India. Though August 15, the day of independence, came with more than the usual painful travail of birth, presaged by terrible bloodshed and the tragedy of a divided country, it was a day of triumph. Evelyn shared in the rejoicing to the full. Even the colours seemed sharper, shot through with the clear sunlight of freedom. The flowers in the mission compound where Christians gathered for the celebration blazed with golds and yellows, purples and blues and crimsons. When the brave tri-colour flag of the new free country, saffron and green and white, was hoisted, a great shout ascended with it.

"*Jai Hind*! *Jai Hind*! Victory to India!" Evelyn yelled and jumped about as excitedly joyful as the hostel children, no doubt shocking and embarrassing her staider colleagues as she had once done Connie.

New life also for the hopeless and rejected victims of one of India's dread diseases, for it was in 1947 that Dr. Paul Brand paid a memorable visit with Dr. Cochrane to a leprosy sanatorium, a short journey which changed his life and that of thousands of others. For, smitten by the sight of ravaged faces, stumps of fingers and toes, clawed hands—especially the clawed hands—he began the long research and experimentation in pioneer surgery and rehabilitation which were to revolutionise the treatment of leprosy throughout the world.

New life certainly for his mother, Evelyn. Came the mission conference of 1947 and the day of her retirement. A pity, she reflected, that Mr. Morling could not be there to mingle his "goodbye" with those of all the others! He would be so relieved to see her go. The thought brought no bitterness. Before his death in 1942 they had resolved their differences and parted as the good friends they had once been. She sensed relief in other mission leaders who for years had endured her constant harping on the needs of the hills. Though their regretful farewells were undoubtedly sincere, she knew they would rest more easily in their beds knowing there was no longer a gadfly to prick their consciences and buzz about their ears. They gave her a beautiful lamp as a farewell present, not so useful a gadget in the places where she was going. A hurricane lantern would have been a better choice for the type of work she was going to do.

Now . . . she was free. Life begins at forty? No, at seventy, she thought gleefully as she made her preparations. Elizabeth, her faithful Bible woman, would go with her. It would take no impressive caravan of coolies to carry their *saman*, baggage. Their needs would be simple at first. Already there, waiting, was the mud hut with the thatched roof which the *dhori*, local ruler, had built for her for about sixty rupees. They could manage until the builder whom she had already hired could put up the small bungalow which Paul had designed.

At last they were ready. The tearful goodbyes were said, the dismayed protests of her shocked fellow missionaries once more endured. "But—my dear, you're nearly seventy years old!" . . . "To go up into those jungles, among those primitive people, a woman almost alone!" . . . "You were to work only one more year, remember?" . . . "Heaven help you, and if you must go, God go with you!"

"He will," Evelyn retorted confidently. That is, she might have added, if I do what I should have done long, long ago!

They crossed the plain in a *jutka*, then took two *dholis* for the trip up the mountain. It might have been her wedding night, except that it was not the Kollis they were climbing but the Kalryans. Which was exactly what she and Jesse had planned. "First the Kollis, then the Kalryans, then . . ." She could almost hear his voice. Never in the nearly twenty years of her loneliness had he seemed so close, so—*alive*. As they mounted higher and higher, the rapidly cooling air filling her lungs with heady energy, the manoeuvres of the coolies on the steep uneven path swinging and rolling and grinding her between the carrying poles, the years seemed to slip away, thirty-five of them. She was that young eager bride riding up, up, with the new life just beginning, knowing that Jesse was travelling just ahead. A sudden drenching shower which turned the *dholi* into a bathtub made the illusion even more real. She laughed aloud.

"I'm coming, Jess," her heart cried silently. "At last I'm coming!"

2

IT WAS ALL to do over again, what they had accomplished in fifteen years on the Kollis. She had chosen well for the site of her little hut, a hill high up sloping to surrounding valleys, which were in turn encircled by higher upthrusts of the same range. A place as near to heaven as possible, with a grandstand seat for viewing the blazing monsoon sunsets which were her meat and drink. If to her zestful thirst of youth the Yorkshire becks had been as the waters of Bethlehem to David, to the deeper hungers of her more mature spirit those mountain sunsets were a thanksgiving feast.

The tiny hut differed little from those of native tribes in the surrounding villages, made of woven bamboo strips overlaid with mud and whitewashed, surmounted by a high thickly thatched peaked roof. Later, with the coming of two retired Indian workers to live with her, she would add an extra room, but now there were only Elizabeth and, for a time, her daughter Ruth and her husband John Michael.

As soon as labourers could be secured and the building materials brought from the plains she had the long-planned-for bungalow erected, an unpretentious little house consisting of two small rooms and a porch, with a tiny narrow cooking space and bathing cubicle at the rear. Only the simplest of furnishings, a table, a cot, a few chairs, cooking vessels such as any villager might buy in the bazaar, no luxuries, not even a mirror. The little portable hut could be set up on the porch to protect from mosquitoes. This was to be her home for the next fifteen years.

Seven years it had taken for their first convert on the Kollis. She had learned to wait now with a small degree of patience, knowing that if one planted the seed and tended it carefully, the harvest would come in time. Surely all that was expected of you was to love people so intensely that you had to meet as many of their needs as possible, spiritual, mental, physical.

The physical offered the most immediate challenge. Already on her camping trips the villagers had profited from her medical skills. Now they came flocking. Her day began as usual before dawn, when she would hasten to her private retreat for prayers. Even before she had had *chota*, morning tea, people would be there, begging with outstretched hands, "*Marandhu*, medicine!" Many would be suffering from poochies, ring worm, round worm. They came with sore eyes, ulcers which had eaten to the bone, scabies, dysentery, skin infections. And always there was malaria. Even though her homeopathic training eschewed the use of drugs, she found the new sulfa medicines a godsend in treating pneumonia.

Of course, the villagers did not all come to her. She went to them, ferreting out needy cases on her camping trips, going where-ever and whenever she was called. No distance was too great, no amount of labour too exacting. Sometimes, it seemed, by sheer persistence and stubborn will-power she performed near miracles. Called to Coopan's house, she found the man's brother so ill with pneumonia that the relatives were squatting outside the hut waiting for the funeral. *"Poi-varungal,"* she told them firmly after one look at the patient. "Go and come again. He will not die." And until she was sure that the crisis was past, she did not leave his side.

She was determined to abolish one of the villagers' worst health hazards, guinea worm. This was a long, slender, round parasite, something like a fiddle string, varying in length from five or six inches to twice as many feet. It was usually found in the legs and thighs of villagers who had gone down into infected wells, or, if the victim was a woman, it might be in the hip, where she carried her earthen water pot. The symptoms might be itching of the parts affected, sensation of something creeping under the skin, sometimes a cord like a ridge which could be felt. At length a little boil would appear, out of which the head of the parasite would protrude. Then the worm had to be wound out on a little roll of plaster, turned as often as possible without breaking. The incidence of the disease on the Kalryans was appalling. Evelyn treated one woman with eight guinea worms, one of the ugly little heads protruding from her cheek. She fought the pestilence with all her fierce energy, instructing the women, urging all to keep their limbs out of the step-wells and to strain the water, badgering the men to clean the village wells, petitioning govern-ment to stock them with fish, planning for a deep new well on her own compound. It would take time, but before the fifteen years had passed she would have almost eradicated guinea worm from the Kalryans.

Her medical work was diverse and manifold. She pulled teeth —with a swift jerk which did not spare pain but made it brief. She applied sulphur ointment for itch, and gave treatment for scabies, those tiny parasites that burrowed under the skin.

"Ayoh! Bathe child first, *ammal,* much *tunnee,* hot water. Then for three nights, *murunthu,* three, rub on this stuff. No bathe. On fourth morning, *nahlu,* four, wash body, everything,

even clothes. *Amma*, yes, understand?" It was not enough to tell. Usually she had to go herself to see that it was done.

She battled epidemics fearlessly, typhoid, dengue, even cholera. During one of the latter scourges her *dholi* carriers set her down a furlong from an infected village, while she went into it alone. And of course she delivered babies. When called, she hurried frantically to arrive in time. It was a popular belief that the baby must be removed before the mother died, or transmigration would be interrupted. She often arrived to find the mother still alive but with her body frightfully hacked. Then she would battle with all her modest skill and fervent faith, for days and nights on end if necessary, to save the patient's life.

Babies! How she loved them, whether Paul's new daughter Mary, born in 1948 in the sterile safety of a hospital, or little waifs thrown out on a village rubbish pit. One day a man arrived at the bungalow, desperately ill, with two children in tow. All three showed effects of neglect, with the tell-tale stomachs of malnutrition and intestinal worms. The man was beyond help. She arranged for *dholis* to carry them all down to the hospital on the plains. As the man left, he turned back and begged pathetically, "Do not forget my children." But burdened with other cares Evelyn did forget.

Months later she was camping at an out-station, Munglepetti. She saw a poor ragged waif begging from house to house. "*Ammal*," said the *dhori*, the village headman, always ready to shift responsibility. "You should look after this child. She has neither father nor mother."

When Evelyn brought her back to the Kunnur bungalow Elizabeth exclaimed in surprise, "*Ammal*, don't you know who she is? Remember that terribly sick man and his children? This is the little girl."

Of course. Immediately Pushpam, as they called her, meaning "Flower", became one of the family. Asked about her brother, she said, "He stayed in the village when I ran away." Almost before the words were spoken Evelyn was on her little horse riding back to Munglepetti. Another five miles, and she was in Pushpam's village. "Where is the little brother of the girl who has come to me?" she enquired. "Sick," was the answer. "Where is he?" she persisted. They pointed towards a house. Evelyn found him leaning against the fence, a pathetic little figure, almost a skeleton, wasted with dysentery.

Trembling with shock and anger, she turned to the group that had followed her. "*Ayoh*, what's this? You know we keep medicine. Why didn't you bring him to me? In another few days he would have been dead."

151

They looked back at her sullenly. "We have enough earth to bury him," one of them muttered. Evelyn understood—too well. The child's relatives were hoping for his death, for they wanted his bit of ancestral land. Pushpam they had willingly let go, for no hill woman inherited anything, even from her husband. Immediately they began frightening the boy with tales of the dire treatment he would receive if he went with her. Evelyn ordered her horse to be brought to the edge of the village. "Bring the boy to me," she told one of the relatives when she had mounted. Prepared for his protests, she was happily surprised when the little fellow held out his small hands asking to be taken.

Andrew she named him. He was four and Pushpam three when she took them. They became two more in the long succession of her adopted children, a burden now to nurse and teach and worry over, but some of her greatest comforts in years to come. Few satisfactions in her life would equal the joy at seeing Andrew return strong and healthy after long treatment at Vellore for intestinal tuberculosis or of hearing twelve year old Pushpam announce eagerly, "Mother, I'd like to be a doctor."

Even on the Kollis, with Jesse's genius and tremendous energy and the helpers supplied by the mission board, progress had been painfully slow. Here, almost alone and without his dynamic skills, she found the pace agonising. Schools? For interminable months there was no one to teach but herself, no schoolroom except the tiny portable hut where, in camp after camp, she would gather the children about her inside the mosquito netting, teaching them to read and write by the light of a hurricane lantern. An orphanage, a demonstration garden, a dispensary, a chapel? All dreams. Justice for the poor villagers oppressed by the *dhoris*? The English had once been called *dhoris*. Now the headman had appropriated the term, together with many of the foreigners' dominating qualities.

On the Kollis local rule was in the hands of village elders who formed Panchayats, at least five men with power to act. On the Kalryans the *dhori* had more power. The story went that a hundred years or so before, a Hill Gounder (approved as their leader) was taken to London where Queen Victoria gave him jurisdiction over all the Kalryans. There was an imposing tomb in memory of this man, a great-grandfather of the Big *Dhori* who now lived in the "Palace". The hills were divided into five districts, or Nadus, each with its own smaller *dhori*. Each villager must pay tribute not only to his *dhori* but to the Big *Dhori*, who claimed all the land and could fix the prices. Like many wielders of such power, this ruler had become a greedy and corrupt despot. Jesse perhaps would have known how to challenge him and would have had the courage to do so.

And the boldest, most elusive dream of all, winning this second of their five mountain ranges for Christ? How, when? With no one but herself and Elizabeth and sometimes Ruth or Santhoshi or another of her Kolli girls, to tell the story of the saving Yesu-swami, to sing the hymns, show the pictures, play the Tamil records, pray unceasingly for converts!

Dreams, all of them? No. Articles of faith. The promise had been given her long ago, on a day before her wedding, when, weak and broken and uncertain, she had cried for guidance. She had stepped into the church at Kotagiri and heard the words which had been her strength ever since : "Said I not unto thee that if thou wouldst believe thou shouldst see the glory of God?"

3

IT WAS 1952. In Vellore Evelyn's son Paul had been making medical history, performing the first surgery ever attempted for leprosy. Operating on a patient afflicted with the deformity known as the claw hand, a stiff flexing of the fingers due to paralysis of certain muscles, he had taken a good muscle tendon from the young man's forearm and transplanted it in the palm of his hand, substituting it for the paralysed intrinsic muscles. It was a type of operation which he had seen in London, used to correct similar disabilities from war injuries or polio. The result had seemed a miracle. The hand was made usable again, opening and closing with almost normal action.

Dr. Paul's further research and experimentation had resulted in conclusions which had overturned some of the oldest concepts of leprosy, establishing the fact that most of the mutilations commonly ascribed to the disease, such as missing or shortened fingers and toes, were due instead to accidents caused by the lack of feeling in the patient's extremities. He had also established on an edge of Dr. Ida Scudder's college campus the world's first rehabilitation centre for patients who have had surgical help to restore them to some kind of normality, *Nava Jeeva Nilayam*, the New Life Centre. Here patients with reconstructed hands and feet were taught the intense care necessary to keep them from accidents, also new skills to make them self-sufficient.

Margaret also had found new avenues of service, joining the staff of Schell Hospital, the eye department at Vellore. Already she was acquiring the knowledge and skill which would enable her in time to become as expert in treating the eye ailments of leprosy patients as Paul in reconstructing their hands and feet.

Evelyn had seen them only briefly during the five years. There had been a few short holidays together in one of the hill stations. To get to Vellore she had to go fifteen miles by horseback or *dholi* down the mountains, transfer to a bus, then to a train, then to a bus again. But she managed a trip there occasionally and was visiting a hospital ward talking, as always, about the needs of the hills when one of the patients, a pastor, said, "I know two young women in Bangalore who are looking for untouched areas to work."

Evelyn pounced on this welcome news. Immediately she consulted Mr. Watts, who had evidenced a new interest in unevangelised fields. Soon after her return to the mountains he came up to her bungalow at Kunnur with the two young women.

"This is just what we are looking for!" one of them exclaimed eagerly, sinking into a chair after a tiring tour of the compound. "When can we come?"

"Now!" replied Evelyn instantly. She was jubilant. What might not be done with these two healthy young enthusiasts as her helpers!

But first they had to return to the plains to make preparations. Presently a message came. "We are sending up several loads of *saman*." Evelyn gasped. She had no cupboards or storage space in the tiny bungalow, not even much living space. The first loads arrived. It took eight men to carry them. There would be more later.

Hastily she made plans. There was another small building where the men workers stayed. They would put a box room on the back of that for storage. She set all the coolies to work putting up the addition and worked hard with them. Its mud walls were raised by the time the next loads arrived . . . tinned meats, ironing boards, beautiful soft white blankets, even toilet paper! Shelves had to be built.

The young women came, with even more of their paraphernalia. In spite of their addiction to such luxuries, they adjusted to the new life with some facility. They were even willing to wash their own clothes in the pool at the "wet" gardens. Evelyn took them on a camping trip and was overjoyed with the effectiveness of their Christian witness. Victory at last, in spite of the surplus of unnecessary gadgets! Surely God had sent them in answer to her prayers.

But she had reckoned without that deadly enemy, malaria. While one of the girls was away on the plains the other came down with a severe attack of fever. Evelyn tried to nurse her through the torturing chills and sweatings, but unfortunately she herself developed a dangerously septic finger. They made a ludicrous pair, Evelyn administering quinine, the girl giving her injections when able, if not, Evelyn giving them to herself. The attack of fever waned, and the girl improved. Not Evelyn. She decided at last that to save her life she must go to Vellore. Though reluctant to leave her patient, the girl did seem better, and she would only be a burden if she stayed.

She started down the hill in a *dholi*. So used had she become to being carried that she had grown careless, neglecting to hold firmly to the side poles. Suddenly one of the bearers fell, and she pitched forward, landing head first on a rock. Overcome with pain, she could only lie there, groaning. "Must go back," urged the terrified bearer. No, it was impossible. To go back would mean an insupportable burden to a girl already ill, and it might well cost Evelyn her life. She must go on. How she did so she would never know. The further miles by *dholi*, the bus ride across the plain, the jolting, swaying hundred mile trip by rail, more miles in a sweltering, crowded bus . . . The pain in her swollen finger was but a minor undertone to the throbbing, pounding, jangling in her bruised back and aching head. But somehow, in a daze, she arrived at the Vellore Hospital.

Paul was not there. He and the family had gone home to England on furlough. It would have been a blessed experience to be cared for by him. But Dr. McPherson treated her septic finger skilfully. Other physicians took X-rays of her injured spine and pronounced the damage not too great. However, they did not discover the full seriousness of the injury. She would never recover completely from the fall.

She returned to find that the girl had been carried down to the plains and that her companion, also afflicted with malaria, had been taken to a hospital. It was the end of their work on the mountains. They were not fit for mountain life.

4

EVEN THOUGH SHE had seen Paul and his family so seldom, still she felt strangely lonely knowing they were no longer in India. Loneliness! It was the one necessity of her Spartan life which was most difficult to bear.

Strange that with a doctor son assigned to India, two of her most serious accidents should come when he was away on furlough!

She was completely alone in her little bungalow that night in February, 1953 when she had the second fall. She had sent Elizabeth away to a distant village. A jug of milk in one hand and a lamp in the other, she managed to trip over the door sill and went "smash down", harder than necessary to keep from breaking the lamp and spilling the milk. She couldn't get up. She knew that nobody would be coming near the house until morning. She dragged herself to her room, lay there in agony on the floor through the night, thankful that the lamp had merely been extinguished and had not set the place afire. So great was the pain that she could not even sing, only pray.

In the morning one of the workmen found her. He sent for Elizabeth, and she sent a message to Atur to Mr. Nevis, a missionary recently stationed there, asking him to bring his jeep to the foot of the hills. Evelyn could not ride in a *dholi*. It was obvious that her hip was broken. Lifting her carefully to an Indian *charpoy*, string cot, the bearers carried her down the mountain. Brother Nevis had brought his jeep not only to the hill-foot terminus but he had pressed on into the jungle. They were able to transfer her in a lying position to the car, and she travelled the hundred miles over rough roads to Vellore, gritting her teeth to keep from crying out in pain.

Again no Paul. But Dr. Somervell, a famous British orthopaedic surgeon, was her competent physician. It was a compacted break. Though he thought at one time of operating and putting a pin in it, the doctor soon realised the near impossibility of trying to restrain her. Finally he treated her by bed rest, trusting the bone to heal itself, and trying to maintain the length of the leg. Bed rest? One might as well have expected to confine a gazelle with a little string. Within days she was making the rounds of the rooms in M Ward Block in a wheelchair, talking to patients and preaching to them, telling them over and over the story of Christ. Then, because she could not always wait for anyone to take her in a wheelchair, she would sit on a little mat on the floor, and propel herself along the corridors, using her arms like the oars of a boat. A strange sight, undoubtedly eliciting many stares and smiles, but appearance mattered not a whit to Evelyn Brand. The sudden appearance in people's rooms of this tiny gnome-like figure, arms akimbo, straight grey hair haloing the wrinkled features, eyes aglow with an almost fanatic eagerness, was at first startling, but not for long. Patients gratefully waited for her coming. To those very ill or awaiting operations she seemed an angel of cheer and compassion.

She could not tolerate idleness or lassitude. Every day, every hour must be used for something worthwhile. Often she would be found on the floor of a veranda painting the flowers in the garden. Her bright pictures and beautifully illustrated texts were soon adorning the walls of many of the rooms. She was the despair of all the staff who believed rules were meant to be obeyed, but most were soon her indulgent champions, especially one nurse, Effie Wallace, who became her special friend.

Paul had been making successful experiments on the feet as well as the hands of leprosy patients, and special shoes were being made, moulded to fit the needs of the individual and designed to prevent the ulcers and other deformities likely to occur in feet which had no feeling. Learning that Evelyn had difficulty walking, Paul's cohorts designed and constructed such a pair of shoes for her. Patiently she yielded to their kind ministrations and promised to use the shoes faithfully.

She remained in the hospital less than three months. To the doctor's surprise her bones healed far more quickly than those of patients who had been supine, perhaps by sheer will power, she was so anxious to get back on her mountains. Since her accidents walking had become increasingly harder and would continue to be so. The new shoes were splendid, and for a time she used them, especially when climbing the hill paths, but little shoe sandals were so much easier to slip on! Presently the shoes were hanging on the wall, a paper protecting them from dust, and there they were to remain. At Vellore they had made her leather gaiters, too, for riding horseback, when she could not avoid the thorns of the lantana bushes, causing trickles of blood to run down her legs after pushing through narrow cow tracks, and these she wore gratefully.

For others, if not for herself, Evelyn Brand took full advantage of her brilliant son's techniques. On her horse rides over the mountains she found victims of leprosy who she felt would benefit from Paul's skills in surgery and rehabilitation. There was Karuninasan.

157

She found him on one of her camping trips, huddled in a wreck of a shed outside his village, turned out because of his leprosy. As she passed he held out his hands and spoke in the shrill whine so common to beggars. "*Ammal, ammal*—pity, pity!" Evelyn stopped, of course. She looked hard at the outstretched hands, fingers bent rigidly at the knuckles, at the bare feet with their uneven stumps of toes and suppurating ulcers.

"*Ayoh*! You poor boy! What you need, brother, is not pity, or even food, or coins. What you need is the treatment my son Dr. Paul Brand can give you, and I'm going to see that you get it!"

She herself took Karuninasan down to the plains, travelled with him third class the hundred and more miles to Vellore, and presented him to her son. "See, Paul, this poor boy! I found him begging because he can't do anything else. Paralysis of both feet and hands, and ulcers on both feet."

Paul examined them, the hands that would not open, the feet that were being slowly destroyed by huge open sores; then one by one Karuninasan had operations which restored first one hand, then the other, then one foot, then the other. He was in the hospital for more than a year. One of the patients taught him to read, and when he learned the story of Jesus, he came to have a new hope and faith. His feet were fitted to some moulded shoes, and he was told he must wear them constantly.

"If you walk barefoot or in a flat shoe," they warned him, "the same old ulcers will come back."

Proud and pleased, Karuninasan returned to his benefactor in the mountains. Evelyn sent him back to his village with new clothes to start his new life. Since he no longer bore the tell-tale marks of leprosy and was a burned-out case, he was no longer an outcast. Finding himself the only man in the village who could read, he started a little night school, working in the fields during the day. He was one of the growing number of hill people to be baptised and each Sunday he rode on a little pony to attend the church service which Evelyn and her helpers conducted.

One day when Paul was visiting his mother he went with her over the rocky paths to Karuninasan's village. The youth met them joyfully, showed them his hands, his school, his books. Then Paul looked at his feet. "Why are you wearing those bandages?" he asked. Removing them, he found the ugly sores returned, the bones exposed. "Karuninasan, where are your shoes?"

"Oh, I have them!" He took Paul into the house and pointed to a little shelf. There were the shoes wrapped in brown paper. Proudly he undid them. "See? I have kept them so carefully. I wear them on Sundays when I go to church."

Sternly Paul admonished his patient and convinced him of the necessity of wearing the shoes constantly. He was not so successful with his mother.

Karuninasan was by no means the only leprosy patient Evelyn brought to her son during those years on the Kalryans. At least two or three times each year she would turn up at the hospital with one or more victims discovered at her little dispensary or on her horseback rounds. Beds for such patients were at a premium, and there was often no room for additions. Moreover, Paul and his team had to be selective in their choice of candidates for surgery, and his mother's entrants did not always fit the qualifications.

Evelyn had no respect for qualifications. She had people who needed help, and she meant to get it for them. If Paul was not there—away on furlough or on a trip to Africa or some other region demonstrating the new skills—she might employ a high-handed technique, drawing herself up to her full five feet slightly plus and, in spite of her shapeless bag of a dress and short stringy white hair, managing to look like a duchess.

"No room? I think you don't know who I am. Dr. Paul Brand is my son, understand? And these are his very special patients."

Or, if Paul was there she might become sweetly wheedling. "Look, dear boy. I have quite a lot of patients with me this time."

"But, mother, there are no beds!"

"Oh, you'll find beds," she would toss back airily. "Just say it's for your old mother. Or put them on the floor. They won't mind."

She did not confine either of these techniques, threats or persuasion, to doctors, nurses, and orderlies. Train guards were by no means hospitable to passengers afflicted with obvious leprosy. On one occasion when she had smuggled a man with badly deformed hands into a crowded third-class compartment, a guard tried to evict the undesirable passenger in no uncertain language. "Get out of here, son of a pig! Out, you filthy—"

He stopped short, faced suddenly with an avenging fury rearing up from the floor where she had been lying. "Don't you dare touch my patient! I'm taking him to my son Dr. Brand in Vellore, Dr. *Paul* Brand, do you hear?" Unable to cope with this Nemesis, the guard hastily backed out of the compartment.

5

THE WORK WAS growing. Slowly a few hill people, like Karuninasan, were becoming Christians. Some endured genuine persecution. There was David, a young man from the village nearest the compound, who had been stirred by a campaign in Madras and offered himself for baptism. The Big *Dhori*, hearing of the defection of the young Hindu, came from Koilputhur, his official residence, and with the boy's father and mother sternly denounced him. "You can draw no more water from the village well. In fact, you can no longer stay in your village." So dire were the threats that poor David was frightened into denying his new faith. He had been baptised, he declared, just for fun. One of the teachers who had been baptised was likewise intimidated. But Karuninasan remained firm and brought several of his family and some of his neighbours to Christ, so there was a congregation in his village.

In fact, Evelyn had workers in four different stations. Jungle lands had been cleared to make way for fruit trees and vegetable gardens. In Madras she consulted with the horticultural department of the government and persuaded the officials to provide five acres of "wet" gardens, demonstration plots for such crops as citrus, tapioca, limes, bananas, which could supplement the staple foods of the villagers. And of course there were flowers and shrubs as on the Kollis, some of them rare varieties which she had appropriated when on holiday in more sophisticated mountain areas—orchids, roses, passion fruit. With official cooperation she was also establishing schools, the government agreeing to pay the salaries of teachers and build the schools if the villagers were persuaded to furnish the land. Often this latter was bought with her own meagre funds.

Some of her projects were not so successful, like the well. When it was being dug a cyclone came, bringing water pouring down the hill, and undoing all the digging; bringing a wildcat, too, which got into her henhouse and killed thirteen hens! But the well was finally finished. In 1954 she put up a windmill to pump water from the well to the house, which was up high, of course, to provide a breeze and a view. The windmill was never too satisfactory, and the well ran dry after two years.

The workers she chose were sometimes as disappointing as the well and windmill. In spite of her keen nose for sin in the lives of her Christian converts, she could be trusting to the point of gullibility. One day in 1955 a white-robed, bearded man arrived on the compound. She was alone, since three of her helpers had gone to Madras to attend the Billy Graham meetings. The stranger was of imposing appearance and called himself a "Swamiar", the Indian name for a teacher of religion. They had a long conversation, and she found him—or thought she did—a true follower of Yesu-swami. When he made no move to continue his travels, she asked, "Where do you go from here, and when do you leave?"

"God has sent me," he replied simply. "I am not leaving."

Thankfully she welcomed him into the fellowship of workers and arranged with friends on the plains for his support. Truly now the seeds so long planted and carefully tended were bearing fruit. There were several baptisms. A small but devout congregation assembled each Sabbath in the little shed used for worship. But Swamiar, if such he could be called, was more wily than holy. Whatever may have been his motive at the beginning, he was prone to temptation. Discovering Mother Brand's Achilles' heel, her weakness in keeping accounts, he took full advantage of it.

"You should have your deeds to the lands up here registered," he told her helpfully. "Otherwise they might be appropriated by strangers."

By himself, he might have added. She handed them over to him to take to the office of the registrar on the plains, and he duly brought them back. She did not bother to read them. It would have taken too much time to decipher the Tamil words. Later she would find that one house had been registered in his own name, and, since the fraud was then three years old, she could do nothing about it.

When one of the villages suffered a destructive fire and her friends sent funds to alleviate the suffering, Swamiar convinced the people that she had kept much of the money for herself. Finally he wrote a letter in the name of a large number of villagers, signed with their thumb prints and stating that they did not want her as their leader. They wanted the Swamiar. But here his scheming backfired. Many of the hill people began to see him in his true light.

Evelyn was one of the last to admit his duplicity. One day she was with him in a village when the local *dhori* came with a big crowd, some of whom he had brought from the plains. To her surprise many of the group were carrying guns. They are turning against us, she thought with dismay. Halfway through the meeting at which the Swamiar was speaking there was a great uproar, and the crowd surged towards him. Evelyn managed to place herself in their path. "Why are you all against us?" she asked the leaders. "You are all right," they shouted back. "We have nothing against you." The Swamiar discreetly escaped before the crowd could reach him.

Stupid she had been, she berated herself when she finally realised the truth. She had made an unpardonable mistake, and a costly one. For many of those incipient Christians who had trusted the Swamiar turned away from the new faith and returned to their caste loyalties. In one village only one family, living up a wild hill, remained faithful. But the damage was irreparable, and it had been all her fault. Not that she would cease trusting people, and whenever she detected sin in her converts she would always blame herself. It must have been something wrong in *her* which had caused it to happen. She could forgive Swamiar. He had only been a tool of his own weakness and ambition. Herself she could not forgive.

6

SHE MIGHT BE "Mother Brand" to her people on the hills, but to Paul and Margaret and their children, to Connie's children in Africa, and to a growing number of friends and acquaintances at Vellore, yes, even in England, she was getting to be known as Grandmother Brand, or simply "Granny". Like it or not, for she was always averse to any concession to her advancing years, she was obliged to accept it.

Of course, the fact of being "Granny" brought many compensations. She revelled in the opportunities, infrequent though they were, to be near Paul's children. Occasionally she would permit herself the luxury of spending a brief holiday with them in whatever mountain resort they chose in the Nilgiris to flee from the worst heat of the plains. It was always a long trip—*dholi*, railway, numerous buses—and, since her moves were likely to be unpredictable, arrangements for her arrival were somewhat haphazard. Once, Margaret met Granny's bus to find her terribly ill with malaria after what must have been a most miserable journey. Unable even to walk, Granny collapsed in the ditch beside the road, and Margaret had to find a ricksha to take her to the little mission hospital, where she was treated.

When the announcement was made, "Granny is coming", the

children were not one hundred per cent enthusiastic. Her visits always meant a variation in their life style. Of course they loved her, but once she arrived and each child had been welcomed and hugged and loved, things began to change. They would get into trouble if found playing with things she regarded as tabu but which their parents didn't feel were wrong, like harmless card games. When a visit was expected they exchanged meaningful glances. But soon all such drawbacks were forgotten. Walks with Granny were tremendously exciting. She drew their attention to beautiful colour combinations, formation of flowers and rocks and trees, helped them to observe and love beauty. She encouraged them to express themselves in art, and if they could teach her a new chorus or recite a verse of scripture, her radiant commendation was enough to cancel all memories of deprivations. As her visit went by the sense of communion would grow between her and the children, and her departure would bring tears. For a few days something would seem to be lacking, and they would even be loath to return to those pastimes forbidden in her presence.

One of her arrivals, however, strained their loyalties to the utmost. Paul had returned to his work and Margaret was keeping house for the children before returning with the younger ones to Vellore, leaving the older ones in boarding school. Word came suddenly that Granny was coming, and the children returned from day school to find her there. Welcomes were brief, for it was a hungry moment, and they were ravenous for the bread and butter laid out for tea. With one accord they fell upon it.

"Wait!" Granny's voice, loud and incisive, cut the action like a knife. "Aren't you going to say thank you?"

Mouths open, hands still clutching the coveted viands, the children froze into unwilling immobility. Grace for meals, yes, but surely just a snack while standing around the table did not demand official thanksgiving! They were certainly acting thankful enough. Not so with Granny. Teatime, such a beautiful time, she thought, deserved a special thank you. Not just "Thank you, God, for this nice bread. Amen". She had just arrived from her beloved hills, and she had been thinking about them on her long trip, persons in the far out-stations, the coolies who had helped her get to the bus, and one by one in a long intercessory prayer she presented them to her Lord. Meanwhile the children, restlessly shifting from foot to foot, the bread moving closer and closer to their mouths (they could smell it even if they couldn't taste it!), waited hopefully for the terminal "Amen". When it came, they joined in fervently. Then there was absolute silence while they stuffed their mouths.

(Paul also had known the awkwardness occasioned by his

mother's insistence on official thanksgiving on all occasions. Once at a meal attended by a huge mixed group of various faiths, few of them Christians, just as they were about to eat Granny had admonished in a loud voice, "Pa-au-l! *Grace*!")

That particular visit to the family in the mountains produced other complications. The rented house was small, unadapted to a crowd. Granny slept on a little glazed veranda next to a small room occupied by Mary and a visiting friend. About three in the morning Margaret was wakened by the sound of much bumping, followed by suppressed giggles. She rose to see what was the trouble. No trouble! Granny had merely wakened, and usually when she woke up it was morning, so she just assumed it was morning, time for everybody to get up. Of course she must have her quiet time just as dawn was breaking. No seeing the sun rise this morning, for the skies were weeping. Still, she must get out of doors, just in case.

She had forgotten that doors in the little veranda were locked and furniture placed against them, to keep out prowlers. The owner of the house had insisted. It was not the way Granny wanted it. She hated a door that she couldn't go through, especially one leading to the free outdoors. She became claustrophobic, and roused Mary and her friend. "Children, you've got to come and help me. Come quickly!" They rushed to see what was the matter. Then she had them help her move all the furniture, hence the sound of bumping. But when she got to the door there was no key, so she could do little about the quandary—except sing hymns. Margaret was not too delighted with choruses at three in the morning, but all the children except Pauline, the baby, were wide awake.

"Come!" urged Granny when the door was finally unlocked. "Get dressed. Put on boots and raincoats. We'll all go for a walk in the garden!"

They did, just about at break of dawn. Jolly good fun, they agreed with Granny. They hadn't had such a lark in a long while. It was only their stuffy old mother who could not see the joke.

Even Granny's visits to the more sophisticated Vellore produced small crises. One of the few luxuries she permitted herself was a little alarm clock. She brought it to the Vellore bungalow, and it stood on a table by her bed. One of the children was playing in her room and accidentally knocked the clock off the table, and it crashed to the floor. Its mechanism was badly upset. So was Granny.

"How am I going to tell the time when I'm up in my hills again?" she worried.

"Does your clock ever stop?" enquired Margaret.

"Why, of course it stops when I forget to wind it!"

"Then how do you know what time to set it?" asked the child who had caused the trouble.

"Why," replied Granny impatiently, as if it were a stupid question, "I go outside and look at the sun, of course."

Like the rest of the hill people, she might have added. Even their language for time was adjusted to the sun and other elements of nature. If the milkman wanted to tell you that his buffalo had been milked early in the afternoon, he would point to a spot high up in the west, saying, "Milked at that time." The average villager referred to any hour in the morning as "daybreak", to all others of the day as "evening." Very early morning might be "cock crowing" or "rolling-time", the latter referring literally to the time when people began to roll over in bed before getting up.

Of course, thought Margaret, Granny had her sun, calling her to get up, warming her at noontime, setting in a blaze of her beloved colours, almost telling her when to go to bed. She didn't really need an alarm clock. She had a built-in one timed with the sun, the roosters, and a deep sense of "time to rise and praise the Lord". The children, being more adventurous and less inured to luxuries, could appreciate this basic down-to-earth sense of life when they visited her in the Kalryans. Miss the sophisticated things of Vellore? Hardly. They enjoyed the novelty of visits to the little outhouse. They thought it fun to have a bath in Granny's tiny lean-to shed. They loved the chances to ride her pony. They enjoyed taking the ducks to water. They revelled in seeing the windmill go clanking around. And because these were a part of Granny's life they became even closer to her.

She seldom came to Vellore except for such emergencies as broken bones. It was in 1958, with the November mists swirling about the mountains, that she fell again and fractured her wrist. This time it was to Regina Hansen that she sent a message, a missionary located at the foot of the hills, labouring among the gypsies. Miss Hansen met her *dholi* at the bottom of the hill and took her to Vellore in her car. *Santhosham*, happiness! Paul was there to take care of his old mother. She refused even to take an aspirin when he set the bone and placed the arm in a cast. But then the trouble began. The pain was severe, but the restraint of the cast was worse. It gave her a feeling of claustrophobia. She came to Paul. "You must take this thing off. I can't keep it on. It's pressing on a nerve." He spoke as firmly as to a child. No help there. Meekly she returned to her hospital bed. The next day she went and sat in the office of Dr. Selvapandiam. "If you'll just take this little bit off—" she begged when her turn came. She persuaded one after the other doctor or nurse to remove a small portion until she got her thumb loose. Then the pain was even worse.

Will Paul be angry with me? she wondered. He was. The thumb was again restrained, and she was adjured even more sternly to leave the cast alone. She went back to the hills with it and was under the care of her niece, Dr. Ruth. "You must take it off," she began all over again. "I can't keep this thing on." Rather than have her rip it off Ruth split the cast, then bandaged it around, changing the bandage every day. More than anyone else she understood Granny's rebellion against any form of confinement, whether of body or spirit.

"You ought not to let your people in the medical college work in basements," Granny scolded Paul on one of her visits to the hospital. "They ought to be up in the air."

It was about this time that Paul and Dr. Chandy, the competent neurologist at Vellore, tried to diagnose the physical weakness which made it increasingly difficult for her to walk. She was unable to lift her toes and had to raise her knees at each step to prevent them from catching on the ground. They found her spine in a seriously weakened condition, affecting her limbs with a sort of creeping paralysis and increasing loss of sensation.

"It's those falls I've had," she turned the matter off with no apparent concern. "Probably the time I tumbled out of the *dholi*, or that other time when I was riding down a steep slope and went over the horse head first onto all those rocks and broke a few ribs."

They fitted her with braces, but she found them almost as repellent as the cast. However, they did help with the walking, and she wore them most of the time, further assisting her progress, especially over the rough mountain terrain, with a pair of bamboo sticks. It was a nuisance, of course, not being able to tramp the long trails, wade through the lantana bushes, maintain her balance on long stretches of rice field bunds. But on most trips she needed a mount, anyway, for covering long distances, fording all the streams, manoeuvering up and down stony precipices like the kind of enlarged mountain goat the horses of the hills resembled. And *stottherum*, praise! She could still ride a horse!

7

It was in 1959, Granny's eightieth year and the thirtieth of her loneliness, that one of her fondest dreams was fulfilled. With all four children in boarding school, two in England, two in Africa, Connie was able to make a long-anticipated trip to India. It was almost more than Granny could have hoped for, that she and Paul and Connie could go back once more to the Kollis together.

The hill people, even many who were not Christians, gave them a *tamasha* of a welcome, constructing an archway for their triumphal entry, loading them with garlands, bringing brass trays, the covers of their water vessels, filled with fruits, flowers, coconuts. They sang special hymns and Tamil songs. They crowded into the chapel for a worship service, sitting on the mats such as Paul had once laid. Even after thirty years there were many who remembered Paul and Connie, marvelled over their growing up, shyly reminded them of episodes in their babyhood. The little wooden house was full of memories. Connie packed a box of her father's books to send to David in Nigeria.

For Evelyn Brand the following days with Connie on the Kalryans were bliss beyond compare. To have a kindred spirit to share with, to talk with, best of all to *laugh* with! For her that was one of the worst drawbacks of loneliness, to have no one to laugh with, for she had always enjoyed a joke, especially one on herself.

"It's the loneliness of her life that worries me," wrote Connie to David. "There are no educated Indian Christians on these hills except pastor and wife, and they live three miles away and seldom see Mother. But she will not leave here if she can possibly help it until there is someone ready and able to take over."

Even between mother and daughter communication was not always easy. "Mother is firmly convinced that I am fifteen years old, but I don't mind, for I really expected it, and she also has a deep-rooted feeling that if I made a bit of an effort I could understand and converse in Tamil! It is really awfully funny how she simply can't say a whole sentence in English when Indians are around, and she always imagines that I have followed the conversations that go on all around me."

But it took no knowledge of Tamil for Connie to share all the joys and frustrations of her mother's daily labours. They went on a camping trip to Munglepetti, where they were greeted by bright school children and the *dhori*, who showed signs of wanting to become Christian, but where the teacher, Paul, was in danger of turning back to Hinduism. From there they visited Karuninasan's village and were led to a string cot under a shelter of palm and banana leaves, while the school children recited texts, brought gifts of fruit and eggs and coconut milk, and hung them with bright garlands. Camping in a little wooden hut in Munglepetti, Connie felt like an animal in a zoo, with curious faces pressed constantly against the screening which formed the top half of the walls. "Never have I seen people with such penetrating, inquisitive, bold stares, and I found it a struggle to smile in return!" She shared her mother's grief when the elusive teacher Paul failed to show up and her joy when he finally appeared and after a long talk admitted his faults and promised to try again.

They travelled many miles on horseback visiting villages. In one a young newly converted teacher was holding his school of twenty little pupils under a tree. "Mother collected the village elders and gave them a ticking off for not getting on with the building." They attended a stone-laying ceremony for a new house for the pastor, who had been living in a shack, mud-walled and grass-roofed, which leaked like a sieve. Arriving hot and tired after a long trek in the blazing sunshine, they were invited to sit down and drink tea. "We must get on with the ceremony," they insisted. "If we don't leave soon, it will be dark before we reach home." Hurriedly swallowing the tea, they went out to look for the site. "Over in that field." The pastor waved in the general direction of a plot of land. They streamed across the grass in the hot sunshine. "Now where should the front wall be?" the pastor enquired of Mother Brand, flourishing a piece of rope. She looked nonplussed. They had not even marked the site! "I should think about here for the front of the veranda," she suggested, pointing vaguely with her toe. Several measurements were made to the accompaniment of voluble Tamil. Sitting resignedly on a big stone, they tried not to dwell on the three miles of rough travel separating them from their supper. After a shallow trench had been dug someone began looking for a suitable stone. A fairly square-looking one was produced and set on the edge of the trench. The pastor struck up an Indian hymn, and verse after verse was sung while the visitors kept looking at the setting sun and Connie wondered how long it was possible to go on singing the same hymn. But at last it came to a breathless stop. There was prayer and the reading of scripture. Then Mother Brand knelt and placed the stone in position—temporary, she hoped, if the building was to be on a strong foundation! Fortunately there was a good moon that night.

Connie was assistant as well as observer, helping to extract teeth, bathe the infected eyes of a buffalo, prepare flannelgraph pictures, cook, clean storerooms, chase rats. One night they had an exciting hunt, chasing two of them round and round the dining table until the place looked like the aftermath of an earthquake. At last they killed them, but Connie dreamed that one was running up under her clothes.

Each night she went with her mother down the rocky path to one of the workers' quarters, where all would gather in a circle, read the scriptures by the light of their little hurricane lanterns, and each would pray. Even now that the bamboo sticks were necessary for support, Granny insisted on going to them. She would have gone on her knees if she couldn't have walked.

On Sundays the little veranda of the house became a church. People came from the surrounding villages, held their service there, then enjoyed a common meal of rice and curry made with simple vegetables, lentils, brinjals. Granny provided the food. The workers cooked it. Here also during the week she entertained her constant visitors, many of them non-Christians, providing instruction and entertainment with her gramophone and its Tamil records of Gospel stories and hymns, most of the latter Indian in both music and lyrics. Her religion, Connie knew, had always been pertinent and contemporary. It spoke to such mundane problems as poochies and guinea worms, malnutrition and dirty well water, mosquitoes and unclean midwives and puny babies, lying and stealing and cheating and fornication, as well as to unsaved human souls. The Christ she proclaimed was no pale western modification. He was what he had been in fact: an Oriental villager who trekked mountain paths, wore country men's rough clothes, worked with tools and calloused hands, loved children, healed simple people, lived and died for persons exactly like these whom she loved and served.

Connie marvelled at her mother's complete disregard for comfort.

She has been having an awful cold, but it makes no difference. She rises at dawn and goes out wrapped up in a blanket to pray on the hillside, preaches in a hoarse whisper, and never stops attending to patients and needy folk . . . Yesterday, after treating a succession of patients and talking to them, at lunch she said, "I just long to lie down and go to sleep for a little while." Within a few minutes a message came saying that an old man was very ill. Without any hesitation Mother began to prepare an injection, some milk, medicine, and we set off in the blazing sunshine. We had to go through a sort of pigsty where filthy, stinking black native pigs were rooting about in the mud, and then squat down surrounded by a curious crowd of villagers, flies, hens, dogs, goats, pigs, and vermin, to attend the patient.

At teatime Mother said, "We will go out for a little quiet time together before the sun sets." But a group of people arrived and needed medicine and the Gospel. "We can't go away and leave them," said Mother. "They have come so many miles." The sun had set before they left, and Mother remarked, "It was probably better for my cold for me to stay in." This kind of thing is happening all the time, and yet she says, "The only real sacrifice I have ever made for Christ was when I left my children." She gives away an awful lot of things, and when I told her I felt it was wrong, she said, 'Well, I'm glad the Lord hasn't shown *me* it's wrong!' "

Connie was not the only member of the family who sometimes differed with Granny on the proper limits of Christian responsibility. On at least one occasion her grandchildren felt that her devotion to duty exceeded all practical bounds.

It was December, 1960, almost two years after Connie had returned to Africa, leaving a void of loneliness more bearable, yet more perceptible than she had found. Paul and his family decided to spend Christmas with Granny in the mountains.

"We'll have the best Christmas ever," the parents promised.

The children believed it. Even the trip was an adventure, the hundred and fifty mile ride in the Vanguard to Salem, then twenty miles farther across the plains to the foot of the Kalryans, using a borrowed jeep because the Vanguard was not built to clear the rocks in the road; finally the fifteen miles up the mountains. Granny had sent her pony and two small *dholis*. As they mounted into the cool bracing air at three to four thousand feet, excitement heightened. Finally came the arrival at Granny's settlement, with rows of schoolboys shouting and singing a welcome, waving banners of coloured paper hoisted on long bamboo sticks.

Excitedly the children exhibited to Granny a fine plump turkey bought in Madras, stuffed and roasted and borne tenderly up the mountain, needing only a final heating. They would have it for the evening meal, said Granny. At noon there would be rice and curry, a big *tamasha*, served out of doors to all the workers and their families. The children, disappointed at the delay, ate sparingly and waited impatiently for the major feature. For Paul, fashioning a pair of rocker shoes for Karuninasan and treating other patients, the afternoon was all too short, but not for the children. Finally evening came, the oil lamps were lighted, and exciting odours drifted from the dark narrow back room of Granny's little house.

"Now," they told each other, "it will really be Christmas."

But not yet. First there must be the usual evening *jebbum*, prayer, with the teachers and their families. They came crowding into the little porch, faces beaming. Always fervent in *jebbum*, at Christmas Granny overflowed with her "*Stottherums*". The prayers went on and on, the flame in the hurricane lantern flickering across the dark intent faces. Then came carols, in Tamil, in English, all accompanied by a rhythmic clapping of hands. The younger children fell asleep. Margaret looked helplessly at Paul. She had visions of the beautiful turkey shrivelling.

Suddenly the screen door was pushed open. Six village men in loincloths entered carrying a pole between them, a blanket knotted to it. Out rolled a woman, eyes staring, mouth open, lips dry and cracked.

"Back!" ordered Granny, pushing the men aside.

Before Paul could reach the woman to find out if she was living or dead, Granny had located the feeble pulse and diagnosed the ailment with uncanny accuracy.

"Typhoid. Dehydration. Water!" she commanded one of her helpers. "No, bring me buttermilk. It's more nourishing."

A bowl of buttermilk was brought, with a spoon. Kneeling on the floor, Granny cradled the woman's head in her lap and, holding her face tenderly to one side, began spooning a few drops of fluid into her cheek, encouraging her with a constant flow of Tamil to swallow it. Though the woman seemed unconscious, her throat did appear to move in little swallowing motions. If Granny increased the dosage to a whole spoonful, the patient would choke, so she just sat there, dribbling the liquid between the lips.

"She'll keep it up all night," thought Paul. He caught Margaret's worried glance and touched Granny on the shoulder. "Mother," he said gently, "don't you think perhaps since this is Christmas we could have some turkey with the children and let someone else give this woman her fluid?"

She turned on him a look of absolute fury. "How *dare* you, Paul! How can you talk about turkey when there's a woman here dying!" And back she went to dribbling the milk down the woman's throat.

Quietly Margaret took the children into the little dining room, and by the light of a tiny, smoky hurricane lantern they dismembered the turkey. After they had eaten their little Christmas dinner, they crept off to bed.

Much later Paul persuaded Granny that perhaps there were some competent helpers who could take her place for a bit, and she consented to eat a few scraps of turkey, then went straight back to the woman. Paul also persuaded her that with the children in the house it would be safer to take a typhoid patient elsewhere, so a fire was built on the floor of a new schoolhouse not yet in use. The woman was laid by the fire with someone to tend her constantly. In the morning she was still alive and much better. Paul, the skilled doctor, would have thought in terms of special drugs for typhoid, which could not have been secured in time, but Granny, with her tremendous concern and her instinct for the simple but right remedy, had saved a human life. The children's disappointment was the only casualty.

"Mummy, have we *had* Christmas?" one of them asked the next day.

Yet, looking back, they would remember it as a Christmas far more relevant to the original than the usual tinsel and gift-wrapped variety. In a setting almost as simple as the stable of Bethlehem they had actually seen "love come down at Christmas".

8

IT WAS IN 1959 that Paul, heading a team from Vellore to observe medical work in a rural area, met a young American missionary, a trained teacher and registered nurse, with whom he fell into an interesting conversation.

"I believe you and my mother are kindred spirits," he told her, describing Granny and her work. "You should go up in the hills sometime and visit her."

Soon after that Carolyn Weeber went home on furlough, but she remembered Paul's suggestion and in 1962, after her return to India, she climbed the Kalryans and stayed with Granny for several days. They were indeed kindred spirits, and Granny was loath to see her go. If she had someone like that to work with her, what might be done !

There were several workers who came to the hills during the fifteen years. Three young women under the New Tribes Mission bravely started a station on the Chitteris, one of the five ranges in her plans, seven miles across the plains in sight of her Kalryans. They built a road up the mountain and travelled on it in their jeep, often carrying patients down to the hospital in Salem. Betty Mills, almost as skilful a mechanic as a nurse, was able to take the jeep apart and service it. Her associate, Dorothy

Jacobson, did evangelistic work. A girl from the religious centre at Dohnavur taught in their school. In spite of the bitter opposition of the caste-bound people a few converts were made, and in time they won friendly acceptance. When they wanted to provide a dinner for the wedding of the Dohnavur girl, a whole village participated. Supplies were furnished by the missionaries, and the village women did the cooking, with six fires for the curry and vegetables. At the wedding reception five headmen from the village came with huge trays of bananas, coconuts, and ten rupees!

"The third of our five ranges," thought Granny with satisfaction. "Only two more to go." Except that by now there were seven, not five, ranges in her plan of operations.

But the house the young women built, though nine miles up from the plains, was in the wrong place, water-logged with a big rock behind it, as Granny did not hesitate to tell them. She was right. In 1961 Betty and Dorothy became ill and went down to the Ellen T. Cowin Methodist Hospital in Kolar. Betty, with malignant malaria, felt she should go home. In alarm Granny sent a sixteen-page letter to Dr. Esther Shoemaker, the superintendent of the hospital. "These girls must not go home. Don't let them go down from the hills. They should dismantle their house and build it on top of the hill, where I told them, where the breeze would take away the mosquitoes and there would be no malaria." To her delight Betty did come back although alone, after her second furlough.

Granny also was a patient at one time in the Kolar hospital. Of course she wanted to learn all about its work, but she talked so fast about the needs of the hills that Dr. Shoemaker and her associates could scarcely get a word in edgeways. When she left she did not pay, but promised to send a cheque. When it came it was made out to Miss Ellen T. Cowin (the name of the hospital). Amused, Dr. Shoemaker sent it back. It was returned made out to the same payee. They finally endorsed it, "Ellen T. Cowin Memorial Hospital". The Swamiar had shrewdly pinpointed Granny's Achilles heel. Accounts would never be her strong point.

Already she was casting longing eyes towards another range of mountains, the Pachais, of course, which she and Jesse had visited with such anticipation just before his death. The way was now open for independent workers to claim them as a mission field, and the interest and support of an American organisation, the International Gospel League of Pasadena, California, was making possible an extension of work on the mountains which promised the fulfilment of her most ambitious dreams. She made more than

173

one trip to spy out the Promised Land, like Caleb and Joshua and their ten comrades, thankful for the use of Regina Hansen's van to carry her the long distance across the plains.

On one such trip she was accompanied by a missionary couple looking for an untouched area. Good! The Pachais were certainly untouched, and how she could use their help! Anxious to show them all the intriguing possibilities of this wide-open field of work, she was overjoyed to find a site which seemed to fit all her requirements—a high hill behind one of the villages with a clean sweep of air and a glorious view. Excitedly she set out to explore this "land of milk and honey", spurring her obviously reluctant companions to follow her up the rocky slope to the top. "See!" she bubbled with Caleb–Joshua enthusiasm. "Isn't it marvellous? We couldn't find a healthier spot. Plenty of room for a house, school, dispensary, all the buildings we will need! And just breathe that clean air and look at that view!"

Like the ten discouraging spies, the visitors refrained from favourable comment. Perhaps they also saw "giants in the land", for soon afterwards they settled in Bangalore with its excellent year-round climate and comfortable, even luxurious bungalows. Granny was not surprised. She had had other experiences with helpers whose brief sojourns had elicited from her only caustic comments.

"They didn't do enough to hurt them out here, but they had to go home on furlough to get over it!"

But of her own harshly disciplined, austere, lonely life she would tolerate no eulogies of heroic self-denial. "Hardships! Living here on these glorious hills? It would be horrible to live in those awful cities. I couldn't breathe. Why, just being on the plains gives me claustrophobia!"

9

It was 1963 when Granny left the Kalryans and moved to the Pachais, her third mountain range. Not that she was less concerned for the two left behind. Like the chambered nautilus, she merely added another dimension to her scope of action. A few months later, early in 1964, she made a brief journey which was like a reliving of the past.

Her son Paul arranged the trip. In the party were Howard

Lewis, director of the International Gospel League, Susie Koshi, wife of a Vellore doctor, and an American author who was writing Paul's story and—horrible and utterly distasteful to all Granny's instincts!—had been asked to write hers. It would inspire interest in the mountain work, Mr. Lewis told her, and help his organisation raise funds to extend it. For her mountains Granny would do almost anything, and reluctantly she agreed.

She met the party in Salem, where they stayed overnight in a luxurious hotel. (Useless extravagance!) The next day they climbed the Kollis—no, not climbed. Rode all the way over the beautiful new road in a jeep. Jesse, the first road-builder, had laid out a trail long ago. How he would exult in this paved road! The visitors were obviously nervous at some of the seventy-two hairpin bends, especially when they had to drive straight to the edge of a sheer drop, back up and start around again, to make the curve. They should have climbed it as she did, on her wedding night. The higher they went the more alive she felt. When they stopped once to enjoy the view she was out of the car, hobbling to the edge of the cliff.

"*Stottherum*, praise the Lord! Isn't it wonderful, Paul, to be up here again where you can breathe!"

They came to the green valley and the *nangi kadu*, rice fields, where her feet had slipped into the muddy ooze on her first journey through the rainy dark. And there on the hill, from which the tiny lantern had come bobbing down, was the nearest spot to Paradise on earth. Of course the Christian community, fruits of their fifteen years, was there to greet them. There was the usual archway of greens and flowers, the shouts of welcome as they emerged from the car.

She relived the past while the strangers probed curiously into the results of their years of labour—the little wooden house, still as stout and sturdy as when Jesse had built it with his own hands over half a century before, yet empty now and full of dust and echoes; the dispensary, the schoolhouse, the sheds, the orphanage, the workers' houses, the teachers' and doctors' dwellings, the chapel. So dazzling were its whitewashed walls, inside and out, that it might have been dedicated yesterday instead of on a Christmas Day over forty years before.

They had dinner there, served by Christian women in bright saris with flowers in their smooth hair. A pity these strangers could not see them or their forebears as they had once been, unkempt, sickly, the hopelessness of fear and superstition in their eyes! Not that all those hopefully converted to the Christian faith had remained true either to their first commitment or to her purist standards of conduct. After dinner many came to her from all over the hills, to greet, to complain, to ask advice. Hands were raised palm to palm, eyes fixed with reverent intentness on her face. They squatted on the floor about her, like disciples about a *guru*—no, more like children about a mother, bringing to her their problems, personal, family, community. She listened, sympathised, comforted, advised, admonished, and, when occasion demanded, severely reprimanded.

"Oh, he's naughty," she ended an interview more than once, shaking her head in sorrow.

Indeed, there was as much sorrow as joy in this return to the Kollis. The work had almost been abandoned. In 1957 the board had decided that it was time the hill people became independent of missionary supervision. In 1959 Dr. Ruth Harris, in sympathy with this decision, had left to establish with her sister Monica a dispensary at Belukurichi on the plains at the foot of the northern Kollis, where little had been done either evangelistically or medically. From there she and Monica had done more intensive work on these northern Kollis, sometimes camping for nearly four months at a time, staying in three small thatched mud huts which the people needed only at harvest time, using one of them as a clinic.

Granny had never quite forgiven Dr. Ruth for leaving Vazha-vanthi. While she agreed with the board that responsibility should be given eventually to the hill Christians, she felt they were not yet ready for it. Moreover, she was bitterly opposed to the action of the board in turning over the schools which she and Jesse had established, even some property which they themselves had paid for, to the government and other non-Christian agencies. But Mr. Lewis and his organisation, joining in the formation of a Hill Gospel Fellowship, were bringing hope for the future. In fact, at the chapel service following the dinner plans were discussed for the appointment of a new pastor.

The next day, after a night in Regina's bungalow, they all ascended the Kalryans. Paul drove his jeep as far as the new road went. Road? The visitors obviously considered the name a misnomer, especially the last two miles across dry fields and rice field bunds. They could not guess that, in spite of stones, boulders, ruts, ledges, ridges, perpendicular ups and downs, it seemed to her like a king's highway! Still she was glad to feel the sturdy flanks of her little pony against her knees. There were mounts, too, for the visitors, with *dholis* for the women, who seemed to derive great amusement from the latter strange conveyances.

They stopped at Munglepetti and were served coffee under the small thatched shelter where she had camped so many times. Brother Christadas, who had directed the work on the Kalryans since she left, presented four new converts, lovely young women in clean cotton saris, blue and orange and crimson, and Granny received them joyfully, remembering them as children whom she had often gathered under her little mosquito net shelter and taught hymns and Bible stories. There were speeches, hymns, and of course *jebbum*, as natural and necessary to Granny's daily programme as eating and much more frequent. People swarmed into the spaces between the upright posts—men and boys with turbaned, shaved, or tousled heads, many wearing only the hill man's narrow loincloth with a length of dingy cloth draped over one shoulder; women, girls, babies in all varieties of dress and undress, cleanliness and grime, well being and sickness; in short, that amazing composite of beauty, ugliness, wisdom, ignorance, curiosity, patience, superstition, simplicity, suffering, friendliness, which was one of her beloved Indian villages.

On they went, eight miles more, up to Kunnur. How blessed to be back again, to be greeted by a band of happy school children, all neatly dressed and combed and scrubbed, carrying long poles topped with pennants! They spent the rest of the day and that night there, the visitors exploring, observing, questioning, taking notes; Granny treating sore eyes and abscesses and scabies and big and little worms, advising, scolding, praying; Paul examining twisted hands and feet, bandaging sores, making more new shoes for Karuninasan out of the crude materials he had available. Sitting on the step of a small veranda and using a rough sickle-shaped tool, he carved two wooden rocker shoes and carefully fitted them to the badly shortened feet, then gave detailed instruction for their use. Karuninasan must *always* wear them. He must *always* walk on straight ground. Even when engaged in his daily work of farming, he must constantly think of his feet.

"*Amma*, yes, Doctor *Dhori*!" The hill man nodded soberly, having learned from bitter experience the folly of disobedience.

Down on the plains again they visited Dr. Ruth and Monica in their dispensary, called on Granny's adopted daughter Ruth, who was a village teacher, and her husband John Michael. Granny went on with the party to Vellore to remain for a week while Paul, now working with the British Leprosy Mission with his headquarters in England, departed for a short term of work in Africa, where a rehabilitation centre had been established.

That hateful book! While Granny conferred with the American author, dredged up memories of the past, ransacked an old trunk for letters, pictures, writings of her beloved Jesse, all the time she was rebelling. How could this strange woman possibly tell her story as it really was? She would probably make her out a great heroine, suffering terrible hardships, accomplishing much, when in reality she had been *nothing*, suffered *nothing*, accomplished *nothing*. If story there was, it must be God's and Jesse's, not hers. And who but herself could write it?

The rebellion would grow, become obstinate and irrevocable decision. Later she would write to the troublesome author in America that she had changed her mind. "Dear Sister, I hope you will forgive me, but I know now that I can't possible let you . . ."

Yet it had been good to relive the early years. Back on the Pachais, eager to start work all over again at age eighty-five — the crude hut, the opposition, the making of friends, the slower making of a few converts, the hundreds of miles of horseback riding over stony trails, the fording of streams, the camping out in all kinds of weather, the planting of gardens, the housing of unwanted children — she found herself still looking back.

As I sit here alone on the Pachai Hills, [she wrote] the third range to which God has called me, my eye wanders to a little rough sketch which He has let me paint. It is a parable of my life. It was first sketched when I worked in and around Sendamangalam at the foot of the hills. I could not go there, but I could see them daily, sometimes buried in dark clouds, drenched in rain, but always there to keep me in prayer for them.

It helped me to draw and paint the outlines of our hills where Jesse and I had seen visions and been thrown back through disappointments on the mercy of God. Then it was sketched on a little board covered with canvas. I loved to come back to it, for I had inserted a rainbow and then the words with its reflections, "I will remember." It was a great help to know that although I could not go back yet, He was not forgetting either the hills or me, his poor mourning servant. Later I put the sketch into oils and hung it up when at last I could get back to the hill country.

At last He called me still further, here to the Pachais. I left the picture on that second range. But I was tempted the other day to bring it away here. I took it down, but somehow or other in transit it became soaked and almost obliterated. Just like the work on the Kollis, blurred so often by sin.

The same little board but with no canvas tries to keep me from forgetting, and although it is scarcely the same picture, the words are there, "I will remember", and the rainbow reflected meets me every day. How we both loved the rainbow, the sure sign of His covenant with us, and then those colours at monsoon time around the setting sun.

God alone has led me through fire and water, letting what

seemed wonderful and blessed on the Kollis become defaced, that it may be more meet for the Master's use, like my own life in the hands of the artist Potter. Again and again has the Artist with skilful and loving hand pressed back the marred clay to perform the perfect design He has in mind for me and the hills.

Six

"Make us Thy mountaineers;
We would not linger on the lower slope,
Fill us afresh with hope, O God of Hope,
That undefeated we may climb the hill
As seeing Him who is invisible.
Let us die climbing. . . ."

Amy Carmichael

From *Toward Jerusalem*

1

It was on a day in April, 1965 that Dr. Paul Brand, while lecturing at the annual post-Easter seminar on leprosy at the United States Public Health Hospital in Carville, Louisiana, met a woman from Pennsylvania, a meeting which was to have far-reaching consequences for the work of Evelyn Brand. For this woman was Carolyn Weeber, the nurse who three years before at his suggestion had climbed the eleven miles to Kunnur and spent four days with Granny. During a coffee break in one of the halls after a seminar session Miss Weeber introduced herself as coming from Tamil Nadu, and they recalled their previous meeting. Then over cups of the very strong coffee which accompanied such breaks they began talking about Granny and her work.

"And how is your mother?" asked Carolyn Weeber.

Paul did not answer at once. He seemed lost in thought. It was almost as if he had left behind the buzzing hall and its occupants, even his companion, and slipped away on some wave-length of deep concern to Granny and her mountains.

"I wish," he murmured, apparently thinking aloud, "that I could find someone to go and stay with her!"

"I'll go," said Carolyn Weeber. Her response was as swift and eager as that of Isaiah, given the shining vision in the temple. *Here am I, send me*! She accepted this opportunity without an instant's hesitation as God's will. An interview was arranged with Dr. Lewis of the International Gospel League, and they met over breakfast in Philadelphia, a meal that lasted two hours. Would she be able to go, perhaps in a few months? "I am ready to go now," she responded.

Granny could scarcely believe the good news. It was a miracle, of course, an answer to more than thirty-five years of praying. If ever a person was suited to work on the Mountains of Death and the outreach to the ranges beyond, it was Carol Weeber, a graduate of Geneva College in Beaver Falls, Pennsylvania. Her experience included a master's degree in nursing from Western Reserve University in Cleveland, Ohio, four years of Public Health nursing in Pittsburgh, Pennsylvania, three years as American Red Cross community nurse in North Carolina, a year as Public Health Nursing Instructor at St. Luke's Hospital in Cleveland, and eighteen years as a missionary among Tamil-speaking people in southern India! She spoke and could read and write the language. She was as stalwart in health as in spiritual commitment. Had she been offered the chance to create an ideal helper for the task, Granny could not have conceived such a composite of skills and dedication. Of course God had been able to do a better job!

Arriving in November, 1965 Carol was immediately thrust into the exciting but gruelling task of ministering to the people on five mountain chains. "You must be working under very primitive conditions," commented her Aunt Sadie. Primitive? Yes, one might call it that, like the morning when she was almost up to both knees in mud in the embankment between rice fields, finding that the best way to get out was to walk on all fours. Having spent that Christmas on the Kollis, Carol and Mother Brand had been told that the U.S.A-sponsored malaria eradication department jeep would take them the three miles to where they could get the bus to the plains 4,000 feet below, but the jeep did not come. While four men took Mother Brand in a *dholi*, Carol walked at a quick trot by a short cut. Short? Because of rain the previous night, what she saved in horizontal distance she lost in vertical by sinking into mud. Arriving at the bus stop, she was startled by the sight of Mother Brand perched high above on the pillar of a stone abutment overlooking a precipice, making a sketch on a scrap of paper with a stub of pencil. How an eighty-six year old woman who could not stand alone had got there hobbling on her two sticks Carol could not imagine.

"Praise the Lord we missed the bus," Granny greeted her. "Look at those huge rock pillars over there! One of those hills looks like this." With a few simple strokes and a smudge or two she happily absorbed the hill into her sketch.

Deciding not to worry, Carol turned her attention to her mud-caked feet, wet shoes, and bespattered dress. A man showed her to the bath house of the forest guards' bungalow, and as she started to wash her feet in a bucket of water, she was pleasantly surprised to find it warm. She was learning to enjoy small things taken for granted in less primitive surroundings.

When the bus finally came Granny regretfully stopped sketching. "One—two—three" she counted and, sliding down off the pillar, tottered towards the bus with the aid of her two sticks. As they passed the wash room Carol saw one of the foresters coming out of the wash room with the empty bucket calling for hot water. So the warm bath had been a stolen pleasure. It hadn't been meant for her!

Primitive? Yes. But sacrifice, no. Already Carol was in hearty agreement with Granny's scoffing response whenever "sacrifice" or some word of similar implication was mentioned in her presence. "Sacrifice! Hardships! What hardships?" No synonym of "self-denial" was a part of her vocabulary.

For the first time in more than thirty-five years Evelyn Brand knew the companionship of one as totally committed as herself to the mission on the hills. Yet even this was a companionship savoured only at brief intervals, for Carol's ministry was to all the ranges now in the scope of the Hill Gospel Fellowship, while Granny was for the present concentrating on the Pachais. Distances and difficulties of travel were staggering. For instance, to reach Granny's station on the Pachais from Kunnur on the Kalryans, where Carol was working, one had to walk the eleven miles down to Papanaiyakanpatti on the plains, travel by bus or Regina Hansen's jeep the sixty miles to the foot of the Pachais, then walk up ten miles to the cluster of dwellings where for some years Granny had been living in a leaky shelter, into which the cold winds blew and in the monsoon season dampness seeped up through the earthen floor.

Granny? Carol soon learned that her comrade found the term distasteful, scorning anything that associated her mere eighty-six years with the suggestion of old age. The difference in age made "Evelyn" or "Evie" seem a bit improper. Neither did the hill people's usual mode of address, "Mother Brand" or "Mother" seem to fit the demands of their relationship, for they were more like sisters than mother and daughter. Yet she remained "Mother" or "Mother Brand" to her new associate for some years, until Carol discovered that brother Charlie's pet name for his younger sister had been "Babs", originally short for "Baby", and she appropriated it tentatively. Granny did not seem to mind. In fact, soon after she gave Carol a Tamil Bible for her birthday, in which she signed herself "Babs". Thereafter in the intimacy of their *tête-à-têtes* and the privacy of her diary Granny became "Babs". Yet "Granny" she would remain to her family, to Dr. Lewis, to most of her fellow workers and supporters around the world.

They met more often on the plains than in the mountains. In 1966 a house was built in Papanaiyakanpatti for Fellowship head-quarters with living space in the back for Granny. Ruth, her adopted daughter, and John Michael lived in the front portion, a happy contrast to the windowless one-room mud-wall and thatched hut which had been the only place procurable for rent when Ruth accepted the appointment as teacher in the village government school. Now their son, an X-ray technician, and their daughter, a nurse, both trained at Vellore, could come home on holiday to decent rooms and pukka beds instead of sleeping on the camp cots which Carol had brought with her from America. Granny, however, scorned all such luxuries associated with life on the plains. "Can you imagine my *living there*?" she demanded indignantly. But the new house, she admitted, made a good lodging in transit and an excellent meeting place for the Hill Fellowship.

The first general meeting there was to be held in November, 1966, and she arrived at the house a week early, but merely to stop, not stay. Bound for a congregational meeting in one of the hill stations, she was undeterred by a note which arrived the day of her departure, advising her not to come because the heavy monsoon rains had swollen the streams and made the paths too slippery for her horse. She set out, made the trip safely, then went across the range to Kunnur station, where a new worker, Frances Dhyriam, had consented to work temporarily. A woman over eighty, she had held many responsible positions and was still an honorary magistrate in her native city of Madurai.

The day of the Fellowship meeting brought a steady downpour. Surely Mother Brand would not get down to join them, but knowing her persistence the workers hesitated to begin. Finally they started the opening devotions without her. The meeting was interrupted by the arrival of a postal runner with news that Mother Brand had reached the last and biggest stream where the waters were up to a man's armpits. The four men who were carrying her *dholi* had set her down, refusing to go farther until the waters abated.

"We must go and get her across," several strong young men of the Fellowship decided.

But just as they were setting out along came the four men bearing the *dholi* at a rapid trot. A tiny figure emerged, dripping muddy water. *How?* they marvelled. It was all very simple, Granny explained, nothing to make a fuss about. She had taken off her shoes with their braces, crawled to the edge of the rushing stream, grabbed hold of the rope which was slung across only when the current was at its worst, and let herself down into the turbulent muddy stream. Then her bearers, who hadn't seen her go into the water, had rushed to her aid and carried her across, since the waters had ballooned her loose divided skirt so that she could not move her legs. Just let her have a small wash and a change of clothes, and they would get on with the meeting.

The next day that same stream carried a woman to her death.

The house on the plains was not the only improvement in living quarters. On Granny's Pachais a new two-roomed house was built for her in the same year, a special gift of Dr. and Mrs. Mervin Rosell of the Overseas Crusade. But the fact of a new, more comfortable dwelling was for her of far less interest than the labour which helped build it, for it was the work project of a team of medical students from Vellore.

The first work camp had been held in 1964 on the Kollis. Granny herself had broached the idea to the college chaplain, Reverend A. C. Oommen. The students, she pointed out bluntly, lived in an artificial world, sheltered from the poverty and suffering all about them. It would be good for them to get their hands dirty, to sleep in mud houses under thatch. Why not bring some of them to spend a week with the forsaken Christian families on the Kollis and light up their fading faith? Other such camps had been held but never in such a needy and isolated area. Chaplain Oommen went to inspect the spot and came back satisfied. "This is the place where our services are needed."

They had come, four staff members and six medical students, taking the train to Salem, the bus to Kalanayagampatti at the foot of the hill, another bus for Solaikkadu, four thousand feet above sea level, praying for safety every minute as they negotiated the seventy-two hairpin bends, then walking three miles through green fields, crossing streams, climbing, descending, reaching their camping place at two in the afternoon. They had helped start a model farm, digging trenches and pits, cleaned the surroundings of Jesse's grave and made a garden around it. They had visited the seventeen Christian families, worshipped with them, treated patients each day from four to six in the afternoon, taught them rules of health.

Now in 1966 a team of thirteen students and staff climbed the six miles of narrow footpath to Pattur. For ten days they stayed on the mountain, sleeping in low thatched field huts vacated for their use by villagers. This time their task was to build the foundation for a new house for Granny. Next year, they vowed, if Granny would invite them, they would come back and build a chapel.

Granny accepted her new snug all-weather shelter with her usual indifference to creature comforts. She rejoiced far more in the improvement of buildings for her helpers. One of these was the pastor, Paul Chakkaravarthy, who had joined the work on the Pachais about 1963. He was a vigorous and devoted Christian in his forties, the only one in his family who had accepted the faith. Formerly a Hindu priest of corrupt practices living in an isolated village in the Nilgiris, he had been converted through a missionary couple from Europe. One day on the plains he had met Granny, and she had invited him to visit her on the Pachais. When he came, she had made a near irreparable mistake which had almost lost him to the work. Contrary to her usual habit of naïve trustfulness, she had accused him of stealing money which had disappeared from her cash box.

"You are the only new person here, and of course you took it," she had charged him hotly.

Later it was discovered that other workers had helped themselves from the box, the key to which hung in a readily available spot. Fortunately Paul had been understanding and forgiving when Granny had invited him to come back to the hills. Leaving their children temporarily with relatives on the plains, he and his wife Vethammal had braved the cold mists and heavy rains of October and November to settle on the Pachais. For Granny it had been the happiest of relationships. Paul shared her intense zeal for bringing the Gospel to the hill people. Even more invaluable than his increase of knowledge through further training in Bible courses was his clear insight into the simple truths of the Gospel which often escaped those born into the faith. For the first time since Jesse's death Granny had a fellow-worker with whom she could discuss her problems and aspirations in full sympathy—one, moreover, who had the courage to firmly but gently disagree with her when he felt that her sometimes hasty and defiant decisions were not in the best interest of the work.

Beside Paul Chakkaravarthy and his wife and children on the Pachais, there were Tata, the old man who went down to the plains to fetch her mail, and Lazarus, an uneducated hill man who had come to her with hookworm, that tiny poochie which, invading the body through the skin of a person going barefoot, could wreak such havoc. She had taken him down to a compounder on the plains for medicine and cured him of the ailment through repeated treatments, then provided him with milk powder for his anaemia, since few of the landowners on the Pachais owned cows. Now he and his son fetched her water, tended her horse, and helped in the fields, each receiving a rupee a day.

The new house was finished by August the eighth, her eighty-seventh birthday, when Regina Hansen's van brought Carol and three other workers to the foot of the hill and they walked up the eight miles and surprised her. Since there were not enough chairs, they arranged the table so that two could sit on a long box.

Another welcome surprise on that very day was a letter from Paul and Margaret.

Carol visited Granny on the Pachais about once a month, and occasionally they spent time together on the plains or in other hill stations, though there were so many supervisory and personal problems at the separated stations that they felt it necessary to divide their forces. They spent two long sessions at Vellore where Granny was pursuing her unwelcome task of completing her autobiography. Though the new house on the Pachais remained her headquarters and the work there her major concern, she was almost as migratory as Carol, whose most permanent office for months consisted of a few boxes under a bed in Regina Hansen's house.

Conditions on the Kollis were an increasing source of grief and bitterness. As if it were not enough for the mission to have turned over much of the property at Vazhavanthi for the temporary use of government and other agencies, the little wooden house which Jesse had built and brought her to on their wedding night had been sold, to be dismantled for its wood! The Kolli Christians were as distressed as she was. "You shall not take our father's house," they told the purchaser. But, being poor, they had no means to prevent it. Granny, too, had been powerless to prevent the sale. She had prayed, wept, written blistering letters, all to no avail. Then in 1967 she found to her ineffable joy that the purchaser was willing to sell it back to her! To her humbling acknowledgment also of lack of faith, for had her prayers been answered and the property not been sold, it would of necessity have been transferred with other mission holdings to the Indian Property Committee, and she could not have bought it back!

Travels to other stations, however, were never permitted to interfere with her duties on the Pachais—except once. One Thursday in the spring of 1967 as the bearers were bringing her down from the Kollis by a little-used overgrown trail, her slight body was badly crushed between the bamboo poles. Her fragile bones felt ground to pulp, and every jolt of the swaying *dholi* was like a knife thrust. Meeting Carol at the foot of the hills that Friday morning, she was unable even to joke at her predicament.

"It hurts me to laugh," she confessed. It was agreed that she could not possibly make the sixty mile trip across the plains by car and then ride up the Pachais on horseback. But she had promised to be there for a Sunday School function held regularly when forty children from the government school came to the station each Sunday for teaching.

"I'll go," offered Carol cheerfully, though she had just come down from Kunnur. She started on the long trip that Friday

189

evening, setting out on the bus across the plains to Atur and intending to spend the night there at the lodge. However, arriving there at eight-thirty, she found there was a bus which would take her the thirty miles to Uppiliyapuram, the place on the main road where one turned off for the Pachais. During an intermediate stop she went into a hotel and ordered a *dosai*, one of the delicious thin Indian pancakes, for she had had no supper. She had taken no more than a bite when people started yelling, "The bus is leaving." Grabbing her *dosai* in its banana leaf plate, she paid for it, ran out, and jumped on the moving bus. "Did you have coffee?" enquired her fellow passengers solicitously. No. Though she had ordered it, they had not brought it. They were relieved to learn that she had not paid for it.

Arriving at Uppiliyapuram at ten, she found all the shops closed. Where to sleep? She remembered a family which had let members of the Fellowship use their outdoor toilet when they were *en route* by bus. Would they recognize her? She had seen them only once, months before. She had brought her bed roll, so all she needed was a corner. The house was dark. She tapped on the door (not an Indian custom) and called "*Ammal*" at respectable intervals. Finally a light went on, and the matron of the house appeared with her husband who, seeing the visitor, retreated into a back room.

"*Ammal*," explained Carol in Tamil, "I have come suddenly. I am going to the Pachais tomorrow. I have my own bed roll. May I have a little space to sleep? Please forgive me."

"Come in," said the woman. Taking off her shoes, Carol walked into the long narrow front room of the comfortable home. All the windows were closed, but an electric fan whirled lazily. In the room there were six children sleeping, each on his own light mattress, and three adults. Carol moved at the woman's direction to one end of the room. Next to her was a boy of five who had not wakened and next to him were two girls whom she remembered as high school students. They sat up and watched her as she spread her bed roll and lay down under her cotton blanket. To her surprise the woman brought her a pillow.

She awakened the next morning to the sound of the little boy's happy voice in the next room, and soon one of the girls brought her a glass of coffee. She got up, rolled up her bed, said thank you and goodbye, and went on her way. She found a man with a bicycle who agreed to take her baggage to the room the Fellowship used in the village on the way to the hills. Starting to walk, she thumbed a ride on an oxcart, climbing up by the spokes on one of its two huge wheels and sitting on a bag of chemical fertiliser, which, the driver told her, came from the U.S.A. Finally she met the men who had come down for Granny with the *dholi*, and they took her *saman*. After four hours more of walking she arrived at her destination.

There had been nothing unusual about the trip. Had she not been writing her semi-annual circular letter home to America that weekend on the Pachais, Carol would not have thought its details worth mentioning. For Granny such a sequence had been merely an ordinary day's activity for the past fifty years.

2

As with Rome, the foundations of an even more "eternal city" were slowly being laid on seven hills. In addition to the ranges originally in Jesse's plan there were now the Bothais and the Paithur Hills. In 1967, besides carrying on the work in seven different stations, three new ones were opened and two which had been unmanned were reopened with new workers. Though Granny continued to make her headquarters in the new snug house on the Pachais, she was engaged in activities all over the seven ranges. That year she made fourteen trips up and down on horse or in a *dholi*.

One of these trips, to an isolated area of the northern Kalryans called Aryure Nadu, was the result of four years' intensive concern. She and her workers had visited the place first back in 1963, a three-day trip from Kunnur, she on her small horse, the others walking. They had preached in villages along the way, climbing sheer slopes, descending into wild valleys, camping at night, arriving at last in this distant, long neglected area. With difficulty they had found a shed in which to stay and itinerate with the Gospel. But though they were well received by the common people, they soon sensed an atmosphere of suspicion. Why? Why also did this area so far from civilisation seem so prosperous, the women dressed in fine bright saris, the men obviously well to do? They had discovered why. One day Granny had gone on her horse to look for a shed near a likely village and, finding an ideal place, had sent messengers to the village to tell of her arrival. A crowd of people headed by an old man had come streaming out. Granny had told him her purpose and asked permission to use the shed.

"*Paw, paw*, be off!" he had shouted rudely, waving threatening arms. Then unwisely, perhaps discounting her knowledge of Tamil, he had turned and explained to his followers, "She will discover our *kanja*!"

Kanja! That plant known in the West as marijuana. They had soon discovered how extensive was its illicit cultivation in this particular area of the hills, whose whole economy was based on its illegal sale to a syndicate which exported it to Great Britain and other Western countries. From that day it had become Granny's obsessive purpose to abolish this evil from the area, just as the wonderful spraying machines equipped with Western chemicals had finally eradicated malaria from the mountains. Now, four years later, she felt the time had come for battle. In March, 1967 the established governments were to take over complete control of the hills, dethroning the local *dhoris* and presumably making enforcement of the law more possible, yet somehow the *dhoris* succeeded in securing a delay order. Nevertheless, a second camping trip had been planned for April, and in April it would be.

This time, instead of trekking for three or four days from Kunnur, Granny and Carol made the eighty-mile trip around the mountains in Regina's van, spending the night in a forest bungalow. Granny's little horse was brought to the foot of the northern Kalryans to meet her. Other workers had been sent on ahead. "The path is impossible for a horse," one of them sent back a message. "We are sending men to bring you in a *dholi*." However, canvas for the *dholi* had been left in the forest bungalow, so Granny started up the steep rocky path on her horse. Impossible? Almost. At least once she had to dismount and proceed on foot, aided by her two bamboo sticks, somehow climbing the path strewn with rocks and boulders. Perhaps the torturous climb was partially responsible for the sensation she developed during the following weeks of falling . . . falling especially at night when she would waken suddenly and cry out.

Arriving finally at the village of Kalliparai, travel stained and exhausted, they were heartened by the greetings of five Fellowship workers and two Christian hill men. Jayaraj, who had been a clerical worker in the Air Force, had trekked with his wife for four days from Nagalur, a station without workers until they had joined the Fellowship. Thankappan, an untrained teacher who had been working in a village five miles away, and Archipaul had made arrangements for their camp. The local *dhori* had given the use of his new tiled house with a big veranda on which they held a Sunday service the next day. For the workers' kitchen he had provided a village house of mud and thatch. Carol, of course, had to leave for other duties, returning for visits when she could, but Granny camped for the next eight weeks in a tent near the village, her horseman Kassy living in a smaller tent and doing the cooking and washing.

Stottherum, praise be! This time the rulers at least did not drive them away. Because of the esteem in which Thankappan was held by his pupils and their parents the men of Kalliparai and those of another village half a mile a mile away agreed to build a school and joined in putting up bamboo poles for its walls. Then came the inevitable opposition. One of the head men tried to drive away the would-be builders with threats and curses. Granny climbed the hill from her tent and boldly asked him to go away. He did leave, but his influence was strong and the workers also left. When there came a rumour that other villages were critical, the work was held up for days. Then came whole weeks given up to *swami* feasts, with a decorated bull being led around the village, and during the whole time, of course, no work was done. But finally the new building of bamboo and thatch was finished, ready to be plastered with mud before the cold weather came, and Granny moved into it from her tent with her helper Grace, who had joined her from Kunnur.

The success of the new adventure seemed even more assured when a group from another village in the area, headed by their *dhori*, came asking that a new school be established for them too. "You must come and see the site we are giving!" they told Granny. "I'll be there tomorrow," she agreed joyfully. Accompanied by the other workers she rode there on horseback and was met by a large crowd. A badly burned child was brought to them for treatment. After telling the story of Yesu-swami they were taken to a lovely stream-fed meadow where the new school would be built. Sitting on a grassy bank talking with the eager villagers, Granny pictured the neat new building in the midst of a lovely garden. She returned to camp jubilant. But in the following days she sensed the waning of the villagers' enthusiasm. Presently another delegation came, again headed by the *dhori*. "*Illai*, no, we do not want you in our village. There are ten people who will not allow it." The cultivators, of course. She should have known victory would not be so easy. *Kanja* had won again . . . for the moment. Disappointment, yes, but not defeat. Granny had only begun to fight.

When she left this camp at the beginning of June she found a wondrous surprise waiting at the foot of the mountains. A sturdy jeep, acquired through Carol for the Hill Fellowship! What a blessing, especially now that this new area was opening! True, only one of the twelve stations could be reached by jeep. The others must be walked to—five, eight, eleven miles—but the distances across the plains had made travel slow and burdensome. To Granny's amazement Carol herself proved to be an experienced and capable driver. When they first went up the mountain road to the Kollis with its seventy-two tortuous curves and their hired driver touched a bus in passing, Carol resolved to take over the driving for good. In the first five months the jeep travelled over eleven thousand miles.

In the weeks and months following this visit to Kalliparai her crusade against the illicit drug traffic became Granny's chief obsession. In July she returned to Aryure Nadu with teacher Thankappan and Leelabai, his bride of two months, who faced the formidable journey up the hill with trepidation but soon adjusted to this new station to which her husband was to be transferred. Since she was educated she would be an invaluable help in teaching. In spite of his lack of training Thankappan had run a very successful school in his former post and had won the confidence of the people. When he and his bride were pressed to return to that village on a visit, the people honoured them with a *moyi*, dropping coins large and small into a basin of saffron water, a token of their affection and gratitude. Already the school at Kalliparai was prospering, attendance having reached about forty. But the sight of long lines of men trekking the mountain paths *en route* to market, on their heads bulky sacks of the injurious *kanja*, cancelled any sense of triumph.

The evil of *kanja*, Granny knew well, could not be eradicated by mere teaching and preaching. Nor did the solution lie with officers of the law on the plains, though she visited the District Collectors, the Agricultural Officers and Directors, and found them sympathetic and cooperative. They were too far away to penetrate the inaccessible areas of *kanja* cultivation with effective means of law enforcement. Besides, such coercive measures were no permanent answer. Evil must be replaced by good. You did not take away a man's livelihood without giving him a source of income in return.

Granny was equal to this challenge. She had been developing experimental crops for years. On the Kalryans in cooperation with the Agricultural Department she had planted young banana trees brought from a range 250 miles away; apple trees, pears, mangoes, limes. She had tried rhubarb, beets, tomatoes, cabbage, not too successfully. There had been an acre in the wet lands for rice, which had to survive the hot months of April and May when all the cattle were let free to get food wherever they could find it, the owners having no responsibility for crops that were destroyed. Her experiments had included coffee, cardamom, pineapple. She had fought their enemies, parasites, insects, droughts, predators both animal and human, with the same zeal with which she was now prepared to wage war against the demon *kanja*. The villagers of Kalliparai must be shown that freedom from the harmful and illegal culture could mean not only peace of mind but other productive enterprise and better nourishment for their families.

So in October she went up again taking about 700 pineapple sprouts which had been brought by jeep from the plantings on the Kollis. For some time she remained preaching and distributing the plants, which were hardy and needed little care, though they would take about eighteen months to bear fruit.

Back once more on the plains she persuaded Carol to drive her to the Nilgiris where they visited the Government Pomological Gardens. Touring the nurseries with zestful avidity, she purchased six apple trees, twelve plum trees, twelve peach trees, twelve lime trees. At another government station she bought cocoa trees. Four days later the saplings had been transported down the mountains, the long distance across the plains, and up the tortuous trail to Kalliparai. To Granny's disappointment she fell ill and had to entrust the delivery of the precious cargo to Carol and Paul Chakkaravarthy. Dissatisfied with the report they gave her, she managed to curb her impatience through a Thanksgiving dinner at Regina's, three Americans, two English citizens, and two Indians partaking with equal enthusiasm of an American collation of turkey, cranberry sauce, and pumpkin pie; then immediately gave orders for her own trip up the hills. Paul Chakkaravarthy arranged to go ahead and prepare the way. Two mornings later when she and Carol arrived by jeep at the foothills, two men had been sent down for their luggage, four men to carry her up in a *dholi*, and two others, each to carry six mango saplings up the steep path in a basket on his head.

Pitifully small it seemed after all the expense and exertion, this planting of a few dozen trees by a handful of interested villagers. A puny combatant to send against the huge fields of *kanja* with their fantastic profits! Like a grain of mustard seed in a bushel of corn, or a small boy going out to face a giant! But a mustard seed could grow into a tree, and a David, with faith, could conquer a Goliath.

On one of their trips to these hills they found Valliyan, a young man in a nearby village who had fallen from a high tree which he had climbed to shake down tamarind fruit. His friends had run to his rescue and carried him down the hill to the government hospital, then as he received no help there, had brought him back home. His back was broken, and he was paralysed from the waist down. Granny found him there, a broken heap, helpless, hopeless.

"You must let us take him to Vellore," she told his parents, describing the miracles that were performed at the great Christian Medical Centre. Both he and his parents refused, preferring to pay much money to the swami to perform *mantrams*. Granny visited him again and again, heartsick each time to see him pulled out of the dark hut by his feet for her to talk with him. They had reckoned without her powers of insistence, or they might have agreed sooner. In July they let him be carried down the hill in a cloth borne by two men. Granny and Carol took him the 130 miles to Vellore in the jeep, where after two weeks in the hospital he was installed in the Rehabilitation Institute, whose director, Dr. Mary Verghese, was herself a paraplegic.*

That autumn Granny was in Vellore spending as much time as possible with her son Paul, who, on tour for the American and British Leprosy Missions, spent two weeks in India from October 22 to November 4, sharing his techniques in surgery and rehabilitation for leprosy with workers from all over Asia. Of course she visited Valliyan. She would not have recognised him. Not only were the sullenness and discouragement gone, but he looked actually happy. Fitted with calipers, he was standing at a work table where each day he made brushes of rope net or bags with plastic wire.

"You know," Granny reminded him, "it is Yesu-swami and his followers who have made all this possible."

Valliyan nodded gravely. After seven months at Vellore he was able to return home where, being only a mile from one of the schools, it was possible for a Christian teacher to keep in touch with him. His family erected a bamboo railing, against which he could lean and along which he could walk with the aid of his calipers. The work he had learned at Vellore made it possible for him to earn a small income, in addition, Granny reflected, to the amount his family derived from their participation in the *kanja* traffic. What a difference from the wreck of impotence and despair that had once been pulled out of the tent by its inert legs!

She must fight the evil of *kanja*, yes. But while waiting for the mustard seed to turn into a tree or one of the children in the new schools to grow into a conquering David, there were plenty of Valliyans pleading for survival. They came crowding about her in every village.

"I couldn't help being amused," she finished one letter to Dr.

*Her dramatic story has been told by Dorothy Clarke Wilson in *Take My Hands*, Hodder & Stoughton.

196

Lewis, "while I was washing and dressing an Indian's stinking and gangrenous foot. Three or four young women were standing outside the door holding cloths over their noses. Of course the smell was awful . . . But why stand around holding your nose when the Lord has so much for us to do?"

3

FOR YEARS IT had been Granny's dream to find a doctor who would respond to the call of the mountains. When in Vellore she was usually invited to speak to the medical students and staff at the college chapel. Always she painted a graphic picture of the needs of the hills and pleaded that some young doctor might see the vision and join the team. Whenever she saw an intent look in a listener's eyes she would say to herself, "I must work on him," and of course she did, drawing him aside and urging, "You must come to the mountains and spend some time with our team."

She talked to medical students on the college campus, at the Evangelical Fellowship Union Meetings which she attended every Sunday when in Vellore, in the hospital, even stopping them on the streets to enquire about their plans, to describe with glowing eyes the God-given opportunities which awaited any young person brave enough to accept the most compelling challenges of human need. And of course in the Vellore work camps she looked ceaselessly for signs of kindled interest and commitment.

It was in the camp of 1968 on the Pachais that she found it. There was a team of eighteen, comprising junior doctors, nursing staff, and both medical and nursing students. After a night in the forest bungalow, a hurried breakfast and worship before sunrise, they started up the six miles of mountain. Granny had sent down a team of twelve porters to help those who could not carry their *saman*, and she was at the top to welcome them. Her eyes were drawn immediately to the face of one young man. His face was familiar. She had talked to him somewhere about the work, and he had revealed a special interest. Perhaps he had heard her speak at one of the chapel services, and she had noticed the look of intent concern in his eyes. Perhaps she had talked to him on the street. It did not matter. Suddenly she knew why her attention was so drawn to him, and her heart leaped. He reminded her of

Jesse. Surely, if the spirit of Jesse lived within that vigorous young body, those compassionate eyes, he must catch Jesse's vision of the hills. Though they had many talks together, she knew she must not pressure him. She would only show him, pray, and leave the rest to God.

The young man was Dr. David Lister, an Englishman who had grown up in a family of physicians. Father, grandfather, uncles were all doctors, and one of his great uncles, Sir Joseph Lister, called the Father of Modern Surgery, had developed the theory of antisepsis. David, a graduate of Cambridge, had received his medical training in a large hospital in London, then had come to India to continue his medical work, studying for specialisation in Asiatic diseases and obstetrics. The scope and excellency of the great medical centre at Vellore had brought him there for both study and practice. Before coming to India he had visited countries in Africa and throughout Asia looking for the place where God wanted him to serve. In Granny he recognised a quality of selfless dedication akin to his own.

"She was happier and more alive than anyone I had ever met," he was to confess later. "When she looks at you, it's as if she could see right through you."

It was a wonderful work camp. The village school lent its building so the men of the group could stay right in the heart of the village with people, pigs, cattle, chickens, and all their by-products. Those who had attended in 1966 were overjoyed to find Granny's house completed and furnished, and the girls occupied one part of it. Granny turned the first spadeful of sod for the new chapel and declared the camp opened. The foundation was already laid, and the group started filling the space with earth from a nearby area. A strange, eye-opening experience for young people, most of whom had never seen such tasks performed except by coolies! Working with villagers, they learned to understand their problems and aspirations.

They were at work by six fifteen in the morning, after coffee and worship with Granny on her veranda; an hour's work before breakfast; work again until the second break, about one, then a welcome dip in the local swimming pool, a tank dug for irrigation in the fields; lunch and rest until three-thirty, then discussion over tea, followed by time to see patients; after supper an hour of Bible study, using the book of Nehemiah, which came alive not only because of their work of building but because the book portrayed the problems, oppositions, challenges facing those who attempted to live the way of Christian discipleship. And Granny, ceaselessly proclaiming the needs of her beloved hills, was the greatest challenge of all.

By the time the camp ended on June 7 the rafters for the new chapel were raised. Only the thatching remained for the place to be ready for worship. And Granny was hopeful that the earnest young doctor had seen the vision, even though he had made no commitment. In the months that followed she continued to hope . . . and wait, for her the hardest of all disciplines. Then in November of that year when she and Carol came down from the Nilgiris with the saplings, they found Dr. Lister waiting at Regina Hansen's. He wanted to go up and see the Kollis. Carol did not stop to remove her luggage from the jeep but started with him at once for Paul Chakkaravarthy's home forty miles away.

Paul, Granny considered, had become responsible for the work on the Kollis. Always first of all concerned for the congregation which she and Jesse had started, she would have been satisfied for him to have it as his sole responsibility, but there was such need of supervision in the other hill stations that he was often called by the various workers to guide them in situations where his leadership was important. Making his headquarters in a fairly central place, he was able not only to visit the Kollis but to assist in the work on other ranges as needed. His four children were receiving the excellent education which he himself had never been able to acquire.

When Carol and Dr. Lister arrived at his house late that night the family had gone to bed, but Paul wakened at her knocking and opened the door. Yes, he would be glad to take the doctor to the Kollis in the morning. Carol returned to Regina's by bus, but the others drove up the road with its seventy-two hairpin bends and back again the same day. The doctor left for Vellore by train that evening. Granny endured tortures of regret because she had been too ill to go with him. She could only pray that those keen young eyes had been wide open to the human needs and possibilities which she would have so liked to show him. Her prayer was answered.

"God wants me here," decided young David Lister. "The need is the call."

In January 1969 he came back to become the only physician and surgeon among the thousands of people on the six ranges, most of whom had never seen a doctor. The Kollis had their own Health Centre with a physician in charge, as well as the frequent services of Dr. Ruth Harris. Dr. Lister settled at Munglepetti on the Kalryans.

Trust and Triumph! The title of Granny's little autobiography seemed even more appropriate with this realisation of her long-time dream. July of that year, 1968 found her in Vellore working furiously with the help of Susie Koshi and Eira Dalton, a professional writer, to finish it. Meanwhile Carol struggled with the red tape, delays, and procrastinations so typical of the Indian economy in getting an all-weather house built for the new doctor on the Kalryans. It took four months to secure a mason. She placed an order for asbestos roofing and cement, but could not get them because the monthly cheque from America didn't come and didn't come . . . and didn't come. It had been lost in the mails. Another cheque had to be issued. But the house was finally in process of building. Not that such externals of comfort and convenience would prove of importance to Dr. Lister. Like Granny, he would have been perfectly content with a shelter of mud and thatch. In fact, it was part of his philosophy to live as nearly as possible like the people he had come to serve. When he asked for eighty-five dollars for a kerosene refrigerator, it was not for his own comfort but for the medicines he was obliged to store. At first he even refused to accept a horse.

"About the horse," he wrote Dr. Lewis. "I am a little undecided because of the business of identifying oneself with the people here. It again emphasises the material resources which we have, and, as they walk everywhere I think it best at the present to walk also until at any rate I know them better."

Not until he had been on the mountains for a year and won the people's love and confidence would he accept this quicker means of transportation which would make him of greater service.

He was appalled as well as challenged by the magnitude of the task he faced.

"These mountain people," a visitor said to him, "must be a hundred years behind the general condition of the people of India."

"Yes," he replied, "much more than a hundred years. You have to see them to believe that such needs actually exist in this world."

But the young doctor was undaunted by this enormity of need. "There is no doubt in my mind," he expressed his purpose in words that Granny herself might have spoken, "that I am in the very centre of the will of God on these mountain ranges."

4

GRANNY COULD NOT stay long in Vellore. Though the medical college was surrounded by mountains, no valley could contain her long. As soon as the last section of the troublesome book had been given to the writer who would put it into final shape, she was ready to move on. Carol had come to Vellore with five patients who needed treatment, one of them Karuninasan, who had been called back for an evaluation of the results of his hand surgery. Several days would elapse before the final conference on Granny's manuscript.

"We can't stay here," she fumed. "Let's visit Kalliparai and come back. That's our nearest station to Vellore." Nearest, yes, but still over a hundred miles away.

Karuninasan went with them. They arrived at the forest bungalow at the foot of the Kalryans to spend the night. Previously they had planned to go up the next day, after putting Karuninasan on the bus for the trip around the hills to the foot of his own mountain. But in Vellore, seeing him clumsily climb into the back of the jeep, Granny changed her mind. Though Dr. Paul's surgical skill had done much to increase the use of his hands, he still had the scars of leprosy which, in spite of the scientific conclusions that the disease was even less contagious than tuberculosis, still suffered the age-old stigma of fear and superstition.

"No," decided Granny. "He might not be given a place on the bus if he travelled alone. Someone must go with him."

The someone, of course, was Carol. Leaving Granny and her companion Grace at the forest bungalow, she boarded the bus with Karuninasan at six in the morning, rode with him the sixty miles to Salem, and there saw that he got a seat on the bus to the foot of the hill, from where four men would carry him up in a *dholi*. Returning to the forest bungalow, the next day she accompanied Granny up the northern Kalryans to Kalliparai, where they camped for five days, depressed by the continued illicit cultivation of *kanja* but cheered by the day school of twelve eager little boys, plus a jolly session at night for those who herded cattle or goats during the day.

While Carol was trekking twenty miles to the two nearby stations Granny decided she must visit Valliyan, the young paraplegic who, after his fall from a tree, had been treated for seven months at the Vellore Rehabilitation Institute. His home was a good mile and a half from the school. All the workers tried to dissuade her. There were no bearers to carry her, and she certainly could not walk. All refused to be party to any such foolishness.

"Very well,' she replied calmly. "I shall go alone." And she started out determinedly, tottering along over the uneven rocky path with the aid of her two sticks. Of course after she had gone some distance they relented and hastened to help her. Somewhat chastened by the experience Granny had to confess that she could not have walked home except for a man on either side, fairly lifting her along. But she had had her way and seen Valliyan, who had taken the name Visuvasam (Faith) after becoming a Christian. She would gladly have *crawled* both ways if possible to give him comfort and encouragement, for she had found him depressed. Though he was still making a few baskets out of plastic wire, the cost of the materials was becoming so high that his new skills were proving useless. Moreover, he was developing ulcers on his feet.

"We must get Dr. Lister to look at him," she decided.

She was back in Vellore on 8th August, 1968, for her eighty-ninth birthday, and at last the manuscript of her little book was finalised and made ready for mailing to Dr. Lewis for publication by the International Gospel League. Good! A disagreeable business finished. She had found the whole idea of parading the events of her life before curious, even loyally interested readers, extremely distasteful. But at least it had not been done by some stranger who would doubtless magnify her few poor labours into heroic achievement. She hoped she had made it plain that all credit for her slight accomplishment belonged to God and to Jesse. Still, there had been spiritual therapy in the process of remembering. The tragedy of Jesse's going and the long years of loneliness, even the bitterness over the seeming betrayal of their work on the Kollis, receded into clearer and kindlier perspective. It was like climbing a Mount Nebo where she could look back over the barren wilderness trails and see the whole pattern of her journeying toward the Promised Land. She could write at the end of her little life story :

> Why did You have to break me first,
> Why did you take my all away
> Before you satisfied my thirst?
> Why must I sink in deepest deep
> Before the promises to know?
> I realize now it had to be
> Before He taught my soul to pray,
> Before the glory I could see,
> The glory that He promised me.

Already there were glimpses of the glory. There were now thirty-three people, including herself and Carol and Dr. Lister, manning sixteen stations on the seven hills. Three of the men workers were getting married, bringing their wives to serve with them. Christians in many parts of the world were dedicating support to this work which could not exist without financial help from concerned persons in other countries . . . such as the Indian male nurse working in Arabia who, after visiting the hill work years ago, had committed himself to sending 150 rupees each month, enough to pay the salaries of two workers. And Granny herself was rapidly fulfilling the old dream of preaching the Gospel on the five ranges, plus two others. By the end of 1967 she had left the new snug all-weather house on the Pachais and moved on to other hills to live again under leaking roofs in bamboo sheds with mud floors.

Even the *kanja* area, her obsessive concern, was showing faint signs of hope. On 15th August, 1968, the twenty-first anniversary of India's independence, there was a flag-raising in Kalliparai. The teacher asked the *dhori*, who had just succeeded to the hereditary post, to give the address. His father, according to practice, had set fire to a field before ploughing, but being addicted to drunkenness had disregarded the rules of time and weather always observed by the illiterate villagers, and had caused the neighbouring village to be burned to the ground. Hence he had been ousted from his position. The new *dhori* was a young man who had studied through high school and, though he had failed the government examination, was highly educated in the hills where illiteracy approached one hundred per cent. He gave the address on the history of independence and the Indian flag. The school children sang the national anthem. A faint chance that this meeting might lift the eyes of these law-breaking citizens to the claims of patriotism, especially since the new *dhori* who was himself engaged in the nefarious traffic, had been in hiding from the police and was accepting bribes from an agent to whom the illicit produce was being directed! Still, Granny snatched eagerly at every straw of hope.

Her efforts to correct the evil never faltered. The following year she even wrote a letter to the Prime Minister, Indira Gandhi.

Dear Madame, I hope this is the right way to address you. I know you are so busy with all your political duties, but I feel you only can help me. I have so great a burden on my mind, too hard to bear alone . . . My great burden is the persistent cultivation by the poor hill people year after year of the evil weed called *kanja*. They make it into that bad drug which at

200 rupees is taken down in loads, smuggled to Bombay and shipped to England and other countries where the stupid teen-agers are teased into smoking it . . . Dear Sister, help me save them. The police try but as they all make money out of it no one raises a hand to stop it. I have been to the authorities who ought to care. They are tired of sending up loads of police who catch the offenders, keep them in jail a few months, then send them back to go on with it. I have a feeling that you care and have love in your heart to stir up your Congress to action. Government with the help of American DDT have completely wiped out the deadly malaria. Then why not try to stay this awful smuggling of harmful drugs? Is it hopeless? I am praying.

That same year, Granny's ninetieth, ushered in harvest as well as famine in the work. The Fellowship was able to purchase a trailer for the jeep. A new road was opened by the government to Dr. Lister's hill station. The women workers were led in a week of Bible study, to the final meeting of which the men workers came from their fifteen stations scattered over seven hills. April brought the fifth Vellore work camp to the mountains, this time to lay the foundation of a new house for Dr. Lister. One of the doctors in the group drove the jeep with the trailer to a brick kiln which had been fired a month before, then returned to the site with a load of pukka bricks. This same doctor had met his wife in a work camp four years before. It had been a love marriage, unusual for India. Now she was here with him, slinging bricks down the line in this land where manual labour was still considered undignified.

The famine was literal as well as figurative. They saw great fields of yellow stalks, prematurely dying because of rain failure. Prices rose to staggering levels. Grain, oil, milk powders came from abroad, and one of the stations was a distributing centre, but this was not for the workers. Eight of them had babies under eighteen months to whom milk was not often available. In her letters home Carol pleaded for packets of milk powder to keep these children and others healthy.

"You must have great joy in being part of the developing work," one of her friends wrote her. Joy? Suddenly she realised that she had let joy become almost submerged in the frustrations of pioneer work in this land of patient suffering and agonisingly slow motion. Not Granny, she noted with a swift humility. "Babs" seemed to have become more youthfully buoyant than ever.

"Mother Brand has that joy," Carol wrote back, "from her wonderful faith in Jesus Christ, and the Lord has granted her long life so that she sees with her eyes what she saw long ago with eyes of faith. I praise the Lord for this witness through her to me."

Granny's joys were human as well as spiritual. Early in 1970 Connie flew to India, not this time from Nigeria but from England, where she and David had gone to facilitate the education of their five children. Granny had not seen her daughter for eleven years. Whetting her keen delight in the reunion was an unanticipated treat in a bit of England which Connie had brought with her— jonquils, daffodils, violets, snow drops, all as fresh as if they had just been picked.

"I never thought I would see a daffodil again!" she exclaimed. "And these have more of a surprised look than I remembered. I suppose they are more surprised than usual to find themselves in India."

They travelled by jeep to Dr. Lister's station. From there they went to Kunnur, the centre on the Kalryans settled by Granny after she "retired" at sixty-nine, more than twenty years before. Connie rode the pony while Granny travelled by *dholi*. Then they had a weekend together on the Kollis, sleeping in the old wooden bungalow, which Granny had bought just three years before. It was empty now of furnishings but filled with a host of memories.

Somewhat to Granny's surprise the memories were unmarred by bitterness. Her long resentment against the mission board which, from her point of view, had neglected, compromised, jeopardised the work she and Jesse had started, the property they had so dearly purchased, had receded into the past. Her niece Dr. Ruth had long tried to convince her that the board's apparent neglect had been due not to lack of interest but to conviction that the Christian community on the Kollis should be encouraged in its maturity to become more independent.

"And you must admit," Ruth would remind her, "that the board officials have always responded to requests for visitations and special ministries. And they have certainly supported our work on the northern Kollis. Believe me, they still have a keen interest in the Kolli Hills people, and there is much prayer for the work there."

Though Granny was ready to make no such wholesale admissions, at least the old bitterness was gone. The matter had become unimportant.

Paul, visiting India a few months before, had noticed this change, sensed in his mother a spiritual strength which she had not shown before. He had written to Margaret, "I found her distinctly younger than she was a year ago." Yet when he tried to define the change he was at first puzzled. She was not physically any stronger. She was no better able to walk, nor had her memory, for some years hazy, improved. Then he put his finger on it. In previous years her passionate love for her hill people had been striving within her with an anger towards those who had been hindering the work. The result had been stress and strain. Now it seemed that she had been able to extend her love a little further, to include those who may have deserved criticism. In this broadening and deepening of her love had come a serenity and peace that brightened her smile and gave her new inner strength.

"This is how to grow old," he had written. "Allow everything else to fall away, until those around you see just love. They will also see your own life renewed and they will recognise the love to be the love of God."

5

SHE WAS NINETY-ONE. Old? Yes, of course. And infirm. Years ago they had told her in Vellore that several of the vertebrae in her spine had partially collapsed and that, seen in X-ray, her bones were very faint and sort of ghostly. But she could still see to read for short periods without glasses. And *stottherum*, she could still travel!

She proved it soon after her ninety-first birthday in August when she and three companions ventured on a trip by truck. Some years before a young man had travelled four hundred miles from the south to help as an untrained teacher in an isolated hill village. To reach his station had been a three-day trek. Now a lorry could drive within two miles of his village on a road built to take down loads of bamboo. Deciding to take this "short cut", they travelled with two company lorries, Granny and her companions in the second one, she and Carol riding in the cabin while Grace and Asirvatham were with the bamboo workers in the back. The lorry in front was prepared to wait for them whenever they got too far behind. After bumping along for about three hours up and down grades, as they descended one hill they could see an amazing near-perpendicular ascent ahead.

"Who was your engineer?" Carol asked their driver.

"We didn't have an engineer," he replied with obvious pride. "The Bamboo Company workers did it."

Confident that he could not understand English, Carol remarked to Granny, "I thought they couldn't have had an engineer. No engineer would allow this!"

206

Descending to a small stream before the breath-taking ascent, the lorry was stopped and big boulders lifted into the area above the back wheels. There was no traction, explained the driver, so the weight kept the wheels from spinning—somewhat. Not far up the steep incline the lorry stalled at a curve, and attempts to get it started only landed it in a soft shoulder of the finest dirt. What to do? Walk, of course, up a grade as steep as a staircase, to the lorry which had preceded them. Granny started, propped up by her two sticks and supported on either side by Grace and Asirvatham. Not by Carol. They had had a bit of a squabble, so she was not acceptable as a helper. Granny sat down often on the roadside, and near the top she even hung her feet over the edge of the abyss and sketched the outline of distant hills. It was a third of a mile to the forward lorry, but she reached it, got in, and promptly fell asleep.

Three hours later, when it was beginning to get dark, the lorry finally accomplished the long climb, all hands tugging on a stout rope and all yelling at the tops of their voices to encourage each other to maximum effort. Two miles later the party of four were dumped out in the dark, the lorry going on to the bamboo piles, prepared to make the return trip with full loads the next day. Fortunately a message sent by a casual passerby got through to their co-workers, a young married couple with a five month old baby. They sent down men who carried Granny up the rock-strewn path to the station by *dholi*. After supper of soup and cocoa from American packets, with sliced bread and butter bought in Salem, followed by family prayers led by Granny, they lay down on mats on the mud floor, covered themselves with the bedding they had brought, and slept.

The next day they travelled on to another station, where Granny stayed on with her helper Grace, ministering to a constant stream of patients and other visitors. After going down to visit other stations and catch up on her administrative work Carol came back for them in the jeep, preferring the eighty-mile trip around to the foot of the hill to taking the "short cut".

By 1971 there were twenty stations on the seven hills. A small hospital was being built for Dr. Lister at Munglepetti, now known as Kumminkurichy, where a Vellore work camp in 1969 had laid the foundation for his terrace roof house. In that same year the doctor had been hospitalised at Vellore, much against his will, for an attack of hepatitis, but he had recovered and returned to his post.

It was Dr. Lister who had enlisted the services for the Fellowship of a talented young couple who were making an invaluable contribution to the work on the mountains, Devaraj and his wife

Cathy. Devaraj, a high school graduate with agricultural training, had come to the Danish Mission Leprosy Hospital at Vedathorasalur, on one of the routes to Vellore from Salem. Though he had come for treatment, his was an arrested case of leprosy which had left no stigmata. He had been employed in a government ceramics project when at a routine medical examination it was discovered that he had symptoms of Hansen's disease, and he had lost his job. At Vedathorasalur he was working in the department of occupational therapy when he met Cathy, an occupational therapist from England. They fell in love and were married in October, 1970.

Dr. Lister, who attended their wedding, had already contacted Dr. Lewis and the leaders of the Fellowship and arranged for their assignment to his own station, Kumminkurichy, where they were already rendering valuable service. Cathy, whose training in occupational therapy gave her something of the medical background necessary to assist Dr. Lister, was an invaluable addition to his work, especially as he could give her instructions in English. Devaraj developed the agricultural work Granny had started and aided the villagers in improving their methods of farming.

There were other encouraging developments in the work. The League in California had purchased for Dr. Lister a large van at a cost of $4300, a unique and practical vehicle, for it had a four-wheel drive which enabled him to travel even the roughest roads. It was equipped with necessary facilities for emergency work along the lonely mountain trails, much of the equipment designed by Dr. Lister himself. Jesse had painfully blazed paths through the wilderness. Now, in the past six years the government had built roads into three of the hills and paved other roads leading to the foot of the ranges. How he would rejoice, exulted Granny. But of course the work was barely begun. There were hundreds of villages still unreached.

While Carol Weeber was away for four months on furlough, Granny's companion was Frances Dhyriam, the forthright Indian woman in her eighties. Granny stayed in the most inaccessible station, making several camping trips to other ranges in an attempt to settle grievous problems. On 2nd August, the day after Carol's return, she came down to the plains by *dholi*, delighted not only by her friend's arrival but by the gift the Gospel League had sent back with her, a cassette player with some of her favourite albums for use on the hills.

"When I flew out of Thailand and was given customs forms," said Carol, "and saw that among the dutiable items, regardless of allowable quota, were cassette players, I was dismayed, knowing how high duties on such things can be. Then I saw the rest of the sentence—'unless battery operated'." Of course, the League had known that there was no electricity on most of the hills.

As usual when on the plains, Granny was restless for the mountains. It was difficult to keep her there until the following Sunday, her ninety-second birthday. A feast was arranged for noon on Saturday, with about seventy people attending. They sat on the floor according to hill custom, eating the rice and curry with their fingers. Carol was amazed to note that the man who supervised the cooking and then went around from guest to guest scooping food from the big brass vessels onto their plantain leaves was none other than the landlord who rented them the house, a Mohammedan! The next day in Denmark Dr. David Lister was being married to Dr. Jonna Boonevie, whom he had met in Vedathorasalur when she came to India under a medical student programme. All over the hills people were demanding eagerly, "When is our doctor coming back?"

Granny could stay on the plains no longer. Two days after her birthday she and Carol set out for the Green Hills (the Pachais). They were excited to find that since their last visit the road which zig-zagged up the hill had been cut the whole way to the top. But it was not yet ready for the jeep. Three quarters of the way up men were waiting to carry Granny in a *dholi*. Carol completed the four-mile journey alone at a slower pace, arriving an hour later than the others. After two glasses of fruit juice and a cup of coffee she lay down on the long wooden box which was always her bed at this station. She was completely exhausted. Not so Granny. Spry after her hour's rest, she was already sitting on the edge of her cot, ready to go.

"You can't expect me to sit here and do nothing!" she complained.

In the next five days they visited three sub-stations, Granny in her *dholi*, Carol chalking up twenty-six miles of walking. In one station, where the co-worker was a qualified teacher, they ate their lunch amid a bombardment of swarming flies, a common experience in a village with no sanitary facilities, where pigs, goats, chickens, cattle lived in close proximity to the dwellings. While Granny took a nap on the veranda and teacher Pragash prepared a delicious roast chicken for their supper, Carol led the children out of earshot, playing "follow-the-leader", then set up races and games for them. After supper Granny attended the night school, composed mostly of boys who had had a few years of schooling but had stopped to help with the family farming.

Granny took an impassioned interest in all such schools, whether run by her colleagues or by government, and no detail of their management escaped her critical eye. In 1964, sixteen years after she had started literacy classes on the Kalryans, the Government Welfare Department had started a boarding school on land she had given adjoining her little bungalow. By now the school, which went through the fifth standard, consisted of three buildings with an enrolment of over sixty and a staff of three teachers. Because it was a Welfare School the pupils, almost all boys, were entitled to not only free board and books but also free uniforms and blankets. Yet months after the term started the pupils might be without books and blankets, though the money for them had doubtless been granted. The hills were far from the main offices of government, and, as in the old days of British dominance, hill men could still be victims of neglect and even exploitation. Though there was now no Jesse to act as mediary, Granny had long since appropriated many of his techniques.

Camping at Kunnur in the spring of 1973, she thought constantly of the children close by, shivering at night, lying with little covering on a cement floor where great patches had no cement at all. Letters to the Welfare Officer accomplished little. But since the children's leave came at the end of May and the weather soon became warm enough for little or no covering, she agreed to wait for the beginning of the new term before attending to the problem personally. Wait, yes, but not cease praying several times each day and talking constantly, even to chance visitors, about conditions in the hostel for which she felt responsible. She was even more distressed that morning and evening prayers, conducted by the Christian couple in charge of the station, had not been permitted for a long time, and the children's attendance at Sunday service had been stopped.

"But you can't expect those privileges in a government school!" her friends pointed out.

"I'm praying about it," she would reply obstinately.

In June she hurried up to Kunnur to be there when school started. Conditions had not improved. She insisted immediately on taking the strenuous trip down to approach—not the welfare officer—but the Collector, the highest official in the district. Arriving at Regina's house on the plains at Saturday noon, she would have proceeded the twenty-three miles to Salem immediately if they had not persuaded her that the Collector might not welcome a visit on Saturday afternoon. "You are always putting things off till tomorrow," she accused Carol more than once that weekend.

On Monday morning early they set out and went straight to the home of the Collector, a smiling, energetic young man recently appointed to the position. After listening to Granny's terse but graphic account of conditions in the school, he picked up the phone and called the welfare officer. "Do you have a school in the Kalryan hills at the place called Kunnur? . . . You know Mrs. Brand, who lives at Kunnur, of course. She is in my office and says that the buildings are in a very bad condition and that the children need blankets. I am sending her over to you."

At the welfare office Granny discarded her two bamboo poles and swung down the narrow aisle between two rows of desks by supporting herself on each desk as she passed, greeting each clerk with a beaming smile. Heading straight for the desk of the welfare officer which dominated the room, she bestowed another smile and greeting. "I am sorry, sir," she began, her English perhaps a little more British than usual, "but I had to go to the Collector, since you did not answer my letters. He kindly arranged for me to come and see you."

The officer listened with respect to her story, then called a subordinate who took charge, promising to bring four men to Kunnur the following Tuesday to make an investigation. Granny returned to Kunnur immediately to be ready when the delegation came.

From the point to which the jeep would go they would have a six-mile hike and would have to stay overnight. On Wednesday Jayasingh, the driver, picked up the men, six of them not four, for they were taking along contractors to estimate the cost of the needed repairs.

The visit was a success. Evening prayers and attendance at Sunday services were permitted. Repairs were started. Blankets were promised and arrived later. The required books were ordered. Granny felt satisfaction but not triumph. Like Jesse who more than a half century before had led his four hundred hill men to the plains to win justice, she thanked God for the solution to this problem. She had prayed much about it, yes. But she knew very well that going to God with such a matter was not enough. One must go also to the world's Collectors.

6

She was ninety-four, so frail and tenuous of body that it seemed bone and flesh must be consumed in the intensity of inner zeal. It was as if physical strength were being slowly muted into pure spiritual vigour. Not only had walking become increasingly difficult, but she now was unable to rise to a standing posture without help, especially from her favourite sitting position on the floor. It was becoming harder to remember recent events and names and faces, though she had an uncanny memory of the hill Christians who continued to come to her with their problems, pinpointing both virtues and sins with unerring accuracy and dispensing blessing, advice, or caustic criticism with sympathy and love to all alike. And not only her hill people . . .

Her son Paul, observing her on his frequent trips to India in these later years, was amazed at the influence she exerted on the young medical students both in their work camps and on her visits to the college at Vellore. One would have thought that because of her failing memory and tendency towards repetition, they would be impatient with her, pity her as a doddering creature in her dotage. But no such thing. Students would gather about her on the floor, hang on her words, bring her their problems. In response she never minced words, always gave them the truth as she saw it, straight from the shoulder. Like all youth, they respected absolute sincerity. It was the testimony of a completely dedicated, single-minded life that so impressed them.

It was so in the tenth work camp, held in April, 1974 at Kalli-parai, the first time the Vellore group had climbed to this isolated village in the *kanja* area. Granny went up to the station early to prepare for their coming. There were twenty-two of them, most of them medical students, under the leadership of Dr. Benjamin, head of the Public Health Department of the medical centre. They helped a mason lay two rows of stone on a foundation which had been completed two years before. The building was badly needed for a school and chapel to relieve the congestion in the small room of the teacher's residence, which was presently being used. On the last day of camp a runner came twenty-one miles from the station where the medical centre was being developed with news that a terrific wind had lifted and flung afar thirty asbestos sheets and timber, dropping debris on three smaller houses and damaging the roofs. But no persons were injured, and all the workers moved thankfully into the house of Dr. Lister, who was still away.

Granny took part in all camp proceedings, though protesting when it was insisted that she ride in a *dholi* on this last day to the shady spot where noon prayers were to be held. In spite of her complaints that walking was extremely painful, she persisted in dragging her poor legs over all sorts of terrain, via helping hands and her two ill-mated sticks. She clapped joyfully to the singing of stirring new songs from the Vellore song book sung to the twang of a guitar, and punctuated the prayers of each person in the circle with vociferous "*stottherums*."

There was no visiting Valliyan, now known as Visuvasam, on this trip. At Granny's urging Dr. Lister had given him an examination and had recommended amputation of the ulcerated foot. However, the patient had refused surgery. In 1971 his foot had become so infected that he had had himself carried over to Kumminkurichy in a *dholi*. Dr. Lister had driven him to Vellore in the new van, and the amputation had been performed before the doctor departed for England. Now Visuvasam was back at the Rehabilitation Centre for treatment of a persistent ulcer on his other foot. When in Vellore the preceding January, Granny had suggested that he learn tailoring. Dr. Mary Verghese had been doubtful of his ability, but Granny and Carol had purchased for him an Indian-manufactured sewing machine, hand powered, and he had shown a surprising aptitude for the work.

"He is an entirely different person," Dr. Mary reported with high praise for his accomplishment, "completely changed. He doesn't even look like the old Valliyan."

With the price of plastic wire making his previous craft prohibitive, Visuvasam could return to his hills with another lucrative profession. True, like almost everybody in the area, he had long been involved in the illegal *kanja* production and might continue to be. Granny would never give up the fight to end the nefarious traffic and her definitions of right and wrong, always in blacks and whites, had never altered.

Nor did she have the slightest inhibition about attacking error wherever she found it. Whether to unlettered hill Christian or to eminent medical specialist, Granny felt it her duty to warn of the dire consequences of her idea of sins both major and minor. She had ceaselessly berated Dr. John Carman, the skilled surgeon who for many years was Director of the Vellore Medical College and Hospital, for his habit of smoking, even smacking his hand and telling him he should be ashamed of himself. He had good-naturedly agreed, admitting that the advice was in the interest of health, yet he had been unable to break the habit. When Dr. Carman's son Bob, a pathologist, had come to Vellore with his lovely wife Lou, Granny had immediately demanded, "Does he smoke? Does he take after his father?" Delighted to discover that this evil had not been passed on from father to son, Granny had praised Dr. Bob heartily and told him how happy she was that he did not smoke. They had often laughed about it together.

It had been some years since she had seen the young Carmans, for they had been away on furlough in America. Now, in Vellore with Paul in March, 1974, she was invited to go with him to a big party at one of the staff bungalows. Though desperately tired, she wanted to spend every minute possible with her son and insisted on going. Never had she felt older and less able to confront a crowd of people, most of whom she found difficult to remember. Her leg was paining her and, though she tried to sleep in the jeep on her way from Karigiri to the college, it was impossible.

"You know," she said, dragging herself out of the jeep, "I think I am really too old for these things now." It was the first time Paul had ever heard her admit to being old. The party will be sad, he thought, with her feeling like this. But with all the guests gathering around and greeting her, Granny rallied a bit and tried to respond, even though she was able to recognise only a few and could not recall even their names. Then she was confronted by a personable young man.

"Well, Granny, do you remember me? I'm Bob."

"Bob?" She studied his features vaguely.

"Bob Carman."

"Oh!" Her face lit up. "I know you. You don't smoke!"

The words erupted with such joyous spontaneity that everybody within earshot burst out laughing. Bob was delighted. Thereafter Granny was completely her old self, cracking jokes, participating in conversation on a variety of subjects, fatigue and old age completely forgotten.

These brief rendezvous with Paul were for Granny compensation for all her life of loneliness apart from her children. From his headquarters at the United States Public Health Hospital in Carville, Louisiana he came to Vellore once or twice a year to spend a week or ten days at Karigiri, the leprosy research sanatorium connected with Vellore. She never let other duties interfere with her joining him there. The preceding spring, in 1973, she had even deserted a twelve-day Bible Conference for the women workers, one of her special delights, in order to meet him. Monica Harris, Dr. Brand's cousin, had organised these gatherings of women workers five years before, and Dr. Ruth and other members of Granny's old mission had taught the Bible courses. Nothing but a meeting with Paul could have enticed Granny away.

This visit of his in March, 1974 offered a special inducement, for his daughter Jean was with him. Graduate of the London Bible College and St. Thomas Hospital School of Nursing, she had chosen to work in India, driving there in a Land Rover ambulance which was scheduled for delivery in Nepal. She had crossed the mountain passes of Afghanistan in mid-winter and was now working in Bombay in various communities, teaching.

Though Granny had never seen many of her grandchildren, her concern for them, especially their spiritual growth, was constant and intense. She delighted that some of them had chosen medicine—Connie's Andrew and Paul's Tricia, as well as Mary's husband Jim; that Christopher with a master's degree in food science was working in the deserts of Mexico; that Jessica had done voluntary service overseas for three years and had married a doctor. She eagerly followed the plans of Connie's Elizabeth, Timothy, Stephen, and Paul's Estelle and Pauline. And Jean, here in India, was her greatest joy. In both conversations and letters she bombarded Connie and Paul with questions. How many of them were going to be missionaries? Were they all pledged to follow Jesus? Were there any romances brewing? She wrote a long letter to them jointly, a bit incoherent like all her letters these days, but full of warning and encouragement.

Dear Ones and Grandchildren . . . Do, darlings, all first make sure of your love for Christ, then if the one you think might be your one and only Chum, if he or she are also in love with your Saviour . . . My married life, altho' all too short was so full of joy . . . I want you all to have the same union . . . Oh, do have the same joy Jess and I had. Pray about the future . . . Don't think I am a stupid old woman . . .

The meetings with Paul were both joyful and frustrating. Sometimes he seemed more like a visiting colleague than like her own son. "Brother . . ." she found herself inadvertently addressing him, her usual salutation to fellow workers. A bit amusing to a chance listener, hearing Paul address her as "Granny"!

"It's been wonderful having him here," she wrote once, "but in a way rather sad! You know what it is like seeing the thing you want and love, but at a distance."

True, she always stayed at the guest house at Karigiri when he came, but he was always so terribly busy—operating, teaching trainees from all over the world, lecturing, presiding at Karigiri Council meetings! Yet one brief time in the day became hers alone. As always, she would get up before dawn and make her way to the top of the flight of steps leading down into the garden. From there she could look out over the plain and towards the mountains. About dawn Paul would come and join her. Perhaps they would read from the Bible together. Perhaps they would talk about the family. He might tell her about his work in leprosy and ask her advice. She might tell him about problems on the hills. But most of the time they would just sit there together in silent communion. It was almost as if Jesse had come back to her.

"The thing so good about these times," Paul would remember, "was the way she was able to be completely at peace."

7

THE PAST AND future were becoming almost more real than the present. Carol was reading to her from old family letters which had long been stored in a tin trunk in the Big Bungalow at Vellore, letters from Jesse to his children, from Paul dating from the time she left him in England until he came to India, from Connie almost every week for fifty years, from her father.

"My sweet Evelyn," read Carol; then, another salutation, "My precious Evelyn." In a birthday letter her father had written, "I long to kiss you as I kissed you on the day you were born, as I kissed the eight who preceded you and the two who came after." In one letter he had enclosed a snowdrop, still there over half a century later, the dried pieces and the stains of it on the paper and a postscript on the side: "Eunice, Mother, and I have kissed the snowdrop."

"And people think those of his generation didn't express affection!" marvelled Carol.

She had seen many evidences of it in Granny. She remembered a letter "Babs" had written to Connie in answer to her daughter's question as to whether she could cut her hair. "Not now, please. I kiss each braid . . ."

Once after a difficult climb to join Granny on the Pachai Hills, Carol had sat wearily drinking coffee. "Babs" had risen, seized her two sticks, and hobbled towards her. "I haven't kissed you yet," she had said tenderly.

The letters brought memories flooding. Granny even felt wistful nostalgia. There were mirrors at Vellore, bringing her suddenly face to face with the ravages of time. This furrowed face, seamed as a dry river bed, was it the same that artists had begged to paint, that had once been portrayed, it was rumoured, on an Australian capital as a model for Britannia, that her father and Jesse and she herself had thought so beautiful? When Paul tried to take her picture these days she tried to hide her face, murmuring, "Horrible now!"

Word came that spring that her brother Charlie had gone on Easter Sunday, bringing the past still more poignantly alive. Of the eleven children now she alone was left. Though not one of the "three little ones", he had been very close to her in age and in affection. She had called him "Chol", and he had called her "Babs".

"Please," she said now to Carol, "don't call me by that name any more."

Carol obeyed. Thereafter she never used the pet name which for some years had been a bond of affection between them. Even in the intimacy of her diary, where "Babs" had frequently appeared, she wrote now of "Mother", "ECB", or "Mother Brand".

As if the last tenuous link with the past had been broken, Granny returned with even more than her usual furious intensity to the present. Time was getting short. The "golden bowl" symbolising old age in Ecclesiastes was becoming scarred and cracked. The "silver cord" was much frayed. And heaven knew the "keepers of the house" had long been trembling and the "strong men" unable to bear her weight. The "grinders", though still fairly efficient, were of little consequence. With prices soaring and the poor of India heartbreakingly close to starvation—rice over 300 rupees a bag and goat flesh ten rupees a kilo—by firm choice there was little meat to chew.

As for the "doors", whether interpreted as lips or ears, both remained wide open. At the Family Camp of the Fellowship that year, a wonderful new adventure where she attended a class every session, sometimes the women's, sometimes the men's, she was an avid listener. The afternoon class for men became her favourite where the students took turns presenting a sermon and their talks were then evaluated by Pastor Wilfred Kurht, a former colleague in her Mission, now an eminent Bible teacher in the Tamil language. When the jeep was there they carried her over the field, but one day when Carol was away from camp and all had gone to classes she appeared in the chapel where the class was being held, having walked the considerable distance, each step a Herculean effort. After class the men hurried for the *dholi*, and for once she was willing to get in and be carried back. After one sermon Mr. Kurht suggested that the student should have spoken more softly. His voice had been regulated to outdoor rather than chapel speaking.

"I don't agree," interposed Granny in a voice fully as loud. "I could hear every word with no straining at all. I like a loud sermon."

Her own speech suffered no inhibition with advancing age. As one friend laughingly commented, "You can't put a cork in Granny Brand." At the midnight communion service the preceding New Year the congregation had gone up front, a procedure which Granny with her foot drop and lack of balance was unable to follow. "Brother," she had called out loudly and clearly, "I want some of that."

217

In fact, she wanted something of all that was happening. Just as long ago being one of "the three little ones" had been cause for resentment, so now she demanded to have a part in all the Fellowship activities, sometimes finding it difficult to delegate the responsibilities which had been hers alone for years on end. When at the General Meeting in March of that year Pastor Paul Raj was not present at the afternoon session and Carol went up front to preside, Granny was obviously irked by her colleague's presumption. She was mollified only when a chair was brought up front for her to share the posture of authority.

Yes, time was short. True, the work had been blessed beyond hers and Jesse's early dreams. Of the promise given long ago in the church in Kotagiri she had received many bright flashes of fulfilment. *Said I not unto thee that if thou wouldst believe thou shouldst see the glory of God?* Seven hills where the Gospel was being preached. Thirty national workers now involved in the constantly increasing task. A new jeep and new roads to conquer the wild remote outreaches of the isolated Mountains of Death and other ranges. But the roads were still unfinished, hundreds of villages still unreached, tens of thousands of her hill people still slaves to disease, ignorance, paganism. And on the far fastnesses of the Kalryans the hated *kanja* was still being grown and sold.

In May she was in Kalliparai, healing, preaching, going out on camping trips in her *dholi*, fighting to supplant the injurious *kanja* with more healthful, if less lucrative crops. In June she was on the Kollis with her faithful helper Grace *Ammal*. July found her on the Bothais camping in the Fellowship hut. August . . .

She was ninety-five. In the Fellowship house on the plains she was given a big *tamash*. There was a crowd even for breakfast when they served 150 dough cakes with honey, tomato ketchup, jelly. At about ten a prayer session was started in the *pandal*. More food was served about twelve. Then Granny had her nap in her usual favourite spot on the floor. There were thirty for tea, with a birthday cake decorated with much-used candles. All day workers and friends kept coming—Devaraj and Cathy with their twins Simon and Steven and their new baby Jonathan, born on furlough in England; Dr. Ruth Harris, A. K. Annamal, Ruth and John Michael, Miss Dhyriam. There were telegrams, gifts, letters, cards. But the most satisfying gift was the knowledge that all over the world, the result of an appeal by the International Gospel Fellowship, people were praying for the work on the mountains.

What can you give [wrote her son Paul not long before her birthday] to someone who has EVERYTHING? I was with my mother earlier this year. As always I began to be ashamed that I have a fine house with electric current and water from a tap. I tried, as I have tried before, to find what I could give her that she would not regard as a luxury or not immediately give away to somebody who has less than she has. Mother insists that she has everything . . . She has her treasure where her heart is, and her heart is in the work that God has given her to do. If we want to add to her treasure it can only be if we can help to forward that work and bring glory to her Lord.

In her letter to me this week Mother expresses a fear and a wish that I feel I must pass on to you. She says that her ninety-fifth birthday will soon be here and she feels sure that a lot of kindly people will write and praise her and say how wonderful she is to be working still at ninety-five years of age. I can see the tears in her eyes when she insists, "I am *not* wonderful. I am just a poor old frail and weak woman. God has taken hold of me and he gives me the strength I need each day. He uses me just because I KNOW that I have no strength of my own. Please tell the people to praise God—not me."

Paul was due to come to India again in the autumn, and for Granny the prospect was a shining beacon. Every meeting, she knew, might be their last. She awaited his coming with even more impatience than usual, sensing perhaps that the "silver cord" was near to breaking. Meanwhile she took comfort in the sound of his voice on a tape containing a sermon he had preached at St. Paul's Cathedral in London. Over and over she listened to it, sometimes in the growing confusion of her mind mistaking it for the voice of Jesse.

Not that she spent the days in idleness. She was more restless than ever. Hearing of a scandal on the Kollis—one of the men having got his wife's sister pregnant—she insisted on going there at once, and September found her again in the wooden bungalow. Here on her way to chapel she fell and gashed her head on a corner of the house but refused to turn back. Carol tied up the bleeding wound with a wad of cotton and a scarf and drove her to chapel, where she insisted on speaking as usual. Though her speech these days was sometimes incoherent and inclined to repetition, when giving public testimony she seldom faltered.

From the Kollis they went to the Kalryans, both Kummin-kurichy and Kunnur, where Granny was visited by the usual stream of visitors, including Karuninasan and his wife Rebecca. Granny sent message after message to one of her backsliding Christians, who had abetted an episode of gross immorality in his family; then when he came at her request, approved his being asked to offer prayer at the Sunday service. Shocked, Carol muttered, "Words, words, words" and got up and left. "Mother forgives on the first syllable!" she fumed after the service.

Paul wrote that he would arrive near the end of September.

"I shall of course go to the airport to meet him as usual," announced Granny one morning before cock crow.

"Mother, you never go to the airport to meet him," protested Carol.

"Oh, yes, you don't remember."

There was no use arguing. Granny might be confused as to fact, but strength of will remained unabated. Fortunately by the time they reached Karigiri the insistence had been long forgotten.

Paul arrived a day late, his plane having caught fire half an hour out from Nairobi but managing to return to the airport safely. Granny also had had an accident, falling in her room and injuring her knees, so to her disgust he found her in a wheelchair. His visit of five days was short and frustrating. They had one profitable discussion of her work on the mountains. She heard him give one of his inspiring talks at Bible study. They rode in the jeep to a dinner at the college, where she became so tired she begged to go home early. But they were unable to have as many early morning talks as usual, due both to Granny's physical condition and to Paul's intensely busy programme. Those they did have were doubly precious. Yet when he left on October 5th she felt almost as bereft as on the day she and Jesse had left the children to return to India. She sensed that she would never see him again.

Though the X-ray had showed no bones broken, the ligaments in her knees had been torn, and she suffered much pain on movement. Still she insisted on attending every service within range of jeep or wheelchair and speaking at most of them. One Sunday in October after a long morning of four meetings, on hearing an announcement of another student meeting at eight in the evening, there was nothing for it but she must attend that also! After a fifth service and a hurried supper she and Carol set out for the meeting and found it was held on a terrace roof two flights up. Protesting all the way, Granny was carried up by a tall medical student, but refused to be carried down and walked, a slow process which taxed Carol's patience more than her own feeble strength. On the way home Carol squelched Granny's elation over the day's activity and then felt guiltily, "I have to learn yet to be more gracious to her strong will."

Though impatient to return to the hills Granny made good use of the days at Karigiri, visiting the leprosy patients so frequently that she got to know them individually, even though her eyes were becoming so unperceiving that she often failed to recognise friends and return their greetings, a strange lapse for her. Beth Wilson, one of the workers at the hospital, was amazed at her endurance.

"You do not know me personally," she was to write Connie later, "but I am one of the Karigiri folks that knew and loved your mother, whom I always called Granny. She spent more time with the patients during the last three or four months than ever before, and I believe there will be a lot of fruit; some of it we have already seen, from her talks and prayers with individual patients. I often used to marvel at where she got the energy and strength to keep it up—from eight fifteen a.m., sometimes right up to lunch time."

The day before they planned to leave for the hills in late October Carol wheeled her through all the wards and they gave sweets to the patients, but as they were doing this a man came from the shoe department with news that the new shoes for Karuninasan who was returning with them would not be ready for four days. Again on November 5th they were ready to leave. After attending morning chapel they went to say goodbye to Dr. Fritschi, Paul's close friend and co-worker for many years.

"You shouldn't go now," he advised. "There are cyclone warnings."

Granny was agreeable. This was Tuesday. She had wanted to stay for the Wednesday night prayer meeting. The next day, Wednesday, she fell again. There was much pain, but Dr. Fritschi, immediately summoned, could locate no specific injury.

"The sands of time are sinking fast," Granny quoted, and repeated most of the sixteen stanzas of the long hymn which her niece, Nancy Robbins, had once sent her but which had been mislaid. By a strange coincidence Carol found the complete poem in a current magazine and read it to her several times.

Suddenly on November 11th Granny's speech became jumbled, and she had no memory. She could not even sign her name. Yet surprisingly she ate well and slept better than usual. Though for years her pulse had been irregular and a slow forty, now it became a regular eighty. It was as if she were being given strength for the ascent of her last and most difficult mountain.

Regina Hansen, returning from furlough, stopped at Katpadi, the Vellore railway station, on her way from Madras to Salem and came to Karigiri to see her old friend, arriving at eleven on the morning of December 18th. Granny did not recognise her, but at least Regina was able to see her once more in life. She went on immediately, and at Belur she found a telegram telling of Granny's passing at two fifteen that afternoon. She had gone easily, peacefully, with one deep sigh.

"A last peep at her," Beth Wilson remembered, "after I had

heard the news. She looked so tall and slim and straight, just like a schoolgirl, I thought, her blue-grey silk dress reaching down to her blue-grey woolly socks."

At eight the next morning a Thanksgiving service was held at the Vellore Hospital Chapel; then the jeep and Dr. Fritschi's car set off with Granny, Carol, Chaplain Oommen, and others on the 180-mile trip to the Kollis. Pastor Paul Raj, her niece Dr. Ruth Harris, and other colleagues joined them in another jeep. They arrived at Vazhavanthi at four thirty for a service in the chapel built by Jesse more than sixty years before. Just in time Granny's adopted daughter Ruth and her husband John Michael arrived in a taxi. Monica Harris came walking. At five thirty Evelyn Brand was laid beside her husband in the presence of a sorrowful multitude.

Trust and Triumph! Never had the shining watchword approached more profound reality than in the last days and hours of her life. Her eager spirit had so long been chafing at the bonds of mortality! Increasing weakness, consciousness of the magnitude of her task, had brought almost unbearable frustration. But with a growing awareness of the divine Presence came a fresh assurance of the promise only dimly perceived before. Already she was shaking off limiting mortality. No longer bound by time and space she could see in clearer perspective the final fulfilment of her vision.

Now she had climbed her last and highest mountain. To a view of sunrise glory? No need of paints and brushes to capture the ecstasy of a vague and distant promise. The beauty to which her spirit had been ever attuned was now all-pervasive and eternal.